ESSAYS IN MUSICAL ANALYSIS

ESSAYS IN
MUSICAL ANALYSIS

By

DONALD FRANCIS TOVEY

CONTENTS

ESSAYS IN
MUSICAL ANALYSIS

By

DONALD FRANCIS TOVEY

Volume V

VOCAL MUSIC

LONDON
OXFORD UNIVERSITY PRESS

Oxford University Press, Walton Street, Oxford OX2 6DP

OXFORD LONDON GLASGOW NEW YORK
TORONTO MELBOURNE WELLINGTON CAPE TOWN
IBADAN NAIROBI DAR ES SALAAM LUSAKA
KUALA LUMPUR SINGAPORE JAKARTA HONG KONG TOKYO
DELHI BOMBAY CALCUTTA MADRAS KARACHI

First Published 1937
Twelfth Impression 1980

PRINTED AND BOUND IN GREAT BRITAIN AT
THE CAMELOT PRESS LTD, SOUTHAMPTON

CONTENTS

BRAHMS

JOACHIM

PARRY

ETHEL SMYTH

DEBUSSY

GRANVILLE BANTOCK

GUSTAV HOLST

CXCVI. INTRODUCTION TO VOLUME V

THE essays in this volume concern vocal music. I have not yet had an opportunity of producing any vocal music without words, such as Medtner's Vocal Sonata or Debussy's *Sirènes*, and so I have not gone into the interesting questions that arise when the human voice thrusts all instruments into the background, as it inevitably does, only to disappoint the expectation of human speech.

It matters not whether the composer writes in self-sufficient musical form, or follows the words without attention to musical form, or attends to the musical form without attending to the words, or attends to both and neither alternately: the moment that words are heard or suspected, they inevitably become the key to the situation. If it is the wrong key, that is because the composer is inattentive, and all we can do is to clear away the wards and turn it into a skeleton key. If the composer is attentive, the analysis of his vocal work will consist of two parts, the first an account of his fundamental hypotheses of the treatment of words, *scilicet* his art-forms and general aesthetic system, and the second the words themselves, with a collection of numbered musical quotations and references to these numbers wherever the themes quoted occur. One result of this is that where the composer's hypotheses have been already explained, the musical analysis as such may vanish altogether. Several of my most adequate analyses of Bach and Holst have thus been eliminated from this volume.

Another result is that it is a sure sign of an imperfect musical civilization when a public that does not know a foreign language prefers to hear foreign vocal works in the original. The difficulties of musical translation are notorious, and they have only recently been tackled with a success that commands the respect of English persons who do not understand the problem. It may be news to many such persons, first that in countries with a more continuous musical tradition, performances in alien languages are not very popular except by way of courtesy to foreign singers, and secondly that the standard of musical translation has been no higher than it is in England. There are Germans who still believe that *Figaro* and *Don Giovanni* were set by Mozart in German, and in 1902 I could still hear in Vienna performances of these works with the old translations to which Mozart himself objected on the ground that Figaro and Susanna ought not to speak in the presence of the Count and Countess as if they were addressing pigs. This was odd, because the reputation of the Vienna opera was at the time still on the height to which Mahler had raised it, especially in its productions of Mozart; and, moreover, the Breitkopf and

Härtel critical edition of Mozart's works had long ago supplied a quite tolerable translation. I had evidently had the misfortune to witness the return of the dog to former habits; and my Viennese friends did indeed assure me that such reversions were among the difficulties which Mahler had encountered.

The present volume contains abundant evidence of the appalling difficulties of musical translation: and I shall have no ground of complaint if my own efforts at tinkering raise a smile. Allowance should sometimes be made for the crudeness of the original text. Frederick Jameson's translations of Wagner are easily the most perfect achievements on record in this art, and I am glad that my praise of them in the 11th edition of the *Encyclopædia Britannica* appeared in time to give their author pleasure. You can study Wagner's declamation in them as closely as in the original; and critics who carp at Jameson's diction have a reverence for Wagner's that is upheld mainly by the enchanting distance of their acquaintance with German.

Splendid work has been done in this line by Messrs. Fox Strangways and Steuart Wilson; and I very much regret that it should so happen that the present volume deals with passages in which I have found myself compelled to disagree with them on details. The very existence of these details is a testimony to the high standard to which such scholars and singers have raised the art.

WEELKES

CXCVII. FOUR MADRIGALS

I. *Three Virgin Nymphs*

Three virgin nymphs were walking all alone,
   Till rude Sylvanus chanced to meet them.
Ravished with joy, he leapt and snatch'd at one,
(Ay me,)
   But missing her, thus rudely greets them:
Nymphs of the wood, come back again and kiss me;
Sylvanus calls, come back and bliss me.

II. *Thule, the Period of Cosmography*

1. Thule, the period of Cosmography,
   Doth vaunt of Hecla, whose sulphurious fire
Doth melt the frozen clime and thaw the sky;
   Trinacrian Aetna's flames ascend not higher.
These things seem wondrous, yet more wondrous I,
Whose heart with fear doth freeze, with love doth fry.

2. The Andalusian merchant, that returns
   Laden with cochineal and China dishes,
Reports in Spain how strangely Fogo burns
   Amidst an ocean full of flying fishes.
These things seem wondrous, yet more wondrous I,
Whose heart with fear doth freeze, with love doth fry.

III. *O Care, Thou wilt despatch me*

1. O Care, thou wilt despatch me,
   If music do not match thee.
     Fa la la la.
So deadly dost thou sting me,
Mirth only help can bring me.
     Fa la la la.

2. Hence, Care, thou art too cruel,
   Come, music, sick man's jewel.
     Fa la la la.
His force had well nigh slain me:
But thou must now sustain me.
     Fa la la la.

IV. *Like Two Proud Armies*

Like two proud armies marching in the field,
Joining a thund'ring fight, each scorns to yield;
So in my heart your Beauty and my Reason,
One claims the crown, the other says 'tis treason
But O, your Beauty shineth as the sun,
And dazzled Reason yields as quite undone.

No period of musical history is more important or less adequately brought before the concert-going public of to-day than the sixteenth century, though everybody knows that it is called the Golden Age of Music. In so far as it is true that the exploitation of sudden discords, and the use of instruments in ways not imitative of vocal harmony, put an end to the harmonic purity and self-contained organization of music at the beginning of the new century, the term 'Golden Age' is very appropriate to the unconscious freedom and security with which the masters of the sixteenth century said all that they wished to say. But it gives no clue to the range of the things they said, nor to the depth of their thoughts. Still less clue to these matters is given by the most authoritative theories of sixteenth-century technique; though, as Helmholtz has shown, musical theory has never again been so scientifically correct, nor the musical ear trained in such accurate accordance with the results of modern acoustic experiment as in the days of Palestrina. But in those days the theorist knew his limitations better than would appear from his pontifical manner. He was a grammarian who settled the licence of the 'changing-note', just as Browning's grammarian 'settled *Hoti's* business'. And he was, before all things, a practical man; his scholars did perhaps about ten per cent. of their work on paper, and the rest by singing at sight and extemporizing vocal counterpoint under much the conditions of a very versatile mental arithmetic. I do not know whether M. Dalcroze would call the sixteenth-century musicians Eurhythmists; but, if language has meaning, that is what they were.

The present group of four madrigals should go far to demolish conventional ideas as to the 'limitations' of sixteenth-century music, whether in point of sentiment, or of harmonic and rhythmic freedom. I here offer a specimen of *Paradise Lost*, treated as ordinary methods of barring are apt to treat the rhythms of Palestrina and the madrigalists.

(To be read with strong emphasis on the second and last syllables
of each line.)

> Of Man's first dis
> Obedience and
> The fruit of that
> Forbidden tree,
> Whose mortal taste
> Brought death into
> The world and all.

This is a perfectly fair parallel to the custom of beating four-in-a-bar to sixteenth-century music. It scans, in an ugly fashion, just often enough to make the Byzantine scholiast imagine that it is the places that will not scan that are wrong, instead of the whole scheme that is fictitious.

Our modern rigid bar-rhythms assumed their dominion over music more gradually than we generally realize. Handel's triple time, for example, has an ancient cross-rhythm at every cadence; according to which two bars of 3/4 are accented like one bar of 3/2, so that it is quite a mistake of editors to 'correct' the accentuation of 4

Ex. 1.

and the glo - ry, the glo-ry of the Lord shall be re - veal - ed

since the accents in such a cadence are (for eighteenth-century rhythm) just where the words demand, and not on the first beat of its second 'bar' (i.e. the first syllable of 'revealed') at all. Handel goes a step farther back to the sixteenth century, at the instigation of a very appropriate text, when he disregards the first of the bar in the voices that follow their leader to the words 'And cast away their bonds from us'; a passage which, in half the vocal scores still in print, has been solemnly corrected by an editor who was shocked to find the first syllable of 'away' coinciding with an 'accented' beat. He should have had a course of syncopated spankings when he was a little boy.

Ex. 2.

and cast a - way . . . .

&c.

and cast a - way . . . .

In the present group of madrigals you will find an admirable specimen of the full luxury of sixteenth-century rhythm in that sumptuous text—

Ex. 3.

La - den with co - chi-neal and Chi - na dish-es

(see p. 6). I have marked the accents as the words demand them, without drawing any bar-strokes. Handel's triple-time cadence at once catches the eye; first, three beats ('glo-ry of the'), then six, divided into three pairs ('*Lord* shall *be* re-*vea*led'). But to this you must add the freedom of 'casting away their bonds'. Every voice begins the bill of lading at a different point, so that the accents do not often coincide in any two parts. But Weelkes is a great contrapuntist and his notes are at least as well packed as any Andalusian merchant's China dishes (Ex. 4).

It is obviously quite absurd to call such art primitive or archaic. It may be a lost art; but we cannot afford to let it remain lost, and we cannot recover it by treating it with the complacent patronage of a superior civilization.

Ex. 4.

As it is with the rhythm, so is it with the harmony. And here our orthodoxy is at once better informed and more subtly misled by its information. There is a vast mass of historical information to account for every harmonic fact in any sixteenth-century composition; and most of this information has been constantly given to the public and to choral societies in particular. Almost every bar in these four madrigals of Weelkes has some harmonic trait that historians will refer to one of four causes: (*a*) the use of the ecclesiastical modes, modified by the laws of *musica ficta*; (*b*) the provincial English taste, shared by the young Orlando di Lasso and the less pure stylists of the Netherlands, for collisions between major and minor thirds in the same chord; (*c*) the desire to explore chromatic and other remote modulations, another taste in which Orlando di Lasso in his youth followed the experiments of the Venetian, Cipriano da Rore; and (*d*) the influence of the monodic revolution, i.e. the dramatic pioneer-work of Monteverdi and the beginning of instrumental music. Now this is all very well, and I am just about to give illustrations of three of these points, which will, I hope, materially assist the listener to an unprejudiced enjoyment of Weelkes's music; but the whole information will be nothing but the sourest scholastic twaddle if we fail to realize that we are here applying it to an art that is of consummate and classical maturity. It can, of course, be applied to archaic and also to decadent works; many works by contemporaries of Weelkes are both. Palestrina was dead three years before Weelkes's *First Set of Madrigals* (called by himself 'the first fruits of my barren ground, unripe in regard of time') appeared in 1597, and the monodists were having everything their own way on the Continent by the time Weelkes died, in 1623. But whatever the historic sources of his ideas and habits, he is a mature artist, and what he chooses to do needs no apology and demands a proper respect for its own intentions. I doubt whether, as a matter of fact, Weelkes took account of contemporary musical revolutions on the Continent, which doubt disposes at once of our fourth heading. As to chromatic experiments, if we compare the superb modulations of *Hence, Care, thou art too cruel* with Lasso's early imitations of Cipriano da Rore, we shall see that, whereas Lasso was quite right in his later contempt for the chromatic style as he knew it, Weelkes is producing a chain of modulations which Schubert or Brahms would have been proud to sign. Such a chain would mean exactly the same in the language of Brahms as in the language of Weelkes, but for the fact that it has far more force against a severely modal background than it can possibly have in the complex luxuries of later music.

It now remains to dispose of (*a*) the use of the ecclesiastical modes with the laws of *musica ficta*, and (*b*) the vicious English taste for false relations. *Three Virgin Nymphs* is Ionian or Hypo- -ionian; and the word 'walking' is rendered conspicuous by the flattening of the B in order to avoid a *quinta falsa* in the harmony. *Thule* is Ionian transposed, its first part closing in transposed Mixolydian. At the word 'wondrous' you will find the same flattened note (E flat this time) as at the beginning of *Three Virgin Nymphs*. *O Care* is Hypodorian transposed, with modulations of unprecedented freedom. Here again the laws of *musica ficta* modify the Dorian scale by providing a 'leading note' and a final major third (*tierce de Picardie*) for the final closes. *Like two proud armies* is Hypo-ionian transposed. Now the more we know about these ancient technicalities, the worse off shall we be if we confuse their grammar with their aesthetics. With great artists like Weelkes, Wilbye, Gibbons, Tallis, and Byrd, these technicalities are the grammatical aspects of aesthetic resources as important as are the principles of fugue and concerto-form to Bach, the principles of sonata form to Beethoven, and the principles of operatic orchestration

to Wagner. But in so far as they are the common property of
every sixteenth-century composer who knew his grammar, they
are neither mysteries nor conventions. In the hands of these great
masters, they are one and all reducible to the fact that while the
use of discord was restricted by a highly sensitive musical-nervous
organization, the possible ways of grouping concords were unre-
stricted by our later demands for a rigid expression of key in
what may be metaphorically called a solid musical perspective.
In other words, the harmony of 'key' had much the same kind
of freedom as the rhythm; and the names of the ecclesiastical
modes are the names of various types to which the harmonic
characteristics correspond. To regard them as archaic shackles
is about as silly as to regard the resources of the Greek verb
and the Aeolic and Ionic dialects as shackles to the inspiration
of Homer. Yet, except for choirs conducted by specialists, few
choral societies show much advance on the standards of 1848,
when an editor of the Musical Antiquarian Society quoted the
wonderful opening of Palestrina's *Stabat Mater* as 'a curious
instance of the uncertainty relative to the scale, prevalent in the
time of the author'.

Ex. 5.

Sta - bat Ma - ter do - lo - ro - sa

There remains only (*b*), the vicious English taste for 'false relations', amounting to actual collisions between sharp and natural
thirds in the same chord. These often really disfigure the works of
a great early master, and more often cause the chief historic interest
and all-pervading ugliness of a dull one. Orlando di Lasso, in other
and later developments of his art one of the greatest of composers,
produced two early books of madrigals that are little more than
solid cakes of false relations. All this does not alter my conviction
that the typical specimen Weelkes gives by way of illustrating
'so deadly dost thou sting me' is a mature stroke of genius.

Ex. 6.

It is not so harsh on voices as it is on the pianoforte, where such things are at their very worst, and it may suffice to show that no amount of historic information can relieve us of the task of taking every detail in such art as that of Weelkes independently on its own merits. It also shows another point, with which we may fitly conclude this introduction to Weelkes, since it is the point which above all others may help us to enjoy him intelligently in bulk and in detail. Classical composers of vocal music, from the sixteenth to the eighteenth century inclusive, have always been inveterate illustrators of the words they set, unless they have, like Pergolesi in his rather overrated *Stabat Mater*, relapsed into convention. Whether conventional or unconventional, their methods of illustration are seldom such as would occur to us nowadays; but while great composers have been pre-eminent among artists in their attainment of the ideal of Art for Art's sake, their attainment has been made the easier and more certain by the naïve way in which they have followed the line of least resistance in using every notion the words, taken both singly and in their context, could suggest for rhythm, harmony, melody, or even (at the expense of everything else) the mere appearance of the written notes.

Many of these points seem grotesque, and the results are not always musical; but on the whole they, like the ecclesiastical modes, are rather the habits that set the true artist free than conventions that shackle him. Here I will confine my illustrations to the texts before us. Every single sentence of *Three Virgin Nymphs* is pictorial. The illustration of 'Three' is obvious,

Ex. 7.

so is the contrivance that explains how three can walk 'all alone'; there is no doubt that Sylvanus is not a virgin nymph, nor that he is rude;

Ex. 8.

Till rude Syl - va - nus chanced to meet them,

there is a certain sense of duty in the cries of 'Ay me' which indicates that the nymphs are not really much afraid of Sylvanus, in spite of the rude way in which he leapt and snatch'd at one;

Ex. 9.

he leapt and snatched at one,

and at last it is not Sylvanus who does most of the calling 'come back again'.

In *Thule* the first word looms in semibreves at the top of the octave as large as Iceland (magnified by the exigencies of Mercator's projection) straddling at the top of the cosmographies of Elizabethan and Jacobean days.

Ex. 10.

Sop. 1.
Thu   le,   Sop. 2.
                        Thu   le,

The   per - iod of   Cos - mo - gra - phy

Many of us can remember Hecla's devastating activities in the 'eighties; and Krakatoa burned more strangely in the same decade than Fogo, and far more to the detriment of the flying fishes. The Fogo of Weelkes's madrigal is probably the one still known by that name in the Cape Verde Islands, which would lie well within the call of an Andalusian merchant returning from India. The climate is such as flying fishes like, and Fogo was active as late as 1688. There is another Fogo in the Azores, which are to this day a region of submarine volcanoes; but this is rather far north for flying fishes, and I doubt whether the Virginian settlers did much trade in cochineal and China dishes. What is quite certain is that Weelkes's strangely burning chromatics are well fitted to express the spacious culture of his adventurous age. And bolder than any of them is the strictly Elizabethan abrupt return to his native Ionian on the word 'amidst'.

These chromatics are entirely different in conception from those
of the wonderful modulations of *Hence, Care, thou art too cruel,*
which are essentially diatonic but remote modulations, expressing
no freak of nature but profound human emotion.

Ex. 12.

On no less lofty a plane is the variety of major and minor
melody and harmony which presents the conventional 'Fa la' burden in every shade of mood from the comic despair of 'oh dear,
oh dear, oh dear' to the tragic pathos afterwards so beautifully
realized by Verdi in Rigoletto's 'la la, la la'.

As to *Like two proud armies*, the points range from trumpet-
calls to the Handelian glory of the end. I must illustrate the bass,
with its impressive 'augmentation' of the theme—

Ex. 13.

WILBYE AND PALESTRINA

CXCVIII. FOUR SIXTEENTH-CENTURY MOTETS

1 *O God, the Rock of my whole strength.*
2 *Paucitas dierum meorum.*
3 *Exaltabo te.*
4 *Dum complerentur dies pentecostes.*

The term 'motet' may be as vague or as precise as the term 'sonata'.
Everything depends on the period and circumstances of the work
described. A 'sonata' in the seventeenth century may be merely

a piece or portion that is 'sounded' on instruments instead of being a piece that is sung, *scilicet* 'cantata'. In the eighteenth century it may still be no more, or it may be anything between a regular suite and a kind of concerto without orchestra. From Mozart's time onwards, it is the most definite and highly organized art-form in the history of music: while at the present day it is one of Humpty Dumpty's words that means whatever he chooses to make it mean. For us, who do not sit upon a wall and who cannot afford to pay our words overtime wages, the best plan is to agree to understand terms of art according to their highest classical usage. Thus the world agrees to understand 'sonata' to mean usually what Beethoven meant by it, the earlier and later usages being far less significant and clear; and thus we ought to understand 'motet' to mean usually what Palestrina meant by it, the etymology of the word being quite obscure and earlier usages being artistically prehistoric, while later usages, even by the time of Bach, are quite capricious.

We are slightly stretching this classical meaning of the word in including Wilbye's composition with its English words; since by our criterion a 'motet' is a composition to a scriptural or liturgical Latin text sung at a particular point in the service of the Mass. This, however, is a question of ritual, not of art. Palestrina's *Exaltabo te* comes from his set of Offertories for the whole year, and the offertory is sung at another point of the service than the motet. But only an exhaustive knowledge of liturgical texts would enable any one to tell an offertory from a motet; and no musical expert is pedantic enough to draw the distinction. Similarly Byrd's *Domine, exaudi me* did not cease to be a motet when it became 'Bow Thine ear'; any more than a selection from an oratorio becomes a complete specimen of an Anglican art-form by being sung in 'Quires and places' when 'here followeth the Anthem'.

The fact is that, just as in the period which comprises Haydn and Beethoven the highest musical art may be said to be in the sonata-style, so in the sixteenth century the highest art is in the motet-style. To this style even the madrigals aspire in their highest flights, though there is a distinct madrigal-style, not artistically lower than the motet-style. But there is no higher or greater form of pure polyphony; even the style of the Mass is decidedly less elaborate, except at its climax in the Sanctus, where it rises to what is indistinguishable from the motet-style. As an art-problem, it is mainly a question of how many words and what kind of sentences the sixteenth-century composer has to deal with. Such a text as *Kyrie eleison: Christe eleison: Kyrie eleison* will give him opportunity, or rather necessity, for expanding the words in something like a fugue-style, but the three sections into which it falls cannot be very long, nor can there be any definite reason for varieties of proportion in the flow of the musical paragraphs. On the other hand, so long a text as the Nicene Creed cannot be treated by the sixteenth-century composer's resources except in a comparatively straightforward declamation of most of its clauses, with few repetitions and, in consequence, only rare and special passages in an elaborately polyphonic style.

The ideal opportunity for the sixteenth-century composer is in such texts, or rather in the combination of these, in all their individual characteristics, with the unchanging order of the Mass, which will harmonize with the motet and throw it into relief. For instance *Dum complerentur* is obviously to be sung on Whitsunday, and for that day Palestrina wrote not only this motet but the *Missa Dum complerentur*, a mass *on the same themes*. This is quite a common case, and one composer might write a mass on another composer's motet. Often both mass and motet were written on themes derived from the Gregorian melodies associated with the words of the motet. Thus the whole musical service became full of old familiar meanings to those who took part in it. Not until Lutheran hymns were worked out in Bach's cantatas do we again find so coherent a scheme in church music. For our immediate purpose one inference may be drawn; a concert performance of a motet without the mass (if there is one) associated with it, is perfectly intelligible; for the mass is always a late and diluted commentary on the motet, though the two together may make a perfect scheme. But a concert performance of the mass without the motet is a set of variations without the theme; though I remember such a performance in London, many years ago, of the *Missa O admirabile commercium*; and the analytical programme had the effrontery to refer to the motet, which not a single person in the audience was ever likely to hear. (I have not heard it yet.)

On the whole I question whether the mass is the right art-form to reveal the Golden Age of Music to concert audiences who are not already familiar with sixteenth-century idioms: it seems better to begin with highly individual texts that express unmistakable moods and meanings. This is the more reasonable since some of the deepest and most devout moods are very rarely admitted into practical church music at all. I doubt whether Palestrina's realization of the ultimate depth of Job's despair has ever been sung in church; though a nineteenth-century successor to Palestrina's official position in Rome, Baini, declared his firm and literal belief that it was divinely inspired. It is impossible to find time in an ordinary church service for such broad contrasts as we can obtain in the concert-room by following *Paucitas dierum* with *Exaltabo te*; and one does not go to church to hear the voice of Job's despair unanswered by the voice from out of the whirlwind.

The best analysis for all sixteenth-century music is that which the words themselves will furnish if we follow them. In the motet-style each clause is given a theme to itself, the treatment of many, but not all, of the themes being more or less like a fugue. But there is no question of the different themes being combined, any more than there is of the different texts being arranged in any but their natural sequence: except that the voices overlap, with words as with themes, so that there is neither awkward stoppage nor any lack of effective articulation. Where you hear a new theme you may expect to hear new words, and vice versa. Where the words admit of expansive repetition they will receive it for their own sake and not for any rigid rules of musical form, though of course the musician has a good deal of choice where the climaxes shall come.

The sixteenth century is that period in which we in Great Britain were indisputably as great in music as any continental nation. If Weelkes may be called a romantic among madrigalists, Wilbye is a classic; though as a matter of fact Weelkes is quite as perfect an artist, and the present specimen of Wilbye's work is a masterpiece of modern power of modulation which the theory of the Church Modes utterly fails to explain. Wilbye's *O God, the Rock of my whole strength* is one of his two contributions to Sir William Leighton's *Tears or Lamentacions of a Sorrowfull Soule*, published in 1614. The text is written in the metre of a certain version of the fiftieth Psalm, and Leighton adds that any Psalm in the same metre can be sung to these motets. This does not prevent Wilbye from making his setting suit the words he has before him: there is not a point on which he does not focus his imagination, from the breadth and firmness of the opening (with the unexpected minor harmonies of 'mine anguish') to the profound modulations and tenderness of the last sentence 'lest that I faint, despair and languish', with its remarkable theme, as clear and distinguished as any theme in a classical symphony.

Ex. 1.

Lest that I faint, de - spair and lan - guish,

Lest that I faint, de - spair and lan - guish,

O God, the Rock of my whole strength,
Let thy sweet mercy salve mine anguish,
And grant me grace, O Lord, at length,
Lest that I faint, despair and languish.

It is no mean source of national pride that this composition is not unworthy to precede Palestrina's sublime song of the despair from which Wilbye prays to be protected.

The text of *Paucitas dierum meorum* is the last three verses of the tenth chapter of the Book of Job with an interpolation from the eighth verse. The Vulgate differs in details from our Authorized Version; and where this is so, I give first a translation of what Palestrina sets, and afterwards the Authorized Version in square brackets. The differences are quite enough to make Palestrina's setting appropriate only to the Vulgate version: e.g. *ut plangam paululum dolorem meum.*

Paucitas dierum meorum finietur brevi:
Dimitte me Domine, ut plangam paululum dolorem meum.

My few days shall soon be finished; [*Are* not my days few? cease *then*], let me go, Lord, that I may bewail my sorrow awhile, [*and* let me alone, that I may take comfort a little].

Ex. 2.

ut   plan - gam   pau - lu - lum do - lo - rem me - um.

Antequam vadam ad terram tenebrosam et opertam mortis caligine.

Before I go to the land of shadows, covered by the darkness of death. [Before I go *whence* I shall not return, *even* to the land of darkness and the shadow of death.]

Ex. 3.

et   o - per - tam   mor - tis   ca - li - gi - ne,

et   o - per - tam   mor - tis   ca - li - gi - ne.

Manus tuae, Domine, fecerunt me et plasmaverunt me totum in circuitu; et sic repente praecipitas me.

Antequam vadam (*da capo*).

Thy hands (O Lord) have made me and fashioned me together round about: and thus thou dost suddenly hurl me down. [yet dost thou destroy me.]
Before I go (*da capo*).

It will be noticed that there is no logical connexion in the words
at the da capo of *Antequam vadam*, &c. This must not be ascribed
to an oversight on the composer's part. The Roman liturgy is full
of such cases: it is not often that a *Responsorium* of which the ver-
sicle that is repeated makes a perfect logical connexion with the
sentence after which it is resumed. Nor is the object or manner of
these utterances any logical narrative: it is something quite as
natural and, rightly understood, more impressive. The stories,
emotions, poetry, prophecies, whatever their form, are all ancient
and ever-present history told by people not bent on giving information, but repeating the familiar words like inspired children,
to whom no impulse is more irresistible than to hark back to just
that point in the story where the *ipsissima verba* (always of inviolable sanctity to children) are most impressive.

After Job's despair, we turn to one of the most famous of
Palestrina's works, the offertorium *Exaltabo te*, for the Eleventh
Sunday after Whitsunday. The much-abused Burney, for all his
insufferable dandified patronage of music prior to the one truly
civilized art of Italian opera, knew how to select the right things
for his *History of Music*; and he saw enough of the splendour of
this composition to score it in the right mode when the source
from which he transcribed it gave it in the wrong. Here again the
words are the best guide; and where, as in the theme of *quoniam
suscepisti me*, you miss the support of rigid modern rhythms, you
have only to forget them, and see for yourself how naturally and
heartily those words are uttered in the rhythm of Palestrina's
music (Ex. 4).

Ex. 4.

quo - ni - am   su - sce - pi - sti   me

The lively flourish on *delectasti*, followed by the weightier rhythm
of *inimicos meos*, has an effect which can be found elsewhere in
Palestrina (notably in the offertorium *Domine, in auxilium*), a subtle
irony towards the enemy who has presumed on divine favour (Ex. 5).

Ex. 5.

nec   de - lec - ta-. . . .

nec   de - lec - ta-. . . .

The main stroke of genius is the entry of the bass on an unexpected chord with the words *Domine, clamavi ad te*—one of the outstanding great moments in classical music.

Ex. 6.

Tenor, imitated by upper voice.

in - i-mi-cos me - os   su - per   me.

Bass.

Do - mi - ne   &c.

Do - mi - ne,   cla - ma - vi ad   te

Exaltabo te, Domine; quoniam suscepisti me, nec delectasti inimicos meos super me.

Domine, clamavi ad te, et sanasti me.

I will extol thee, O Lord; for thou hast lifted me up and hast not favoured my foes before me [hast not made my foes to rejoice over me].

O Lord [my God], I cried unto thee, and thou hast healed me. Ps. xxx. 1, 2.

Yet Palestrina knows of higher joys than this answer to human prayers and triumph over human foes. Like Spinoza, he is God-intoxicated; and the Feast of Pentecost is his spiritual birthday. In *Dum complerentur* there is no attempt at a connected narrative. The cloven tongues of fire are not mentioned, though the last *Alleluia* clearly illustrates them. On the other hand a verse from the Gospel of St. John is interpolated for the sole purpose of making merry over that long-forgotten 'fear of the Jews' which compelled the first Christians to meet like conspirators.

Ex. 7.

pro - pter   me - tum   Ju - dae - o - rum

The Christmas-carol triple rhythm at that point is very characteristic; so is the dramatic and sharply rhythmic simplicity of junctures like *et subito* and *tanquam spiritus*; while nowhere, even in the sixteenth century, has rhythm been led such a whirling dance as in the three *Alleluias*, which are all different from each other and from the rest of the motet.

Ex. 8.

Al - le - lu - ia . . . .

Ex. 9.

Al - le - lu - ia . . . .

Ex. 10.

Al . . . . le . . . . . .

Al . . . . le - lu . . . .

lu . . . . ia.

. . . . ia.

Dum complerentur dies pentecostes erant omnes pariter,	(Acts ii. 1) And when the day of Pentecost was fully come they were all with one accord . . . (saying Alleluia!)
dicentes Alleluia!	
Et subito factus est sonus de coelo :—Alleluia !	2. And suddenly there came a sound from heaven,—(Alleluia!)
tanquam spiritus vehementis, et replevit totam domum. Alleluia!	as of a mighty rushing wind, and it filled all the house . . . (Alleluia!)
Dum ergo essent in unum discipuli congregati, propter metum Judaeorum,	St. John xx. 19. When . . . (therefore) . . . the disciples were assembled together for fear of the Jews,—
sonus repente de coelo, venit super eos;	Acts ii (?) a sound suddenly from heaven came upon them
tanquam spiritus, etc	as of a mighty rushing wind, &c.

J. S. BACH

CXCIX. MASS IN B MINOR

TEXT

As arranged by Bach (hence slight deviations from the English Prayer Book version). With references to the musical examples.

1. KYRIE

1.

Exx. 1–2. *Chorus.* Kyrie eleison.
Exx. 3–4. *Duet.* Christe eleison.
Exx. 5–8. *Chorus.* Kyrie eleison.

Lord, have mercy upon us.
Christ, have mercy upon us.
Lord, have mercy upon us.

2. GLORIA

2.

Ex. 9. *Chorus.* Gloria in excelsis Deo.

Glory be to God on high,

Ex. 10. *Chorus.* Et in terra pax hominibus bonae voluntatis.

and on earth peace to men of good will.

Ex. 11. *Aria.* Laudamus Te; benedicimus Te; adoramus Te; glorificamus Te:

We praise Thee; we bless Thee; we worship Thee; we glorify Thee:

Exx. 12–14. *Chorus.* Gratias agimus Tibi propter magnam gloriam tuam.

we give thanks to Thee for Thy great glory.

Exx. 15–16. *Duet.* Domine Deus, Rex coelestis, Deus Pater omnipotens; Domine Fili unigenite Jesu Christe altissime! Domine Deus, agnus Dei, Filius Patris!

O Lord God, heavenly King, God the Father Almighty; O Lord the only begotten Son, Jesu Christ, most high; O Lord God, Lamb of God, Son of the Father.

Ex. 17. *Chorus.* Qui tollis peccata mundi, miserere nobis: Qui tollis peccata mundi, suscipe deprecationem nostram:

Thou who takest away the sins of the world, have mercy upon us: Thou who takest away the sins of the world, receive our prayer:

Ex. 18. *Aria.* Qui sedes ad dexteram Patris, miserere nobis:

Thou who sittest at the right hand of the Father, have mercy upon us.

Exx. 19–21. *Aria.* Quoniam Tu solus sanctus, Tu solus Dominus, Tu solus altissimus.

For Thou only art holy; Thou only art Lord; Thou only art most high—

Exx. 22–4. *Chorus.* Cum Sancto Spiritu in gloria Dei Patris. Amen.

with the Holy Spirit in the glory of God the Father. Amen.

3. CREDO

3.

Exx. 25–7. *Chorus.* Credo in unum Deum.

I believe in one God,

Exx. 28–9 *Chorus.* Patrem omnipotentem, factorem coeli et terrae, visibilium omnium et invisibilium:

Exx. 30–1. *Duet.* Et in unum Dominum, Jesum Christum, Filium Dei unigenitum, et ex Patre natum ante omnia saecula: Deum de Deo, lumen de lumine, Deum verum de Deo vero genitum, non factum, consubstantialem Patri, per quem omnia facta sunt;

Qui propter nos homines et propter nostram salutem descendit de coelis:

Ex. 32. *Chorus.* Et incarnatus est de Spiritu Sancto ex Maria Virgine, et homo factus est;

Exx. 33–4. *Chorus.* Crucifixus etiam pro nobis sub Pontio Pilato, passus et sepultus est:

Ex. 35. *Chorus.* Et resurrexit tertia die secundum Scripturas; et ascendit in coelum; sedet ad dexteram Patris, et iterum venturus est cum gloria judicare vivos et mortuos, cujus regni non erit finis;

Ex. 36. *Aria.* Et in Spiritum Sanctum, Dominum et vivificantem, qui ex Patre et Filio procedit, qui cum Patre et Filio simul adoratur et conglorificatur; qui locutus est per Prophetas: Et in unam sanctam catholicam et apostolicam ecclesiam.

Exx. 37–9. *Chorus.* Confiteor unum baptisma in remissionem peccatorum, et exspecto—

Exx. 40–2. *Chorus.* resurrectionem mortuorum, et vitam venturi saeculi. Amen.

4. SANCTUS

Ex. 43. *Chorus.* Sanctus, sanctus, sanctus, Dominus Deus Sabaoth.

The Father omnipotent, Maker of heaven and earth, and of all things visible and invisible:

And in one Lord Jesus Christ, the only begotten Son of God, born of the Father before all worlds: God of God, Light of Light, Very God begotten of Very God,* not created, being of one substance with the Father, by Whom all things were made:
Who for us men and for our salvation descended from heaven;

And was incarnate by the Holy Ghost of the Virgin Mary, And was made man,

And was crucified also for us under Pontius Pilate. He suffered and was buried.

And the third day He rose again according to the Scriptures, And ascended into heaven, And sitteth on the right hand of God the Father. And He shall come again with glory to judge both the quick and the dead: Whose kingdom shall have no end.

And I believe in the Holy Ghost, the Lord and Giver of life, Who proceedeth from the Father and the Son, Who with the Father and the Son together is worshipped and glorified, Who spoke by the Prophets: And I believe one Catholic and Apostolic Church.

I acknowledge one Baptism for the remission of sins. And I look for—

the Resurrection of the dead, And the life of the world to come. Amen.

4.

Holy, holy, holy, Lord God of hosts.

* This is according to Bach's punctuation.

Exx. 44–5. *Chorus.* Pleni sunt coeli et terrae gloria ejus.[1]	Heaven and earth are full of His glory.
Exx. 46–9. *Chorus.* Hosanna in excelsis.	Hosanna in the highest.
Aria. Benedictus qui venit in nomine Domini.	Blessed is he that cometh in the name of the Lord.
Hosanna in excelsis, *da capo.*	

5. AGNUS DEI   5

| Exx. 50–1. *Aria.* Agnus Dei qui tollis peccata mundi, miserere nobis. | O Lamb of God, Who takest away the sins of the world, have mercy upon us. |
| Exx. 52–4. *Chorus.* Dona nobis pacem. | Grant us peace. |

The Kyrie and Gloria of this enormous work were sent by Bach to the Kurfürst of Saxony in 1733, with a request to be appointed to his court. The request was not granted until 1736. By 1738 Bach had finished the Mass, but he did not send the rest of it to the Kurfürst, though that prince was a Roman Catholic. According to Lutheran usage a Kyrie and Gloria comprised all the music required for a Mass; and Bach's four short Masses contain nothing else. He accordingly had already given the title of Mass to the portion sent to his prince in 1733. He was evidently not encouraged by its reception, and the four short Masses afterwards written for Dresden contain between them only five movements not known to be arrangements, sometimes very perfunctory and sometimes absurdly inappropriate, from Church Cantatas.

In the B minor Mass itself the adaptations from earlier work begin at the *Gratias*, and become more and more frequent as the Mass proceeds. But it would be a hasty inference from this that Bach lost interest in the work. The Agnus Dei is no mere adaptation of the beautiful aria 'Ach bleibe doch' that has the same ritornello in the Cantata *Lobet Gott in seinen Reichen.* The aria in the cantata is longer by three-eighths, and for two-thirds of its entirety different in material. A new composition could not have cost Bach more trouble than the Agnus Dei. And the changes imply no dissatisfaction with the original aria: they are dictated by the altogether different structure of the new text. The theme common to both compositions remains, because it is the right thing in both places.

The case of the *Dona nobis pacem* is less clear. No doctrinal or symbolical reason can be plausibly given for its being set to the same music as the *Gratias*, and there is a manifest artificiality in singing to a single clause a double fugue whose two subjects were originally made for two clauses. Yet even here there is a certain

---

[1] sic: instead of the liturgical reading *tua*.

fitness in ending with this particular movement. Only in the pure
vocal polyphony of the sixteenth century does a Mass end with
a natural musical finality. As soon as orchestral ideas heighten
the values, the text of this last section of the Mass forms an anti-
climax which only Beethoven, with his living memories of the
bombardment of Vienna, could turn into something vivid. In
the *Gratias* Bach had something at once monumental and quiet,
the recurrence of which would round off his Mass without violence
to the words, but rather with an expression of confidence that
the peace prayed for would be given to those who seek it. And the
fact that the music had been heard more than an hour ago serves
to perfect its finality.

The other known adaptations in the B minor Mass will be discussed as we come to them. Schweitzer points out that though
Bach writes habitually as a Lutheran, there is a vital sense in which
he conceives this Mass as Catholic. But it ought not to be necessary
to point out that if we criticized it from the point of view of the
Roman liturgy we should soon prove that it was wrong from
beginning to end. In some respects it is almost drastically Protestant; most notably in the Sanctus where Bach is himself beating
time to the angels swinging their censers before the Throne, and
has entirely forgotten the awe-struck mortals kneeling in silence
before the miracle which gives them immortality. But surely the
mere scale of the whole work should have sufficed to prevent anybody from imagining that it was part of a church service. Beethoven
could have designed his Mass in D for the successive installation
of two Royal Archbishops instead of one, if he had been allowed
to work on Bach's scale.[1]

Still, we need not add to Bach's inveterate Protestantism the
mere errors of a performance that ignores the divisions of the
text. Nobody need be a liturgiologist to understand musical
settings of the Mass. But what can anybody be expected to understand, who, being brought up in a civilization at least officially
Christian, does not know where the Nicene Creed ends? Bach

---

[1] I should have thought this paragraph comprehensive enough to satisfy
most people. But it has provoked a surprising amount of protest from
critics and private persons who contrast my 'view that Bach shows
Protestant tendencies' with the view of Schweitzer and Terry that he is
illustrating the Church Universal. The objection seems to be based on
two assumptions: first, that 'the ability would warrant' startling supposi-
tions as to Bach's church and Shakespeare's race; secondly, that Protes-
tants, as such, believe themselves to be cut off from the Church Universal.
No such belief is implied in the historic protest that the practices and
doctrines of the Roman Church needed reform. Hence the terms Protestant and Reformation. It is as indisputable that Bach intended to illustrate
the Church Universal as that he also prayed to be 'preserved from the
murderous cruelty, cunning, and arrogance of the Pope and the Turk'.

has taken special pains to show that the *Resurrexit* is not the end: yet his final ritornello, which so carefully takes the edge off the climax of that chorus and leaves us calm enough to resume the doctrinal thread, is often omitted. The omission is a sign that the performance has been undertaken without the faintest idea of what Bach meant by the great group which he entitles *Symbolum Nicenum*. Accordingly we must put in the forefront of our conception of the B minor Mass the fact of its division into the five sections (sometimes called Hymns) of all normal Masses: viz. Kyrie, Gloria, Credo, Sanctus, and Agnus Dei. The Gloria usually follows the Kyrie with little or no pause. A considerable pause should, in this huge work, separate the Gloria from the Credo. An even longer pause is convenient between the Credo and the Sanctus; for the chorus has to regroup itself for the six-part Sanctus and the antiphonal double-choir Hosanna.

With these two intervals the work falls into its natural divisions, none of which is inordinately long or devoid of refreshing contrasts.

A word is needed as to the art-forms prevalent in Bach's choral music. Fugue is, of course, prominent. But it is not in itself so much a form as a texture, like blank verse, hexameters, heroic couplets, *terza rima*, &c. A piece written entirely in fugue is, then, properly called 'a fugue'. But parts of other pieces may be written *in* fugue of a strictness equal to that of the fugues that are nothing else. The main formal element of Bach's choruses is not fugue, for that has little power to determine a form, but the ritornello, such as constitutes the opening of nearly all concerto movements and the instrumental openings of arias. Most of these choruses of Bach which are not entirely in fugue will be found to be concerto-like amplifications of an opening ritornello; and in several cases where no such ritornello appears, its existence in an earlier version of the composition can be either verified or inferred.

Now the naïve listener, if endowed with a quick and retentive memory, is more likely to appreciate the way in which Bach uses ritornello than the listener who knows something about fugue. My own experience is that I discovered many relatively unimportant points in the structure of the B minor Mass before I realized the folly of regarding the ritornellos as merely introductory. This error the naïve listener does not commit; for him the music begins at the beginning, and so he has the better chance of recognizing the beginning when it recurs in a higher light. For this reason my musical examples outline some of the ritornellos, actual and conjectural, in full.

The ritornello gives the form of a concerto to the whole, and recurs, entire or in sections, at each important close, in various keys, until it has buttressed all sides of the edifice; while the fugue-passage corresponds to the special material which the solo player contributes to the concerto. And in most cases we shall find that in the first fugue-passage the voices are unsupported by the orchestra, which either leaves everything to the continuo or has an independent accompaniment, while in the second fugue-passage the orchestra doubles the voices. The same principle is seen in the fugues in the motets for double-chorus; at first one choir sings the fugue against an independent second choir; afterwards the two choirs unite, voice by voice, as the subject enters in each part. Thus with Bach's small choirs the volume of sound regulated itself. With our large choral societies we have to take care lest this natural scheme should be obliterated. And our orchestras are in one sense too small for big choirs; we do not need larger orchestras on the whole, but we need a dozen oboes and a dozen flutes instead of twenty-four players of ten different kinds of instrument. However, there is no harm in throwing clarinets into unison with the oboes in Bach's tuttis. Not even Berlioz or Mahler knew (as Handel knew) what twelve oboes would sound like; but we do know that their tone becomes darker and actually less pungent by multiplication; and we also know that the precise colour is not so much Bach's object as the power of penetrating so that all parts of the polyphony are heard.

1. KYRIE

The first Kyrie of the B minor Mass is so vast that it seems as if nothing could control its bulk; yet the listener needs no analysis to confirm his instinctive impression that it reaches its last note with an astronomical punctuality. The foundation of this impression is that the form is such as will seem ridiculously simple when it is correctly described. Helmholtz has prettily illustrated the capacity of the ear to analyse into component sounds the inextricable complexities of the waves that reach it. All depends on the point of view. If you are bathing in the sea you will not have much success in analysing the corrugations of the wave-fronts that break over your eyes. But if you are looking down on Brodick Bay from the shoulder of Goatfell you will be able to see all the interlockings of waves from wind, tide, steamers, down to the circles radiating from the diving-bird. Bach's ritornello gives us just such a hill-side view of the wave-system of his Kyrie. After setting the standard for scale and style in four mighty introductory bars for full chorus and orchestra, the ritornello begins. Its theme is a fugue-subject, confined at first to the upper voices. The whole matter of the ritornello is entrusted to the wood-wind, oboes d'amore in two parts doubled by flutes, until, towards the end, the basses enter with the subject. Meanwhile the strings have accompanied the whole with a beautiful harmonic halo.

Here is the ritornello—

Ex. 1.
Subject.

The voices enter in the next bar. What will they do with this material? Well, the theme is a fugue-subject; so the five-part chorus begins with a five-part fugue exposition, which necessarily coincides with the ritornello for the first five bars. After this, however, it must diverge, so as to lead to the entries of other voices. The accompaniment is reduced to the two oboes d'amore and the continuo. The last voice to enter is the bass, after an anomalous entry of the first figures in the second soprano. As the bass finishes, the second soprano makes a true entry of the whole subject in the dominant. The orchestra supports this and henceforth the other entries voice by voice until it is supporting the whole chorus. This sixth entry proves to be the beginning of a choral recapitulation of the whole ritornello in the dominant, so that the F sharp minor cadence in bars 9–10 becomes a close in C sharp minor. In the episode the voices add entirely new counterpoints to bars 11–14; a fact which shows the danger of supporting large choirs by small orchestras; for unless the orchestra can assert itself here, the form is lost. At the bar corresponding to 15 the voices reunite with the orchestra and remain reunited until the end of the ritornello.

Now the orchestra has an interlude in which portions of the theme drift in short sequences through various keys, including A major, the only major harmonies in the whole movement. Within eight bars there are four changes of instrumentation. Then the bass enters in the tonic at extreme depth as the beginning of a second exposition of the fugue. The orchestral bass necessarily supports the voice, but the rest of the orchestra is independent, the strings being also independent of the wind. The fugue rises from voice to voice, the tenor being unsupported by the orchestra. But violas support the alto, and violins the first soprano. The last voice to enter is the second soprano; and by entering in the subdominant it inclines the harmonic balance of the whole towards firmly establishing the tonic. The joints of this second fugue are larger than those of the first, and their rhetorical point consists in the advancement of the step marked * in Ex. 1. In the first fugue that step has been pathetically flattened as in Ex. 2 (i). Now it is heightened as in Ex. 2 (ii) and (iii).

Ex. 2.

The natural result of bringing the fifth entry into the subdominant
is that the sixth entry follows in the tonic. It thereupon initiates
a final choral recapitulation of the whole ritornello. No wonder
this huge movement seems after all to end punctually. Notice
that though this form is so absurdly simple, it is so poised that no
human ear can detect the moments when recapitulation begins.
One fugue entry is exactly like another, and, even when marked
by the support of the orchestra, the sixth entry does not immediately give away its secret. Furthermore, there is all the fine
detail, of which Ex. 2 shows the more obvious points.

The *Christe eleison* is a duet for two sopranos, or soprano and
mezzo. The ritornello, given by all the violins of the orchestra—

is on material in which the singers do not share except for one
passage where they use the figure here marked (*a*). For the rest
they are either warbling in thirds with whole-hearted Italian delight
in physical beauty, inspired by Bach's joy in divine glory—

or else pleading in canon—

The second Kyrie is a strict fugue in F sharp minor, in which
the orchestra supports the voices without any independent part
except in the bass. The subject, with its flat supertonic and
diminished third, has a gravity akin to that of the first Kyrie, but
confidence seems to have become stronger.

The small notes indicate the close stretto (or overlap of subject
and answer) in later stages of this fugue. The voices often cross,

producing contrasts of tone which recall certain subtleties in the
styles of Palestrina and Orlando di Lasso.

Ex. 7.

An important imitative episode—

Ex. 8.

adds greatly to the energy of the whole, especially as it is never
brought into combination with the main theme.

And so the first division of the Mass ends in F sharp minor
instead of B minor. From this point onwards neither B minor nor
any other minor key is the fundamental key of the Mass. Everything henceforth is grouped about D major.

2. GLORIA

CHORUS. *Gloria in excelsis Deo.*

Trumpets announce a jubilant ritornello theme beginning
thus—

Ex. 9.

The structure is clear and four-square; nor do the voices obscure
it when they enter and begin it in the tonic in order to lead to
the dominant and, after a short interlude, restate it there. The
completion of a symmetrical design follows, and the movement
closes into something very different but not less joyful. In solemn
sequences the massed voices enter into dialogue with divers
sections of the orchestra in modulations that range over the

darker keys beyond the subdominant, closing into the supertonic minor. Then the orchestra alone carries the sequences into higher regions over a deep pedal and eventually closes in B minor. The figure of these sequences now takes shape as a glorious fugue-subject announced by the first soprano.

Ex. 10.

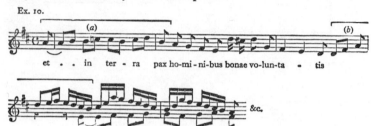

et . . in ter - ra pax ho-mi-ni-bus bonae vo-lun-ta . tis

Before the alto enters with the answer the soprano has begun a florid countersubject, as shown in the quotation. The five voices enter in an exposition which is quite regular until the fifth entry. This, in the second soprano, is a note too high, which lands us in E minor. Thence the initial figure of the first countersubject (*b*) modulates in dialogue with the orchestra, which had hitherto been accompanying the fugue with staccato chords. The former introductory sequences on figure (*a*) of the main theme are now resumed, while the trumpets watch like the kings who

> sate still with awful eye,
> As if they surely knew their sovran Lord was by.

The sequences drift into the whole theme in the tonic. Soprano and alto, disengaging themselves from the full chorus, resume the fugue which is now supported by the orchestra. This time the fifth entry is in its proper tonic position. The episodic sequences follow, in stronger and more tonic positions, until two final entries of the whole subject (alto in dominant, second soprano, and trumpet in tonic) conclude the movement.

ARIA. *Laudamus te*, for Mezzo-Soprano with Violin Solo.

What Schweitzer calls Bach's joy-motives, both rhythmic and melodic, abound in this florid air, which almost anticipates Haydn in its conviction that God will not be angry at being praised cheerfully.

Ex. 11.

The solo movements in the B minor Mass are particularly varied in the relation between the voices and the ritornello. Whereas in the *Christe* the voices were almost entirely independent, here the singer combines new matter most deftly and unexpectedly with that of the solo violin. And as there are no middle sections and da capos in the B minor Mass (unless you count the ritual repetition of the Hosanna), so there are no miscalculations as to the length of these things which Bach has to write out in full. The solos end as punctually as the choruses.

The *Gratias* is a transcription of the first chorus of the cantata *Wir danken dir, Gott* written for the Sunday preceding the municipal elections (Rathswahl) in 1731. As the German text means precisely the same as the Latin, no doubt can exist as to the fitness of the music for its present position. The chorus is a strict fugue in stretto throughout. The orchestra supports the voices (written in four parts), but the trumpets add a fifth and sometimes a sixth part. The fugue-subject is one of the oldest in all music.

Ex. 12.

Gra - - - - ti - as a - - - gi - mus ti - bi

The asterisks mark the points at which answers can overlap. The second clause, *propter magnam gloriam tuam*, has a theme of its own—

Ex. 13.

prop - ter mag - nam glo - - - - - - - ri - am tu - am

which enters as soon as the bass has taken breath after announcing the first subject. It is likewise in close stretto. The first subject is then resumed, with a new rhetorical point in the widening of its main leap.

Ex. 14.

Then the second, or notes to that effect, is combined with it. But such a combination is not the main business of this fugue, and the subjects continue to prefer to develop alternately. So, after an effective counterdevelopment of *propter magnam gloriam* led by the soprano, the real business begins when no less than thirteen entries of the first subject, all on tonic and dominant are piled up without intermission, the trumpets providing the 8th and 9th entries in extra parts. This I believe to be Bach's record in such edifices. The nearest approach to this that I can recollect is a pile of eight overlaps in the first fugue of the Forty-eight.

The second subject reasserts itself after the 13th entry has boomed in the bass, and then a shortened stretto ends the fugue. Small wonder that it should prove a fitting and majestic prayer for peace (why not say peace with honour?) at the end of the Mass.

DUET, for Soprano and Tenor. *Domine Deus.*

The ritornello is for flute in dialogue with muted strings. A later version, in a Latin church cantata (known as Church Cantata No. 191) comprising three numbers of the Gloria (*Gloria in excelsis,* the present movement, and the *Cum Sancto Spiritu*), shows that all the flutes should play. So does the autograph of the Mass.

Ex. 15.

The voices stand in a novel relation to the ritornello, giving a kind of free augmentation of its theme.

Ex. 16.

By a happy device each voice sings a different clause; thus already emphasizing the unity of the Father and Son, which is to be more precisely illustrated in the Credo. They interchange parts, so that no word fails to rise to the surface. A middle section in E minor and B minor deals with the clauses *Domine Deus, Agnus Dei, Filius Patris,* and, by its minor tonality and more supplicating tone, prepares for the *Qui tollis.* Bach is undisturbed by the conscientious scruple which in many other works compels him to complete the design by a da capo, sometimes (as in the Cantata *Es erhub sich ein Streit*) even to the detriment of the sense. Whether a movement closes in its own tonic or leads elsewhere, all the single sections of the B minor Mass are subordinate parts of the five great groups. In the Latin cantata this movement is set to the words *Gloria Patri et Filio et Spiritu Sancto* and has no middle section. In the Mass the *Qui tollis* enters on the fourth beat of the last oar of the middle section; a point very inadequately displayed in the Bachgesellschaft edition, but conspicuous in the autograph.

CHORUS. *Qui tollis.*

The *Qui tollis* is a four-part chorus in B minor, in almost strict canon, with two other florid parts, also freely canonic, for flutes.

Ex. 17.

It is an arrangement of the first movement of the Cantata (46)
Schauet doch und sehet, transposed from D minor and with its
sixteen bars of opening ritornello omitted. In the Cantata it leads
to a great fugue in quicker time. The appropriateness of the music
to its new environment is obvious. What better expression can be
found for the burden of the sins of the world than that which was
designed for the words 'Behold and see if there be any sorrow like
unto My sorrow'?

ARIA, for Alto, with Oboe d'amore. *Qui sedes.*

The words *qui sedes ad dexteram Patris* elicited from Beethoven a tremendous shout, followed by utter collapse. Bach does
not here lift his eyes up to the Throne; his prayer arises from its
native humility and needs no reminder of the insignificance of man.
Widor has finely commented on the delicious notes of the oboe
d'amore, and Schweitzer is characteristically illuminating as to the
gestures of submission in the theme.

Ex. 18.

ARIA, for Bass, with Horn and Bassoons. *Quoniam tu solus sanctus.*

This aria presents extraordinary difficulties in the management
of the continuo; for all the instrumental parts are low, so that the
accompaniment must lie for the most part above them. Nothing
can be more delicious than the colour of the opening—

Ex. 19.

but in the long run it is apt to become indistinct. To disagree
with Schweitzer is dangerously like disagreeing with Bach. But
I have doubts about Schweitzer's suggestion that violoncellos
should join with and sometimes relieve the bassoons, though I
gladly take advantage of a similar device in the *Et in Spiritum
Sanctum* suggested by a note in a strange hand in the autograph.
The bassoon has peculiar acoustic properties. I find that the
violoncello always sounds as a bass to the bassons, even when,
as in bar 3 of Ex. 1, it goes above them. The wind instrument is
more vocal than the stringed, and no voice can ever make a bass to
an instrument. Mozart wrote a sonata for violoncello and bassoon,
and invariably treated the violoncello as the bass, though the
bassoon can go lower. In this *Quoniam* distinctness can be attained
by two precautions. First, the bassoon theme must always be
brought out as a main theme and not treated as an accompaniment.
Secondly, the double-basses must never play with the violoncellos.
The ritornellos may be supported by double-basses without violoncellos, and the vocal passages by violoncellos without double-
basses. The pianoforte (or harpsichord if available) is better for
filling out the harmony here than any stop of the organ. Otherwise Schweitzer relieves a strain on my conscience by his conclusion that Bach required no other keyed instrument than the
organ for his continuo. Nevertheless it is a great convenience to
have something for the purpose that is not a wind instrument.
The voice only dimly alludes to Ex. 19, and derives most of its
material from the next bars.

Ex. 20.

Its own first theme is new.

Ex. 21.

Quo - ni - am tu so - - lus sanc - tus, tu so - lus

sanc - tus, tu   so - lus Do - mi - nus.

CHORUS. *Cum Sancto Spiritu*

The *Quoniam* closes into the final chorus of the Gloria. I am
as sure as I can be of anything that this is an arrangement of a

lost work, and that voices have been adapted to its opening
ritornello, which I conceive to have originally taken the following
shape—

Ex. 22.

continue developing (c)
and (b)

&c.

It is much easier to see how the present result could have been
reached by adding voices to the first and later statements of a formal
ritornello-scheme, than to imagine how the scheme thus modified
could have occurred to Bach at all as a direct setting of the words.
Besides, we see the process in all its stages in the last movement of
the Credo. In the Latin cantata Bach carries the evolution of the
Cum Sancto Spiritu a stage farther. Adapting it to the words,
Sicut erat in principio, &c., he is obliged to add a bar, with a new
figure, at symmetrical distances in his ritornello. In the unknown
original chorus, the vocal theme, represented as follows in the
Mass—

Ex. 23.

Cum Sanc-to   Spi - ri - tu

was probably identical with figure (*a*) in Ex. 22. From the ritor-
nello-material emerges a very energetic fugue—

Ex. 24.

in the treatment of which a salient feature is the frequent anticipa-
tion of its subject in other voices a beat before and a beat behind
the real entries. As usual, the first exposition of this fugue is unsupported by the orchestra. In the Mass the accompaniment is
merely the continuo; but in the Latin cantata Bach afterwards
added a most delightful independent accompaniment mainly
derived from the first notes of the fugue theme. This accompaniment ought unquestionably to be used in performances of the
Mass; it greatly enhances the force of the rhythm, it is full of colour,
and it is quintessentially Bach.

As usual, after the ritornello has intervened in other keys, the
fugue is resumed with the voices doubled by the orchestra, until
everything merges into the framework of Ex. 22 beginning at its
fifth bar.

3. CREDO

CHORUS

Gevaert is unquestionably right in saying that, before the chorus
begins the great Mixolydian fugue with which Bach opens his
setting of the Nicene Creed, a bass voice (or voices) should pronounce its immemorial theme on A, as the priest would intone it
in the service of the Mass. The chorus will thus begin with the
answer. The theme is perhaps the most pregnant of all Gregorian
tones, as it obviously ought to be.

Ex. 25.

Bach treats it as a seven-part fugue over a bass that is in perpetual motion of steady crotchets such as students practise in the
'third species of counterpoint'—thus once more showing the truth
of the modern poet's dictum that 'All is not false that's taught in
public schools'. Of the seven parts in the fugue five are vocal,

and the other two are violin parts differing from the vocal ones only in their higher range. Again I find myself unconvinced by Schweitzer's argument that here and in the *Confiteor* the voices ought to be supported by other instruments besides the organ. Within the ritornello choruses it is self-evident that the structure is actually conditioned by the contrast between unsupported fugue-passages and fugue-passages doubled by orchestra; and I can see no reason, except practical makeshift, why such a contrast should not extend to whole movements in juxtaposition. And a movement like this Mixolydian Credo returns to an old practice of Schütz a century earlier. Schütz would have called each of these violin parts a *Vox Instrumentalis*, and would have written the words under it, not without care as to the division of syllables!

Bach discovers in this Gregorian tone many possibilities of stretto, mostly at strange intervals such as the second. The asterisks in Ex. 25 show where answers overlap the subject, and Ex. 26 shows the archetype of the later stretti.

Ex. 26.

The stretti culminate in a blaze of polyphony over an augmentation of the theme in the vocal bass (the orchestral bass never ceases its march in crotchets). Counting one entry in 6ths as double, and counting also those syncopated entries that have to avoid collisions by clipping a note here and there, the other voices and violins give no less than seven entries of the theme while this augmentation is proceeding. Here is a reduction of the whole stretto, divested of the bar-lines which, in the score, lie across the rhythm and so obscure the reader's view.

Ex. 27.

This Mixolydian fugue serves as introduction to another fugue in plain D major and lively rhythm, freely accompanied by the orchestra. In order to follow the previous Mixolydian close this fugue has to begin with its answer—

Ex. 28.

Pa - trem om - ni - po - ten - tem, fac - to - rem coe - li et ter - rae,

which, led by the bass, is masked by shouts of *Credo in unum Deum* from the other voices. The tenor responds with what is the real subject; and from this point the movement is bar for bar identical with the first chorus of the Church Cantata *Gott, wie dein Name* (171). Here is the theme of the cantata, from which may be seen how subtly and skilfully Bach fits his declamation to the matter in hand. The downward 7th on *omnipotentem* is the very reason why that word coheres and sounds powerful; but it originated in a detached top note which exactly gave the syntactical force of 'so'.

Ex. 29.

Gott, wie dein Na - me so   ist auch dein Ruhm bis an die Welt En - de

The orchestra soon merges into the voice-parts, to which a trumpet adds a fifth part, again happily adapting the theme to its own special needs.

Bach does not check the festive energy in order to express any sense of awe at *et invisibilium*. The *piano*, which many editors insert near the end, is doubtless intended to repair the result of Bach's inattention; but you really cannot ask three trumpets and a kettle-drum to express invisibility by hammering a low D with a lively rub-a-Dub-a-dub-a-DUB!

DUET, for Soprano and Alto. *Et in unum Dominum.*

For Bach to write in free canon is no more remarkable than for Milton to write in blank verse. Hence it would have cost him more effort to avoid illustrating than to illustrate, as he does, the unity of the Father and Son by a canonic theme.

Ex. 30.

This 'neither confounds the Persons nor divides the substance', for the figure that is detached in one voice is slurred in the other!

In a footnote to his delightful essay on Handel the late Lord Balfour gently twits Bach on the quaintness of his symbolism, and supposes that if the whole Trinity had had to be represented Bach would have written a canon three in one in the unison. I cannot at present remember any such illustration of the Trinity by Bach; but Palestrina's Mass *Sanctorum meritis* is entirely permeated by a canon three in one in three tenor parts which are displayed by themselves at *Pleni sunt coeli et terra*. But the canon is not in the unison; it illustrates the *Filioque* clause, and is in the second and third, as '*proceeding* from the Father and the Son'. This is all very quaint, but it does not prevent *Sanctorum meritis* from being among Palestrina's finest works.

Bach's *Et in unum Dominum* illustrates yet more points. What is the meaning of this new feature in the strings after the words *de Deo vero*?

Ex. 31.

At present, nothing in particular; nor can we find any reason but the convenience of a musical pattern why these words, together with *per quem omnia facta sunt*, should be set in a minor key. But the words beginning with *qui propter nos homines* remind us of the Divine Love that endured unspeakable sorrows for our salvation, and so there is no difficulty in seeing why the music here, returning to the home tonic, closes in the minor mode, almost abruptly and with deep pathos. And now we find that Ex. 31 means *descendit de coelis!* So here we have the not uncommon case of a salient detail the meaning of which does not appear until it is heard for the second time. The converse case is equally unobjectionable; if a detail originally illustrated certain precise words, that is no reason why it should not recur symmetrically when those words are no longer present—unless, of course, the ideas are incompatible. Now the *Et in unum* movement originally showed this converse case. As first written it got through the words more quickly, and had reached *qui propter nos homines* where we now have *Deum de Deo*, &c. And so *descendit de coelis* was represented *in situ* by Ex. 31. Then the present return to G major and minor was the *Incarnatus*, the second instrumental descent being now appropriately reminiscent. There is something to be said for returning to Bach's original distribution of the words and over-riding his evident conscientious objection to singing the *Incarnatus* clause in two different settings. But I confess to feeling the force of Bach's scruple.

CHORUS. *Et incarnatus est.*

It is not surprising that Bach came to think it a mistake to include the *Incarnatus* as a mere final section of this duet. This mistake he promptly repaired by setting this central doctrine to a chorus which for simplicity, depth, and mystery cannot be surpassed, though different achievements (such as Beethoven's) may have equal claims to reverence. A violin figure hovers like the Spirit of God moving on the face of the waters, while the orchestral bass throbs slowly and the voices work out a symmetrical movement on imitative sequences of a simple chord-theme, the bottom note of which is often quite other than what we expect.

CHORUS. *Crucifixus*

The first known mention of this wonderful movement is in a letter from Beethoven to his publisher Tobias Haslinger, asking him for any choruses by Bach that can be procured, especially a *Crucifixus* which is said to be very remarkable and to be founded on 'a basso ostinato—like you!' Here Beethoven gives the bass of Bach's *Crucifixus* in F sharp minor, a tone too high. I do not know whether Haslinger was able to send Beethoven the *Crucifixus*; certainly Beethoven never saw the rest of the Mass, nor any of Bach's choral works.

It is evidently a mistake to suppose that any number of such adaptations as this *Crucifixus* could prove that Bach was losing interest in the composition of the B minor Mass. Not all his adaptations are successful or justifiable; but he spent quite as much pains and often as much original inspiration over adaptations as over new works. The original version of the *Crucifixus* is the first chorus of the Cantata *Weinen, Klagen, Sorgen, Zagen* (12), where it is in F minor, and has a middle section without use of the ground-bass. The ground is in minims, which Bach subdivides into crotchets in the Mass, thus producing a more emotional throb. The chromatic descent is Bach's typical motive of grief: it is older than its well-known appearance in Purcell's lament of

Dido, and it is conspicuous in Bach's early *Capriccio on the departure of a beloved brother.*

Ex. 33.

The instrumentation in the Mass is beautified by the antiphonal use of flutes; and a first instrumental statement of the 4-bar ground-period has been added. The voice-parts are hardly altered more than is necessary for the new rhythm of the words. But instead of the final tonic close, Bach is inspired with one of the greatest of all his strokes of genius in the unexpected modulation to G major with a cadence of immeasurable depth.

Ex. 34.

CHORUS. *Et resurrexit*

The resurrection is proclaimed in a phrase of which Schweitzer specially commends the declamation. Nevertheless I believe he would readily entertain the supposition that there is a lost original work behind this chorus. The ritornello I believe to have run more or less as follows:

Ex. 35.

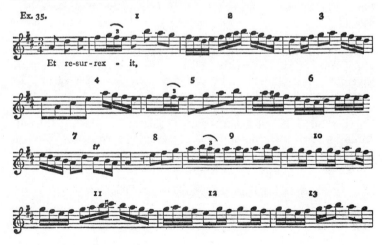

probably longer by 4 bars between 16 and 17

There is no fugue (unless you count a few imitative coloraturas) in this chorus, which perhaps was originally much more formal than it appears now. The passage *et iterum venturus est* I believe to be intended here for a solo voice; and I should expect that the original words would give an excellent reason why this passage was so treated. The autograph is absolutely clear that the accompaniment is *piano*, a nuance which is meaningless here except in relation to a solo voice. As if to give a new musical explanation of the words *non erit finis* Bach concludes with no less than twenty bars of instrumental ritornello, some of it ostentatiously lightly scored. Here again I should expect the original words to show why bars 9–15 of Ex. 35 have hardly any bass. The word *coelum* does not suffice to explain this, for Bach's heaven always rests on a very solid foundation.

I have already given my reasons for considering it a blunder of the first magnitude to omit this ritornello. It is Bach's first step in surmounting the most unmusical part of the Nicene Creed. After we have been stirred to the depths by those miracles of Christianity which all can recognize though none can pretend to understand, we now are asked to find music for the controversial points that were settled at Nicaea by the theologians. For the musician there are several solutions of this really appalling problem. The easiest is to set everything to equally attractive music, as Palestrina set 'Here beginneth the first chapter' and the letters of the Hebrew alphabet, and as Mozart often set all the words of the Mass (including caricatures of the pronunciation of his clerical friends) to equally attractive clichés of opera buffa. The most ingenious method is that by which Beethoven marches to Zion through all these clauses with enthusiastic shouts of 'Credo! Credo!' over the monotone of the lower voices. The most interesting method is that of Ethel Smyth's Mass in D, which is the only Mass I know which might illustrate Manning's aspiration to repair his earlier neglect of the Holy Ghost in his preaching and meditation.

ARIA for Bass.   *Et in Spiritum Sanctum*

Bach's method is more definite than Palestrina's, and more decorous than Mozart's; but in essentials it agrees with both these masters. If doctrine is beyond musical illustration, let us illuminate it with musical decoration. The ritornello of the *Resurrexit* has reduced the emotional tension till we are well in the mood to listen to the most graceful music Bach can give us. Schweitzer regards the key-word of this aria as *vivificantem*; and his explanation amply suffices to justify Bach in his ways here. Who could have thought that the jangle of such Latin as **unam Catholicam et Apostolicam Ecclesiam** could have produced such music?

Ex. 36.

In the autograph a note in a strange handwriting suggests two solo violins as an alternative to the two oboes d'amore. I find that great relief is given to players and listeners by assigning the accompaniment of the vocal passages to the violins and giving the oboes only the ritornellos, with an occasional overlap.

CHORUS. *Confiteor unum baptisma*

Now we draw towards the real climax of the Creed; that which concerns our means of salvation. Bach was too severely orthodox a theologian to dream of concealing the 'acknowledgement of baptism' perfunctorily beneath shouts of 'credo', as Beethoven conceals it. The baptism is the means of the remission of sins; and means and end have each their own theme, first stated separately and afterwards in combination. Here is the combination—

Ex. 37.

Con - fi - te - or, con - fi - - te - or
in re - mis - si - o - - nem pec - ca - to - - rum

Those who are curious in such matters may like to know that this combination is interchangeable in peculiar ways, viz. at the 11th and 13th, besides the usual inversion at the octave. The asterisks show the points at which the themes can be answered in stretto. The orchestral bass is largely independent of the vocal bass, and moves for the most part in crotchets, but not with the perpetual movement of the *Credo in unum Deum*. The resources of the fugue are unfolded steadily. At a certain point the orchestral bass may be heard to pause on the dominant; without however interrupting the flow of the fugue, which continues while we become aware that the text is being declaimed in Gregorian tones by the vocal bass with the alto in canon. Ex. 37 shows the version of this in the second Credo as given in the *Liber Usualis* now issued according to the practice of Solesmes.

Ex. 38.

Con - fi - te - or   u - num bap-tis - ma   in re-mis - si - o - nem pec - ca - to - rum

This differs but slightly from what Bach had before him, which he represents thus—

Ex. 39.

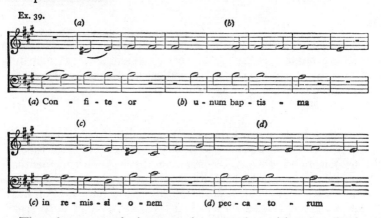

(a) Con - fi - te - or   (b) u - num bap - tis - ma

(c) in re - mis - si - o - nem   (d) pec - ca - to - rum

Then the tenors take it up, not in canon, but with notes of twice the length. The fugue has not come to the end of its resources when the tenors have finished. But suddenly a veil of awful mystery is drawn. Bach's modulations are normally confined to a narrow range of five very directly related keys. Outside this there is a large region which Haydn and Beethoven explored thoroughly, and Beethoven's range extends to a kink in harmonic space. But when Bach goes outside his narrow range he never anticipates Beethoven in treating remoter keys as related; he always heads abruptly to wherever the kink in harmonic space can be found; in other words, he modulates enharmonically. The veil of death is not all darkness to the eye of faith; but the light which shines through it deepens its mystery.

Bach sets the words *Et expecto resurrectionem mortuorum* to
slow modulations each one of which comes as a shock to all
smaller expectations. In the copy of the Bachgesellschaft score
in the Reid Library this page is marked in Oakeley's handwriting
with the words 'This might be engraved on Bach's monument'.

The general trend of the modulations follows a more or less
continual slow descent of the bass.

CHORUS. *Et expecto resurrectionem*

Suddenly the expectation rises from awe to rapture, and
trumpets proclaim the ascension of ransomed souls. The final
chorus of the Credo is another adaptation so ingenious that,
although now widely recognized as such, it escaped the notice of
several Bachgesellschaft editors, including the one who edited
the Cantata *Gott, man lobet Dich in der Stille* (129), of which this
chorus was the original number. It was a very formal and festive
affair with a square-cut opening ritornello, fully repeated as a
closing ritornello, followed by a middle section, and a da capo
in full with both ritornellos.

Here is the original ritornello as in the cantata—

Ex. 40.

In the Mass the notation is *alla breve* in bars of half the length.
The whole chorus in the Mass takes 105 bars which correspond
to 53 of the cantata, or less than twice the ritornello as given in

Ex. 40. Yet Bach has twice inserted 8 new bars, equal, each time, to 4 in the cantata! Clearly then his procedure is extremely terse. Much of the vocal material is new, and the chorus is in five parts instead of four; but the following examples show the two *attacco* themes that have been taken from the cantata and adapted freely to the new words.

And now we learn how to achieve finality. The opening ritornello had been combined with voices and then shortened: the closing ritornello does not exist, though the chorus quotes its last bars (Ex. 40, half-bars 27–28--29). But these it ends quite abruptly with a crotchet, corresponding to a quaver of the original. The finality of the effect is absolute. And with this clear proof that Bach achieved such results with deliberate intention, we may perhaps begin to see the folly of supposing that we can treat him as a formalist.

4. SANCTUS

SIX-PART CHORUS. *Sanctus*

Bach is here conducting the angelic hosts. The strings represent the swinging of censers: the various antiphonal sections of the choir sing to each other like the two seraphim so often represented in the finest sixteenth-century motets for Trinity Sunday on the text that comprises that pious fraud about the Three Witnesses. The threefold 'Trisagion' is well displayed in the theme.

The basses move in giant strides under the mighty sustained chords and rolling themes of the other voices. The architecture is not founded on a ritornello, but is more like that of a great arpeggio prelude, or such a movement as the Organ Toccata in F.

Suddenly the chorus breaks into a new movement in shorter bars.

CHORUS. *Pleni sunt coeli*

This chorus is a fugue with a countersubject that is capable, together with the subject, of being doubled in 3rds.

Ex. 44.

Ple - ni sunt coe-li et ter-rae glo - - - ri - a . . e - jus

Already near the beginning Bach saves time by bringing on two voices at once. Such combinations give rise to great variety of tone-colour according as the themes interlock, or the 3rds become 6ths, or move wide apart. Here, for example, is a position with a trumpet in 3rds removed by three octaves from the bass, while some inner voices move in close 3rds.

Ex. 45.

Another resource is a stretto of the main theme at one bar's distance. An autograph sketch of the theme in crotchets instead of quavers shows that the tempo should be majestic.

DOUBLE CHORUS. *Hosanna in excelsis*

The Hosanna follows immediately. It is an eight-part chorus in double choirs, with the orchestra as a third choir. Bach had just written it as the opening chorus of an Accession-day Cantata for His Majesty Augustus of Saxony, who paid him no less than 50 thalers for the whole cantata. Beyond omitting the opening symphony Bach found few details to alter in turning this into a Hosanna. The scheme, with voices and instruments entering in antiphonal song and dance in all manner of groupings, is better suited to the heavenly hosts than to the poor mortals to whom Bach was beholden for fifty thalers and a court title. The opening displays the antiphonal groupings well. It also contains Bach's only two notes of *genuine* unaccompanied chorus!

Ex. 46.

O - san - na, O - san - na

Another important theme is treated more or less fugally, and runs thus—

Ex. 47.

Meanwhile the trumpet-like hosannas continue, in trumpets and voices; making at one point the following rhetorical climax—

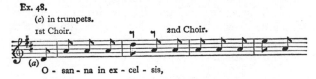

Ex. 48.
(c) in trumpets.
1st Choir.   2nd Choir.

O - san - na in ex - cel - sis,

One of the rare *pianos* which Bach allows to interrupt his jubilation greatly enhances the joyousness of the whole by providing an effect of distant echo. Much as I admire the Hosanna, and perfect as I find it in its place, I can by no means agree with those critics who see in it the climax of the whole Mass. That position I would assign to the Sanctus, if such questions were not vexatious. The Hosanna I regard rather as a deliberate step towards the anticlimax which is inevitable in every orchestral Mass, and which therefore must be made artistically intelligible. Moreover, Bach himself wishes to proceed to the Benedictus, and he therefore retains the final ritornello of the Hosanna though he had deprived it of the introductory one. Before the Benedictus, then, this ritornello should be retained. After the Benedictus the Hosanna is to be repeated. This, perhaps, is a liturgical rather than a musical necessity. But if the Hosanna is repeated, then its effect need not again be weakened by this final ritornello.

ARIA for Tenor. *Benedictus*

Schweitzer finds the declamation of the Benedictus rather artificial, and suspects it of being another adaptation from a lost original. I have heard the voice-part sung too beautifully to leave any trace of artificiality in its declamation. There is no clue as to what the accompanying instrument should be. No one seems to have questioned the decision of the Bachgesellschaft editor that such beautiful music must be for the violin. But I have grave suspicions of violin music that never goes below the compass of the flute, and I do not see any unmistakable violin figure in it, while any of Bach's slow flute solos in minor keys will present constant resemblance to its turns of phrase. Here is its theme, which begins violinistically enough, but is not even there unlike flute music, while the violin character soon disappears. Modern prejudice is sceptical of the flute as an emotional instrument; but this music expresses far more on the flute than on the violin.

Ex. 49.

V. AGNUS DEI

ARIA for Alto. *Agnus Dei*

Of the Agnus Dei in relation to its origin I have already spoken. Here is its main theme with indications in small notes where the cantata version differs—

Ex. 50.

And here is the new theme with which the voice begins—

Ex. 51.

Bach shows no consciousness that the Agnus Dei is properly a threefold petition, twice with *miserere nobis*, and the third time with *Dona nobis pacem*.

CHORUS. *Dona nobis pacem = Gratias agimus tibi*, &c.

Listen to this for its own sake, and you will find it a worthy and peaceful close to Bach's Mass in honour of the Divine Glory.

CC. MÁGNIFICAT

1. *Chorus.* Magnificat anima mea Dominum.
2. *Aria* (Soprano II). Et exsultavit spiritus meus in Deo salutari meo.
3. *Aria* (Soprano I). Quia respexit humilitatem ancillae suae: ecce enim ex hoc beatam me dicent—
4. *Chorus.*—omnes generationes.
5. *Aria* (Bass). Quia fecit mihi magna qui potens est: et sanctum nomen ejus.
6. *Duet* (Alto and Tenor). Et misericordia ejus a progenie in progenies timentibus eum.
7. *Chorus.* Fecit potentiam in brachio suo: dispersit superbos mente cordis sui.
8. *Aria* (Tenor). Deposuit potentes de sede, et exaltavit humiles.
9. *Aria* (Alto). Esurientes implevit bonis: et divites dimisit inanes.
10. *Trio* or *Semi-chorus* (Soprano I, II, and Alto). Suscepit Israel puerum suum, recordatus misericordiae suae.
11. *Chorus.* Sicut locutus est ad patres nostros: Abraham et semini ejus in saecula.
12. *Chorus.* Gloria Patri, et Filio, et Spiritui Sancto: sicut erat in principio, et nunc, et semper, et in saecula saeculorum. Amen.

Bach's *Magnificat* is one of his most comprehensively representative works. From it almost any point in Bach's treatment of words, of musical forms, and of instruments can be brilliantly illustrated. Opinions may differ as to whether it is a representative setting of the Song of the Virgin Mary, or whether that question is important to Bach-lovers. One of the greatest of these, my beloved master Hubert Parry, complained almost angrily that there is nothing feminine in it. On the other hand, a not less impassioned Bach-lover, Widor, quotes the aria *Quia respexit* as a perfect example of the exquisite femininity of the oboe d'amore, inspired by Bach's treatment of the words. And perhaps Bach's defence would be that in setting each verse as a complete sound-picture, he cannot be limited by the consciousness that the words were first pronounced by a woman.

Certainly a feminine treatment of 'He hath shewed strength with His arm' would be disastrous on a large scale. Parry, setting the *Magnificat* as a single design, can retain throughout these words the note of the Virgin adoring the remote power as well as the intimate mercy. In other words, Parry can dramatize the whole text in such a way as to relegate the illustration of its details to a subordinate place.

It is therefore beside the mark to complain that Bach forgets that it was a woman who first sang the words that he illustrates according to their substance. Where the substance and subject are feminine, as in *Quia respexit humilitatem ancillae suae*, he is feminine enough; and it is no mere coincidence that the first words of the whole work are given to the sopranos and altos. Nor is it without conscious purpose that the aria, *Et exsultavit*, as well as the *Quia respexit*, is for a soprano voice. And nobody can mistake the purpose of the stupendous chorus, *Omnes generationes*. The more we emphasize the weight of that chorus, the more deeply do we feel moved at the thought of the innocent singer whom all generations call blessed. With this chorus Bach passes, by a stroke of something akin to dramatic genius, beyond the range of dramatization; and, as if to emphasize this, he sets the next words ('for He that is mighty hath magnified me'—*fecit mihi magna*: 'hath done great things for me') as an aria for a bass voice. One reason for this is that he happened to have five solo singers who each required an aria: another reason is that the aspect of the text that he is illustrating is that of '*qui potens est*'.

It will now be convenient to describe the work theme by theme. As Bach's *Magnificat* is an original work, with no antecedents set to other texts, we shall find Bach's musical symbolism here in its quaintest and most powerful forms. Bach took it for granted, and did not attach to it anything like the importance it is apt to assume in the minds of readers who learn of its rediscovery to-day. Good music was to him a thing that could be used to any good new purpose, regardless of what its details may have symbolized in their first setting. When Hercules had to choose between Pleasure and Virtue, the presumption was that the pleasures of a demigod would not be less refined than those of the Duke for whom Bach was writing a birthday cantata; and so the song of Pleasure enticing Hercules away from the strenuous pursuit of Virtue could serve for the cradle-song of the Virgin in the *Christmas Oratorio*. Sometimes Bach thinks fit to add new symbols, but he seldom troubles to remove old ones merely because they no longer happen to illustrate the words. His symbolism therefore does not relieve us of the task of interpreting his forms as pure music: on the contrary, it is apt to mislead critics who are not strong in their grasp of musical form.

1. *Chorus.* (My soul doth magnify the Lord.)

In the *Magnificat* we see very clearly a treatment of words on a method often found in Bach's choruses. First there is a main theme by which the words are stretched out in coloratura. Then, before our up-to-date critics have time to point out that coloratura is unrealistic, another theme appears in the natural rhythm of the words, and pervades the rest of the design.

Overleaf is given the unquestionably feminine coloratura with which the sopranos and altos begin—

Ex. 1.

Mag - - - - - ni - fi-cat

And here is the natural rhythm of the first word:

Ex. 2.

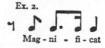

Mag - ni - fi - cat

But there is a third and equally important theme which does **not**
immediately explain itself.

Ex. 3.

Mag - - - - ni - fi - cat

If it had no other purpose, it would justify its existence at the
present day as a drastic refutation of the heresy that Bach's long
phrases are to be sung or blown without change of breath. This
heresy is the ruin of just the best and most enterprising class of
chorus-singers. And it is quite unnecessary. When I first met that
exquisite artist the late Louis Fleury, he astonished me by playing
the greatest of Bach's flute sonatas with a phrasing as free as that
of the finest violinists. When I asked him how he managed never
to chop up the phrases he answered 'by taking breath very often'.
The more often breath is taken the quicker it can be snatched.
I never could detect when Fleury took breath. And, long before
such a consummation is attained, the listener will find that a slight
hiatus after each accented beat (not before) almost immediately
ceases to attract attention. On the other hand, nothing can remedy
the loss of tone towards the end of a phrase that is too long for the
breath. So, if you object to Bach's way of singing 'ma-ha-ha-ha-
ha-ha-ha-ha-ha-ha-gnificat', kindly extend your objection to all
coloratura-singing whatever, and to all things in eighteenth-
century music that would not occur spontaneously to a musician
whose range extended only from *Elijah* to *Götterdämmerung*.

The further purport of Ex. 3 will not appear until much later.
Meanwhile, let us consider the form of this opening chorus. Like
most of those florid choruses of Bach that are not fugues (and like
some that are) it is a concerto in which the chorus-voices play the
part of the solo-instrument. (Bach once turned a movement of the
first Brandenburg Concerto into a chorus, the whole vocal mass
corresponding to the solo violin.) Accordingly the themes are all
grouped into a rounded orchestral paragraph of thirty bars. The

voices repeat the first half of this in their own style, up to the middle close in the dominant. For the second part they substitute a new development, which covers a wider range of key, but is hardly longer than the original second part. When the voices have come to a close in the tonic, the orchestra repeats the last sixteen bars of its paragraph.

Bach's ways of ending a movement form an important subject in musical aesthetics. A final orchestral ritornello is used by him for the express purpose of destroying finality by giving a formal anticlimax to a chorus that would otherwise eclipse what is to follow. Thus in the B minor Mass it is a great mistake to omit the cool ritornello which Bach has so carefully put at the end of the *Et resurrexit*. In spite of its enormous expansion by the treatment of every clause as a separate movement, the Nicene Creed is for Bach, as for all orthodox Christians, a single thing. Finality comes, not after the Resurrection, not even after the Last Judgement, but when the Amen has been sung to the expectation of the life of the world to come. And Bach's most solemn finality is always simply punctual; sometimes to the verge of abruptness, but never otherwise than at the exact end of a melodic phrase. Supplementary chords filling an architectural space apart from formal melody are necessary in a later symphonic and dramatic music which will sound either epigrammatic or archaic if it is deprived of them; but they are inconceivable in Bach's art. If a chorus ends without an orchestral ritornello the voices will still end in the very terms of the ritornello. The only question is whether Bach will see cause, as in this opening chorus, to let the orchestra recapitulate the last paragraph. Apart from this, Bach's last chords, vocal or instrumental, are always written with deliberate purpose as to their length. We find quite short final chords with rests to finish the bar, and a pause clearly placed over the rest instead of over the chord. We find chords that complete or fill the last bar without pause, or with a pause over the double-bar instead of over the chord. Lastly, we find the familiar Handelian pause on a long final chord; but rarely except in fugal choruses where the orchestra is merely supporting the voices. The grand Handelian adagio cadence I cannot remember to have found in any of Bach's choral works, though something like it occurs at the end of his toccatas, and once, very impressively at the end of the first movement of the C major Double Concerto. Ah!—but was I not forgetting '*mente cordis sui*' in this very work? Well, that is rather another story. The rhetoric may be Handelian; indeed, what good rhetoric is not? But here instead of the quintessential expectedness of Handel's adagio cadence, we have something very unexpected indeed. We do not even know what key the whole movement is in until the last moment.

The first chorus has ended with its orchestral ritornello, to which we will *not* add the emergency-brake ritardando which is often supposed to be the only correct way to produce Bach's full closes.

The last chord is short, and Bach puts his pause on a subsequent rest.

2. *Aria*. (And my spirit hath rejoiced in God my Saviour.)

The aria *Et exsultavit* is terse, like all the movements in this highly concentrated work. The orchestra sums it up in the first twelve bars.

Ex. 4.

There is an early version of Bach's *Magnificat* in which some other church songs were inserted, some in German, some in Latin. After this aria came a figured chorale, *Vom Himmel hoch da komm ich her*, one of the very few movements in which Bach, writing ostensibly for unaccompanied chorus, does not show that he is really relying all the time on a sixteen-foot organ bass. The interpolated numbers are well worth performing; but this can be done without making them interrupt the *Magnificat*, which Bach evidently preferred to keep in its integrity.

3. *Aria*. (For He hath regarded the lowliness of his handmaiden: for behold from henceforth . . . shall call me blessed—)

4. *Chorus*. (—all generations.)

Widor's favourite illustration of the modest femininity of the oboe d'amore sums up the first part of the aria *Quia respexit*.

Ex. 5.
Adagio.

It does not sum up the whole; for there is a new tone in the voice-part at *ecce enim ex hoc beatam me dicent*; though the oboe d'amore still accompanies this with the old material. The voice does not quite reach the end of the sentence. This is taken out of the singer's mouth by all the generations that are calling the Virgin blessed while the millennia unroll.

Ex. 6.

om-nes, om-nes gen-e - ra - ti - o - - - - nes

I see no ground, either in tradition or in the musical sense, for the prevalent custom of taking this as a quick movement, or even as one appreciably faster than the aria of which it finishes the words. Be this as it may, nothing need prevent the listener from enjoying the rhetorical points by which Bach keeps the impression of inexhaustible multitude always augmenting. First the theme is given in normal tonic and dominant positions, until, in the first four bars, all the five chorus-parts have had it. Then the voices take it in steps rising up the scale at half-bar distances. Ignoring changes of octave as the theme alternates between male and female voices, the steps are: F sharp: G sharp: A, B, C sharp: D, E, F sharp: with a close in A major. Then the voices enter at intervals of fourths and fifths so contrived as to drift through several keys. When the dominant of the key of the movement is reached, we soon become aware that another scale of rising entries is in progress. This time it has ten steps: G sharp: A, B, C sharp: D, E, F sharp: G sharp: A, B sharp, leading to a close in the dominant. Then the voices concentrate their entries on to the one note of the dominant and gather into a pause thereon. After this all the voices, except the bass, deliver the rhythm of the theme in full harmony, the bass entering with the theme itself half a bar later; upon which an answer in the sopranos brings this tale of generations to an end which symbolizes things not ended here and now.

5. *Aria.* (For He that is mighty hath magnified me: and holy is His name.)

Inspired, as has already been said, by the words *qui potens est,* Bach sets this as an aria for a bass voice. The accompaniment is for continuo alone, and we do not even possess a figured bass to tell us what harmony Bach intends for the superstructure. The common sense of the matter begins with the plain fact that when Bach writes an aria with a merely continuo-bass accompaniment, that bass will, wherever it stands alone without the voice, constitute a main theme in itself. Yet, not only do many commentators express the utmost bewilderment at the 'incompleteness' of Bach's finest continuo-arias, but, conversely, an editor of one of the later Bachgesellschaft volumes has gravely printed an aria in which the bass is obviously a mere bass without the smallest pretensions to a sense of its own; and has let this pass without any hint that something is missing. In the *Magnificat* nothing is missing except the figures, and this lacuna is not unusual in eighteenth-century manuscripts.

This aria is not only a continuo-aria, but it is almost entirely confined to a ground bass which is diversified here and there by little interludes that enable it to change its key. The unwritten superstructure should be smooth; and there are places where it is difficult to find a good construction, in the absence of any help from figures. But it cannot be too simple in its effect; and the bare bass is at all events a main theme which is as fit to stand alone as any other specimen of Bach's glorious 'one-part counterpoint'.

Ex. 7.

In the earlier version a lively figured Chorale, *Freut euch und iubilirt*, follows here.

6. *Duet.* (And His mercy is on them that fear Him, throughout all generations.)

An orchestra of muted strings, with flutes in unison with the violins, gives the gist of this movement in the first four bars.

Ex. 8.

The voices bring a new figure at the words *timentibus eum*; and at the end Bach actually gives a slow vibrato—

to the tenor on the word *timentibus*.

7. *Chorus.* (He hath shewed strength with His arm: He hath scattered the proud in the imagination of His heart) [*sic*: 'mente cordis *sui*', and not in agreement with '*superbos*'.]

Starting on the subdominant side of G major, this chorus gradually reaches the dominant side of D and passes beyond it, until it is brought to a surprising end, reaching its final D major from a distance. A coloratura theme uproots the mountains (figure (*a*)), and brandishes a mighty fist (*b*)—

Ex. 9.

Fe - cit   po - ten - - - - - - - - - - - -

- - - - ti - am in bra - chi - o su - o

while other voices and antiphonal groups in the orchestra give the
natural rhythm of the words—

Ex. 10.

Fe-cit po - ten - ti - am

and the foundations quake unceasingly.

Ex. 11.

The coloratura theme rises in fugue through all the five voices,
and is then taken up by one of Bach's shrill agile trumpets. Meanwhile the chorus is mentioning a particular exercise of the Divine
might. 'Dispersit, dispersit, dispersit . . .' What, or whom? Nothing
of importance. The chorus, accustomed to repeat important words
until fugues have run their course, merely mentions the superbos in
one derisive shout. The earthquake is over, and the sun scatters
the clouds. When the heart of God imagines the proud dispersed,
they are dispersed beyond our reckoning. (Bach, following the
reading sui, is in agreement with the practice of all the liturgical
composers. The Greek Testament is unmistakably in agreement
with our Prayer Book as well as our Authorized Version, in reading
'their hearts'. But this reading would hardly have given Bach the
opportunity for so grand a change at this point.) In the early version a short Latin Gloria in excelsis follows here.

8. Aria. (He hath put down the mighty from their seat: and
hath exalted the humble and meek.)

The opening ritornello gives a general idea of the mood of this
aria—

Ex. 12.

&c.

but the detailed symbolism appears when the voice enters; the violins (the whole body in unison) illustrating *deposuit* thus—

Ex. 13.

while the tenor, as in Handel's 'Every valley', illustrates *exaltavit* by long rising coloraturas.

9. *Aria.* (He hath filled the hungry with good things: and the rich He hath sent empty away.)

Symbolism is at its quaintest in this delightful aria, which ends with a downright practical joke when the flutes omit the resolution of their penultimate notes. The writers of the printed continuo-fillings are desperately afraid of this child-like trait, and they all try to make the continuo contradict it. But may we not ask in all reverence whether this childlike humour does not actually belong to the words? The dethronement of the mighty is a serious matter, which the humble will regard with awe in the midst of their own exaltation. But it is no such tragedy for the rich to be sent empty away while the hungry are filled with good things. There would be something dangerously like malice if there were no humour in the zest with which the Psalmist says that the Lord has prepared a table 'for me in the presence of mine enemies'. Anyhow, Bach does not seem to suppose that the rich have any worse fate than to be sent empty away in respect of their having asked for more than they already possess. This aria expresses the delight of the hungry in the good things. To the rich it only says, 'This is not for you!'

Ex. 14.

In the early version a Latin duet, *Virga Jesse*, is intended to follow here, but is left unfinished. A complete German version of it is found in one of the Cantatas.

10. *Trio* or *Semi-chorus.* (He remembering His mercy hath holpen His servant Israel.)

There is no evidence to show whether this is a trio or a chorus. Bach's solo singers were members of the choir, so that he did not need to specify such details in unpublished works that were always performed under his own direction. I greatly prefer a choral per-formance of this highly imaginative movement. While the feminine voices weave a flowing texture in close polyphony above a bass of high violoncellos, the oboes (tutti in unison) play an old Canto

Fermo used for German settings of the *Magnificat* ('*Meine Seel'* *erhebt den Herrn*')—

Mozart uses this in his Requiem at the words beginning *Te decet hymnus*.

11. *Chorus.* (As He promised to our forefathers, Abraham and his seed for ever.)

A not uncommon mistake in criticism is that of treating a classical composer as if he were a candidate for a musical degree. If a student writes a fugue in which the subject is invariably so harmonized as to make a full close, and the answer invariably enters on a unison with the last note of the subject, it is very unlikely that the examiners, whether internal or external, will suppose that the student knows much about fugues. For no other reason than this so great a Bach-lover as Spitta thought that the G sharp minor Fugue in the first book of the 48 must be an early work, though it is one of the maturest and most beautiful things in the whole collection. Two important facts about full closes are involved here. First, beginners have to begin by mastering full closes because they can do nothing else. Secondly, full closes, if at short and regular distances, will chop up the style and destroy the sense of movement. Very well then; the full closes in this *Sicut locutus* chop up the style and destroy the sense of movement. To which Bach is able to add 'Quod erat faciendum'. Each movement in this *Magnificat* has been wonderfully terse; and each has been independent of the rest in all but the common ground of harmonious contrast. And now all these independent pieces are to be rounded off as parts of a single whole, and rounded off in an astonishingly short, almost abrupt, though perfectly final way. As we listen to the stiff little periods of this simple fugue we feel a new sense of leisure, and we enjoy its sonorous euphony, which

would satisfy even an examiner. Moreover this stodgy style does
take up a certain amount of time, which passes very pleasantly.
Only the organ and the basses support the chorus. At the end there
is an effective climax, with a chain of suspensions in the treble,
and the music draws a longer breath before finally closing with
another regular period.

12. *Chorus.* (Glory be to the Father, and to the Son, and to the
Holy Ghost: as it was in the beginning, is now, and ever shall be,
world without end, Amen.)

After that rigid little fugue, anything in a more free rhythm
would sound big. And the opening of the Gloria sounds gigantic.
First, on the dominant of D there is a mighty shout of the word
Gloria in its natural rhythm, in which the whole orchestra takes
part. Then, over a deep organ pedal-note, the voices arise swarming
in coloratura. With each clause the process is repeated and
developed. Like Browning's Spanish monk, Bach frustrates the
Arian in three sips, putting the words together in this form:
Gloria Patri; Gloria Filio; Gloria et Spiritui Sancto.

All this makes a magnificent introduction—to what? It takes
time, but it covers only introductory ground. There is only one
thing big enough to follow it, and well enough prepared by its
antecedents to be heard without fatigue; and that is the whole
Magnificat! Fortunately the beginning may stand for the whole.
Bach finishes in two-thirds of a minute; and now at last we learn
the meaning of Ex. 3. The text is built up as in the previous verse;
*sicut erat in principio; in principio et nunc; nunc et semper et in
saecula; et in saecula saeculorum. Amen.* The coloratura of Ex. 1
makes a grand climax in the bass on the word '*saeculorum*'; and
the precise meaning of Ex. 3 is 'as it was in the beginning'.

Ex. 17.

Si - cut er - at   in   prin - ci - pi - o

CCI. CHURCH CANTATA, NO. 67, 'HOLD IN AFFECTION JESUS CHRIST!'
FOR THE FIRST SUNDAY AFTER EASTER (SONNTAG QUASIMODOGENITI).

1 *Chorus*—'Hold in affection Jesus Christ!'
2 *Aria for Tenor*—'Christ Jesus is arisen.'
3 *Recitative for Alto*—'Lord Jesus, Thou the sting of death hast drawn,'
                          alternating with
  Chorale—'Come, let us hail this day of days.'
4 *Aria with Chorus*—*Bass.*   'Peace be unto you.'
                      Chorus. 'O joy! Jesus for us fighteth.'
5 *Congregational Choral*—'Lord Christ, Thou art the Prince of Peace.'

The cantata 'Halt im Gedächtniss', No. 67 in the edition of the
Bachgesellschaft, is one of the most perfect and attractive of all

Bach's works. When I chose it for performance at the Reid
Concerts I was surprised to find that it was not among the English
vocal scores of the Bach cantatas. Messrs. Novello, however,
obligingly added it to their series of vocal scores. I heard it, not,
I think, later than 1890, at a concert in London; and then only
from the passage-way to the platform of St. James's Hall. But
Joachim was waiting in that passage, and I well remember how,
when the music of 'Peace be unto you' entered, Joachim whispered
'Isn't it unspeakably beautiful?'

Bach's Church Cantatas must be understood as Church music;
and it is not every cantata that should be given in the concert-
room as a whole. The first editor of the Bachgesellschaft, Moritz
Hauptmann, writing with such insight as could be expected of a
man first discovering the existence of this choral music a century
after Bach's death, commented on the strange phenomenon of an
art-form that usually begins with a fine chorus, follows it with
'a luggage train' of wiggy arias and crabbed recitatives, and then
concludes with one verse of a plain hymn-tune. Hauptmann
obviously did not understand Bach; but it is quite true that a
cantata that happens to be on those lines needs the rest of the
church service to give its form a natural meaning; and we should
do better justice to such works in the concert-room by selecting
choruses from several of them. Otherwise the best cantatas for
transplantation to the concert-room are those which either have no
choruses at all (there are some forty solo cantatas), or which, like
the present example, have two. As to the plain final choral, it will
always make a glorious end, if the audience will consent to accept
Bach's direct invitation to sing the melody. The tunes that his
congregation knew are not always unknown to us, and they are
always easy to learn when a powerful chorus is leading them at
the pace of German congregational singing.

No. 1. Chorus

Hold in affection Jesus Christ!
He now is risen from death's dark prison.

A compact ritornello comprises the theme of the first line, given to
a kind of slide-trumpet, with a glorious florid counterpoint for
two oboes d'amore.

The slide-trumpet, or *corno da tirarsi*, is not the brilliant *clarino*
of the *Magnificat* and the B minor Mass, but an instrument
of moderate range, with a complete diatonic scale obtained by
means of its slide, and capable of playing the main theme of
Ex. 1 (overleaf) an octave lower as well as at the pitch of the
opening.

Ex. 1.

The ritornello is completed in sixteen bars which close into the entry of the chorus. The meaning of the long holding-note of the trumpet is at once revealed by the soprano; it means what it says, namely 'Hold!' With the other voices, Bach puts up with a certain inaccuracy in his word-painting, by repeating 'Hold' thrice; but this matters little, for the real theme is on the surface and comprises the whole clause directly enough. Moreover, the trumpet repeats it in the lower octave. By this time we shall have learnt to fix our attention on it; and so when the basses restate it in E major, there is no great harm in the threefold repetition of 'Halt' appearing on the surface. Once more the trumpet echoes the theme.

A double fugue now follows. The mention of death causes the florid second theme to close in a minor key, imparting a magnificent new depth to the harmonic purport of the first theme.

Ex. 2.

One result of this is that we never know where the combination of themes will arrive next time. This first fugue-passage reaches

the quite remote key of G sharp minor. The accompaniment has
been only the organ and orchestral basses. In G sharp minor the
orchestra re-enters, swinging round easily to E major, the dominant, at the third bar. It now takes in its stride the whole ritornello,
in which the full chorus takes part. Then the orchestra alone again
gives the first phrase of the ritornello, which is answered by the
chorus with the theme in the bass and a new turn of harmony.
This leads to the tonic, where the same antiphonal process is
repeated. The double fugue is then resumed, supported by the
whole orchestra. It eventually leads to the whole ritornello, with
full chorus in the tonic, which concludes the scheme. In every
respect this is typical of those choruses of Bach which comprise a
ritornello and a passage of fugue. I have dealt with Bach's use
of the ritornello, and with other relevant matters of orchestration,
in my analysis of the B minor Mass.

No. 2. *Aria for Tenor*

Christ Jesus is arisen!
Why should I doubt and fear?
The Saviour's triumph well I know;
Yet fear my anxious heart will show.
Lord Christ, with light appear!

In the very first phrase Bach compresses into two bars the
emotions of joy and fear, together with a symbol of resurrection,
the scale-figure (*a*) so often associated by him with the word
'erstanden'. The other figure (*b*), in spite of its broken rhythm,
does at first diminish the joyous expression of the tune, but it is
soon developed into a quiet, consistent and unmistakable allusion
to fear (*'was schreckt mich noch?'*).

In order to find the relation of Bach's Church Cantatas to the
services for which they were designed, it is not always necessary
to make so deep a research as that with which Professor Sanford
Terry has illustrated his monumental translation of the texts of
all Bach's extant cantatas. The English Prayer Book will give
us the Gospel and Epistle for any Sunday or holy day in question.
On the First Sunday after Easter we commemorate the evening
when the doors were shut, where the disciples were assembled
for fear of the Jews'; and the cause of the fear matters little to the
writer of the cantata-text. The word suffices to remind him of
graver fears, and it is fortunate that he gives chapter and verse

for the following recitative, which I confess to having found quite
unintelligible until I looked up Hosea xiii. 14. But that makes the
sense clear; though it would be interesting to know whether either
Bach or his librettist expected any listener to see the allusion, 'O
death, I will be thy plagues; O grave, I will be thy destruction.'

No. 3. *Recitative for Alto*

Lord Jesus, Thou the sting of death hast drawn, and art of
hell become the torment. (Literally "Thou art called the poison
of death, and a pestilence of hell'.)
> Then why should I with fear and doubt be torn?
> For hast Thou not given to our voices
> A victory song the heart rejoices?

Choral (*plain*)—Come, let us hail this day of days,
> Nor stint our song of joy and praise!
> To-day Lord Christ triumphant rose
> And captive led His humbled foes!
> Alleluia!

Recitative—And yet, O Lord, my spirit knows no rest.
> By hosts of hell my peace is still assailed.
> With fear and doubt I'm torn.
> Yet, Lord, for me Thou hast the victory won.

> I pray thee chide me not, Thy child so wayward.
> Lord, soon let faith make us see fully
> That Thou, the Prince of Peace,
> Hast by Thy mighty arm given us release.

And now comes one of the most moving and glorious things
in all Bach's works. The string band displays the fightings and
(symbolized by the rhythmic tremor ♩ ♫ ♪ as in *Fecit potentiam* in the *Magnificat*) the terrors of this world.

Ex. 4.

Suddenly He is in the midst of them.

Ex. 5.

Peace . . . . be un - to you.

This is usually supposed to be a bass solo. But if it be so, why have the choral passages no bass? I believe Bach's intention to be that the voice of Christ should be given by the chorus; and I think it highly probable that he placed the basses of the chorus apart from the rest.

The rest of the chorus then proceeds to sing through the battle symphony.

No. 4 (or 5). *Aria. (Orchestral introduction.)* (Ex. 4.)

Vox Christi—Peace be unto you! (*Thrice.*) (Ex. 5.)

Chorus (Soprano, Alto, and Tenor)—
> O joy! Jesus for us fighteth.
> In the foe no heart remaineth;
> Satan his pride shall rue. (Ex. 4.)

Vox Christi—Peace be unto you! (*Thrice.*)

Chorus—Jesus heavenly peace imparteth;
> From our heart all doubting casteth;
> Faith He doth renew.

Vox Christi—Peace be unto you! (*Thrice, and continued into following chorus.*)

> *Chorus*—O Lord, in Thy strength prevailing,
> And Thy bitter death availing,
> To Thee bid me go!
> *Vox Christi*—Peace be unto you!

I hope some day to produce Bach's A major Mass, a work which, though the Kyrie is probably its only original number, sheds upon its various adaptations a light by no means accidental or unrevealing of new beauties. We do not want to think of anything else while we listen to this sublime mystery; but the A major Mass is well worth hearing, and its Gloria, from the beginning to the *Gratias* (inclusive), is a wonderful re-creation of what we have just heard.

Lord Christ, Thou art the Prince of Peace, True God and Man in One.

E'er strong to help when foes in-crease, Through life and when life's done!

In Thy dear Name our prayers we frame, Thy Father's aid in - vok - ing.

V F

The Cantata ends fitly with a congregational choral. I find that in performance in the concert-room the melody does not lie too high to be sung effectively by the audience if copies of the words and tune have been distributed.

CCII. CHURCH CANTATA, NO. 170, 'VERGNÜGTE RUH',' FOR THE SIXTH SUNDAY AFTER TRINITY

1 *Aria:* 'Vergnügte Ruh', beliebte Seelenlust.'
2 *Recitative:* 'Die Welt, das Sündenhaus.'
3 *Aria:* 'Wie jammern mich doch die verkehrten Herzen.'
4 *Recitative:* 'Wer sollte sich demnach wohl hier zu leben wünschen.'
5 *Aria:* 'Mir ekelt mehr zu leben, drum nimm mich, Jesu, hin.'

Bach's Church Cantatas cannot always be rightly understood in the modern concert-room without reference to their original place in the service of the Lutheran church. This is particularly evident when they begin with a big chorus and end with a plain chorale. Lovers of Bach have become accustomed to accepting such a scheme as in some mysterious way giving a satisfactory climax in a concert-room, but the fact remains that it does not. In its proper environment the plain chorale formed the highest possible climax to a work in which other agencies besides music engaged the attention of a congregation which had been listening first to the Gospel and Epistle for the day, then to half of a cantata the text of which was a poetic commentary thereon, then to a sermon (presumably also relevant), then to the rest of the cantata, which led to a final tune in which all could join.

Some cantatas, however, are less dependent on such an environment; and foremost among these are those solo cantatas that do not end with a plain chorale. *Vergnügte Ruh'* is undoubtedly among the most beautiful and mature of these or of any works by Bach. Anything like it in Bach's purely instrumental music would have become hackneyed long ago. The cantatas, however, are a field so enormous, and of such uniform excellence, that it is the merest fluke which of them gets exploited first, as far as their beauty is concerned. There are many practical questions that often decide for the production of this and the neglect of that. Chief among these are the difficulties of Bach's continuo, i.e. the early eighteenth-century method of supplying the harmonic background. Almost throughout the nineteenth century this problem was evaded by modern orchestration which removed all trace of Bach's feeling for tone without satisfying any modern criterion in return. Fortunately Bach is not so easy to over-paint as Handel; the players have enough to do to tackle their own parts; and when even so facile a contrapuntist as Franz tries to add to Bach's polyphony, the additions (in spite of the reverent admiration they excited when they were new) cut a poor figure. They have had their day; but the old art of filling up figured bass was not to be recovered by mere wishes. From a technique as practical as that of parliamentary debate, it had risen (or fallen) to its present august position of abstract written exercises in 'harmony'—exercises which the writers would never dream of playing at sight even when they have finally acquired perfect ease in writing them. Meanwhile, the task of recovering the practical art of thorough-bass proved to be full of pitfalls; the eighteenth-century theorist did not explain points which their instruments had made too self-evident even for consciousness; while modern theorists and modern artists have too often distrusted or neglected each other's best resources and instincts. It is likely that Bach often used *two* organs (or an organ and a harpsichord, according to circumstances) for his filling out; that one of them accompanied the voices and the other the instruments, and moreover (a feature which is not reproduced here) that the pitch of the one was a whole tone above that of the other! The pianoforte was already regarded by Quantz and by Bach's own sons as much better than the harpsichord for filling-out purposes; and the modern instrument, if played lightly, blends equally well with orchestra and organ.

The words of *Vergnügte Ruh*' are, in terms of eighteenth-century musical symbolism, very faithfully illustrated by Bach, but we should pay him a poor compliment in supposing that they represent all he knew about the Gospel and Epistle for the Sixth Sunday after Trinity. A more wretched commentary on the Scriptures was never delivered by the feeblest of preachers; and its claims to common sense, scholarship, and orthodoxy may be gauged from the fact that the word *Racha* (from the text, 'Whosoever shall say unto his brother, Raca, Raca, shall be in danger of hell-fire') becomes confused in punning fashion with *Rache* ('revenge')!

When Bach sets such stuff to music he goes to head-quarters for his inspiration. Accordingly, instead of distracting the listener by the grotesque original words from which a literal translation can extract neither grammar nor sense, I here present what Bach's audience had before them, the Gospel and Epistle for the Sixth Sunday after Trinity:

THE GOSPEL. St. Matt. v. 20.

Jesus said unto his disciples, Except your righteousness shall exceed the righteousness of the Scribes and Pharisees, ye shall in no case enter into the Kingdom of heaven. Ye have heard that it was said by them of old time, Thou shalt not kill: and whosoever shall kill, shall be in danger of the judgement. But I say unto you, that whosoever is angry with his brother without a cause shall be in danger of the judgement: and whosoever shall say to his brother, Raca, shall be in danger of the council: but whosoever shall say, Thou fool, shall be in danger of hell-fire. Therefore if thou bring thy gift to the altar, and there rememberest that thy brother hath ought against thee; leave there thy gift before the altar, and go thy way, first be reconciled to thy brother, and then come and offer thy gift. Agree with thine adversary quickly, whiles thou art in the way with him; lest at any time the adversary deliver thee to the judge, and the judge deliver thee to the officer, and thou be cast into prison. Verily I say unto thee, Thou shalt by no means come out thence, till thou hast paid the uttermost farthing.

THE EPISTLE. Rom. vi. 3.

Know ye not, that so many of us as were baptized into Jesus Christ were baptized into his death? Therefore we are buried with him by baptism into death; that like as Christ was raised up from the dead by the glory of the Father, even so we also should walk in newness of life. For if we have been planted together in the likeness of his death, we shall be also in the likeness of his resurrection: knowing this, that our old man is crucified with him, that the body of sin might be destroyed, that henceforth we shall not serve sin. For he that is dead is freed from sin. Now if we be dead with Christ, we believe that we shall also live with him; knowing that Christ being raised from the dead dieth no more; death hath no more dominion over him. For in that he died, he died unto sin once; but in that he liveth, he liveth unto God. Likewise reckon ye also yourselves to be dead indeed unto sin, but alive unto God through Jesus Christ our Lord.

Dr. Sophie Weisse has given me a translation of the cantata, which really helps towards understanding Bach's music. By adopting the diction of Christopher Harvey's *Synagogue* (if not of George Herbert's *Temple*), the translator has succeeded in giving a very faithful rendering of what Bach has read into the original text. It is not a translation for singing; but it might well be used as the basis of one.[1]

ARIA.

Fair Peace, the Soul's loved Joy,
Midst hellish Sin no man may find thee,
But only in the Heavenly concord.
Thou comfortest the weary soul,
Fair Peace, the Soul's loved Joy,
Hence in my heart shall virtue only dwell.

RECITATIVE.

The World, that House of Sins,
Breaks out into the songs of hell,

[1] These notes were written before Dr. Sanford Terry solved the problems of performances of Bach's complete vocal works in English.

And seeks by hate and envy
To wear old Satan's image,
Their mouths are full of viper's venom,
Which does the innocent to death,
And finds no word but
'Raca, oh, thou fool!'
Most righteous God, alas, how far
Is man from Thee!
Thou art all Love, and yet his mouth
Doth utter nought but hate and cursing;
And ever doth he seek
To tread his brother under foot.
Alas, what prayers can wash this guilt away?

ARIA.

Ah! woe is me for all these perverse hearts
Which are abhorred of Thee my God,
I tremble and I feel a thousand pangs
While they rejoice in hatred and revenge.
Most righteous God, what are Thy thoughts towards them,
When they, filled only full of Satan's wiles,
Have laughed to scorn Thy sharp command—
Ah! Thou hast doubtless thought to punish them.
Ah! Woe is me for all these perverse hearts.

RECITATIVE.

Who then would wish to live here
When in return for Love
We see but hatred and ill-will?
But since by God's command
I needs must love my foeman as my friend,
My heart flees rage and bitterness
And longs alone to live with God,
Whose Name is Love itself.
Ah! Spirit of Peace, when will He give to Thee
    Thy Heavenly Zion.

ARIA.

It sickens me to live,
Therefore take me, O Jesu, to Thee.
All sin fills me with horror,
Let me find that Heavenly Mansion
Where I at rest may be.

In the first aria (Ex. 1) Bach sings, in his greatest melodies and rhythms, of the peace and heavenly harmony within the soul that has resolved to do right. A literal translation of the text would go far to spoil the music; yet, wherever there is a point that can be

made without showing up the tastelessness of the poet, Bach makes
it. A splendid instance occurs in the middle of this aria, where the
voice, expressing the *resolution* to harbour only good gifts in the
heart, enters abruptly with a monosyllable on a high note before
the ritornello is finished.

Ex. 1.
(*Andante tranquillo.*)

After the first aria there is a recitative in which Bach puts his
own noble indignation into a denunciation of the malice and
slanders of the world. Then comes one of the most singular designs
to be found in music; an aria in which a fugued duet for the two
manuals of the organ is supported only by a kind of free ground-
bass in the violins and violas, all in unison (Ex. 2), while the voice
contributes its own material, besides taking up the fugue theme.
The sentiment is that of sorrow for the perverse souls that reject
God; and the mockery of the ungodly is realistically suggested by
two brilliant passages in the organ obbligato. The whole air, though
perhaps the most difficult movement in all Bach's works, is
extremely picturesque and rich.

Ex. 2.
Adagio.

The following recitative is accompanied by the strings. Their
entry, in sustained harmony, here symbolizes (according to a train
of thought constantly occurring in Bach's religious music) the
releasing of one's thoughts from the slavery of this world to the
freedom of the divine kingdom. In the final aria (Ex. 3) Bach gives
full vent to his habit of expressing all his joy of life in the form of
looking forward to the next world. 'I loathe life,' he sings to a
delightful tritone fourth (D-G sharp), which the old theorists had
solemnly stated to stand for the Devil in music (*Mi contra Fa est
Diabolus in Musica*); 'So take me away'—to the tune of '*Hat man
nicht mit seinen Kindern hundert-tausend Hudelei*', while the organ
warbles contentedly, and this world, with its *Hudelei*, sinks into
oblivion in the childlike perfection of Bach's faith.

Ex. 3.

CCIII. DOUBLE CHORUS, CHURCH CANTATA, NO. 50, 'NUN IST DAS HEIL' ('NOW IS THE GRACE')

Whether this chorus is part of a larger work or not, it is in no sense a fragment. Only by rare accident can there be more than a loose unity in a cantata that is part of a long Divine Service and is interrupted by the sermon and ended by a plain hymn-tune sung by the congregation. It is quite possible that this chorus is the opening of an otherwise lost cantata and that the rest of the cantata consisted of two arias, one recitative, and a plain final verse of a congregational hymn. Such a scheme, outside a church service, is fragmentary as the single chorus is not. But the editor of the miniature score not only persists in regarding the work as a torso but believes that its 'abrupt end' indicates the loss of an introductory and final ritornello. This idea rests first on the common failure of critics with an undeveloped sense of form to recognize that a powerful modulation before the final close in the tonic has already occurred before in a foreign key. (Not one connoisseur in ten realizes that the tremendous harmonic earthquake at the end of the F major Toccata has happened twice before, in D minor and G minor.) Secondly, the notion that the end is abrupt rests on a failure to grasp the simplicity of the whole structure, which gives no material for a ritornello in its subject and countersubject, and leaves no room for any such feature at any point. The whole movement is a 'round-fugue' pure and simple, such as I have discussed in analysing the B minor Mass and the Cantata *Halt im Gedächtniss*, and the 'round' consists of a subject accompanied in round-order by five countersubjects from one of which arises a short episode which leads to a close in F sharp minor, the mediant. The round is then resumed in new positions and the episode is so placed as to close in the home tonic. These forms of Bach's, the description of which proves to be so absurdly simple, always have an inherent quality corresponding to *entasis* in Greek architecture: the lines appear marvellously straight because they are really subtly curved. In the present chorus the phrase-length of the round is eight bars; but each voice enters at the seventh bar.

Here are the words of the Authorized Version:

Now is come salvation, and strength, and the kingdom of our God, and the power of his Christ: for the accuser of our brethren is cast down, which accused them before our God day and night.

REVELATION xii. 10.

And here is the theme with its five countersubjects, swinging clouds of incense before the Throne.

The fifth countersubject is evidently maintaining its identity with
difficulty in the polyphonic stress; but the experienced critic will
not despise the masterly inactivity of the third countersubject,
which contributes enormously to the weight of the harmony and
the transparency of the whole combination, while the fourth

countersubject attracts to itself a mass of plain chords in all the otherwise unoccupied voices. The first trumpet adds to the vocal ensemble a ninth part, with the main theme at a superhuman height. The middle episode deals with the outcast Adversary in terms of figure (*a*) of the main theme; and after the close in F sharp minor the main theme, in plain chords, is divided antiphonally between the two choirs before the counterpoints begin to assemble, which they proceed to do in their original order of succession but a reversed order of pitch, building the harmony from the top downwards instead of from the bottom upwards. From an early stage of the movement the orchestra completes the tone-picture by a Jacob's ladder of jubilant arpeggios, ascending and descending.

CCIV. MOTET, 'JESU, MEINE FREUDE' ('JESU, PRICELESS TREASURE'), FOR FIVE-PART CHORUS

1 *Chorale*, 'Jesu, priceless treasure'.
2 *Chorus*, 'For there is now no condemnation'.
3 *Chorale*, 'In Thine arm I rest me'.
4 *Semi-chorus or Trio (Two Sopranos and Alto)*, 'Thus then, the law of Spirit'.
5 *Chorus*, 'Death, I do not fear thee' (*Chorale-variation*).
6 *Chorus*, 'Ye are not of the flesh'.
7 *Chorale*, 'Hence with earthly treasure'.
8 *Semi-chorus or Trio (Alto, Tenor, and Bass)*, 'If therefore Christ be in you'.
9 *Chorale-variation (Semi-chorus or Trio of Two Sopranos and Tenor, with Chorale in Altos)*, 'Fare thee well that errest'.
10 *Chorus*, 'If by His Spirit' (*resuming No. 2*).
11 *Chorale*, 'Hence all fears and sadness' (*to the music of No. 1*).

Before attempting to describe this, one of the greatest of Bach's choral works, it is necessary to make a statement as to its method of performance. Only five 'unaccompanied' choral works of Bach are extant, nor are any known to have been lost. Of his choral works with organ and orchestra we possess at least two hundred and fifty, and we know that at least another fifty have been lost. These facts alone would prove that the very notion of an unaccompanied chorus had become unfamiliar in Bach's day, even if we had not the still more striking fact that the creator of our standards of choral music, Handel, in all his works (as collected in one hundred volumes by the Händelgesellschaft) never wrote a line of unaccompanied choral music. Bach's five 'Motets' (or works to be sung by the 'Motet-choir' of his church) would thus in any case be an isolated and experimental *tour de force* if it were certain that they were meant to be unaccompanied. He has no such view of choral music as had Palestrina and his army of sixteenth-century fellow-masters, to whom the unaccompanied chorus was the one real instrument

of music, and all artificial instruments the merest crutches. To
Bach the unaccompanied chorus can exist, if it exists at all, only
as a *tour de force* alike for composers and performers. Bach is
capable of a much greater *tour de force*. He can make a single violin
or violoncello support itself throughout entire works on a large
scale without a moment's failure to supply all that is necessary to
suggest its base and its harmony.

But as he never fails in the execution of a genuine *tour de force*,
neither does he waste time over a pointless one. When the conditions of a work are unusual, whether by nature or through custom,
he applies his imagination to the problem and makes common sense
of the solution. Now it is very significant that he has not done this
with the problem of the 'unaccompanied' motet. There are hardly
two consecutive pages in all these five motets without some passage
which proves that Bach has imagined the basses to be supported
by some instrument an octave below them. If he were a capricious
and inexact writer like Haydn, it might be arguable that this means
no more than it does in some of Haydn's early string quartets,
where there are, perhaps for three notes in twenty works, similar
instances of the composer's forgetting that a violoncello is not a
double-bass. But the cases are not parallel. Haydn's early quartets
show the rapid rise of a highly organized chamber-music style out
of the crude theatrical formalities of the small orchestra; and so
the absence of mind (for it is nothing more) that can make him
forget the octave a violoncello plays in, might have been expected
to show itself oftener than it does. With Bach's motets it is quite
inconceivable that the many places in which the tenor goes below
the bass can have been written in absence of mind. There is no
single one of those places in which the tenor makes a really good
support to the harmony. In many it is actually incorrect as
a bass; and in every passage without exception the bass voice-
part, if doubled in the lower octave, is obviously the only real
and intended bass. Well then, it might be said, why not put the
bass voice an octave lower? It is known that these motets (of
which three were written for funerals and so must have been
hurriedly rehearsed) were actually performed by Bach himself
with accompaniment; but was this not a mere makeshift, though
the vocal basses have taken advantage of it; and would not Bach
have been the first to sanction a slight change that brings out the
full perfection of his unaccompanied choral style? Unfortunately
the trouble here is that it is difficult, if not impossible, to find
any good point at which the basses can make their descent to a
lower octave; and, moreover, the loss in tone-colour is very serious.
When all has been said and done, the fact stands out more and more
clearly that Bach not only failed to imagine the incorrect effect of

these passages without an instrumental support in the sixteen-foot octave, but he did magnificently conceive, with all the vividness of his imagination, their effect when so supported.

Let us now turn to the orthodox view as given in the preface to the current English edition. The editor writes: 'The vexed question of the Motets being sung without accompaniment need not be discussed here. A good case can be made for both sides. If by their being accompanied they are likely to be performed by choirs who might otherwise fight shy of them, then by all means let the voices be supported by the organ. But undoubtedly they have their finest effect when sung *a capella*.'

If this is 'making out a good case for both sides', I prefer my bad case! Few choirs can resist the moral pressure to show that they do not 'fight shy' of unaccompanied singing. But where the moral pressure is so formidable we may be allowed to suspect that the material case is weak. My case, I frankly admit, is not moral but grammatical. I would cheerfully join Bach and the Emperor Sigismund in declaring myself *supra grammaticam*, if I could think that Bach's *imagination* was on the side of unaccompanied singing of his motets. But I myself had always held as a pious opinion that their finest effect was *a capella*, until at one of our practices I casually used the organ in order to attack a difficulty with more confidence. With Palestrina the effect of so doing is obviously a makeshift, tolerable only as long as it is needed. With Bach the effect once for all startled me out of any further belief that his motets should be sung *a capella*. If you want *a capella* music, go to the sixteenth century and to Brahms and a few very modern writers (mostly British, Dutch, and Spanish) for it. If you want Bach, use the organ according to eighteenth-century methods.

Of course the organ accompaniment is not a thing to be done by machinery. In the absence of the composer we need a carefully written organ-part in which each passage and each theme is supported or left alone in accordance with the forms of the music and the practice of Bach in all his other works.

A glance at the list of movements in 'Jesu, priceless treasure' shows that they are arranged in a remarkable symmetry. Six verses of a chorale alternate with five passages from the eighth chapter of the Epistle to the Romans; the sixth chorale is set to the same music as the first; of the prose scriptural choruses the last resumes the music of the first, while the two scriptural numbers that are for three-part semi-chorus or solo voices (Bach gives no indication) are at equal distances the one from the beginning and the other from the end.

The third of the six chorale-verses treats the chorale melody so freely and elaborately that it probably was not recognized as a chorale-variation at all until Brahms pointed out the fact. Once pointed out, it is unmistakable, and I have devised my first quotation so as to include the whole original melody, and have placed underneath it note for note the corresponding phrases of this variation.

Ex. 1.

Death,   I do not fear thee

&c.

I follow the example of my master, Sir Walter Parratt, who, when he produced this motet in St. George's Chapel at Windsor, used to give the pitch to the choir by playing on the organ the short chorale prelude on 'Jesu, meine Freude', from the *Orgelbüchlein* (transposed from C minor to the key of the motet); such being undoubtedly one of the purposes for which that collection of preludes was written.

The motet begins with a plain four-part setting of the first verse, as given in Ex. 1.

Jesus, priceless treasure,
Source of purest pleasure,
Truest friend to me;
Ah, how long I've panted,
And my heart hath fainted,
Thirsting, Lord, for Thee!
Thine I am, O spotless Lamb,
I will suffer nought to hide thee:
Nought I ask beside Thee.

Then follows a five-part chorus to the following words (Romans viii. 1):

So there is now no condemnation unto them which are in Jesus Christ: who walk not by the flesh corruptly, but as the Spirit leads.

The first part of this sentence is set as a broad and rhythmic melody ending on a half-close, which is repeated piano. The rest is treated in a form, very characteristic of Bach, which may be described as a 'masked fugue', i.e. a fugue in which the subject, instead of being stated alone by an unaccompanied part, is concealed in a mass of harmony until it rises to the soprano. The *Matthew Passion* is proverbially said to 'have no fugues': as a matter of fact it has rather more than most eighteenth-century works; but they are masked fugues. It is no defect in this form that the subject is not easily heard until it reaches the surface: the surface can do very well without it meanwhile, and what concerns the listener is the flow and balance of the whole musical paragraph. Ex. 2 shows the subject.

Ex. 2.

They who walk not by the flesh

The masked fugue comes to a firm close in the dominant minor, at the words 'but as the Spirit leads'. Then in that key the first clause is again given twice in full (first loud, then soft). Its words are further developed in a more fugato style, leading back to E minor, in which key the fugue ('They who walk not by the flesh') is resumed unmasked and with a new countersubject, and brought to a close in the tonic corresponding with the former close in the dominant. The whole chorus is thus in as solid a musical binary form as any instrumental suite-movement.

No. 3 is a five-part chorale, still plain, but with a good deal of movement and colour in the inner parts, following every suggestion of the words.

> In Thine arm I rest me,
> Foes who would molest me
> Cannot reach me here:
> Though the earth be shaking,
> Every heart be quaking,
> Jesus calms my fear.
> Fires may flash and thunders crash,
> Yea, and sin and hell assail me;
> Jesus will not fail me.

No. 4, a trio or three-part semi-chorus, resumes the Epistle to the Romans.

Thus then, the law of the Spirit of life in Christ abiding, now hath made me free from the law of sin and death.—(Rom. viii. 2).

At the words 'now hath made me free' the rhythm becomes independent of the barring in a style suggested by the words, and distinctly reminiscent of the liberty which musical rhythm enjoyed in earlier centuries.

No. 5 interrupts, in the same tempo, with its vigorous defiance of Death and the powers below. I have been obliged to alter the translation, without any attempt at the impossible task of preserving rhyme.[1] Bach's family traditions remembered the Thirty Years' War; and the preachers of his religion not only believed in Hell but took no pains to avoid the subject; and when they meant Hell they said Hell, or Tophet: not 'Sheol' or 'a future state of punishment'. When these motets were first published, some eighty years after Bach's death, taste had changed, and Bach's texts were adapted to the Christianity of bountiful persons who would probably have ruffled the temper of Bach's widow if they had visited her in the almshouse in which she ended her days. It is these adaptations which underlie the current English version published in Novello's scores: and they do not fit the music. Taste or no taste, rhyme or no rhyme, it is astonishing how much better a chorus can sing when the words fit the notes than when they do not. When the words fit, you will get better results in a language which most of the singers do not speak, provided you explain the sense, than in a 'translation' where 'soar and vanquish Death' is to be sung to a descending *decrescendo* the only possible meaning of which is 'rest in peace'. Again, 'God is God for ever' is a phrase which Bach would have set magnificently if it had been there for him, and he wrote magnificent music in the place where our

[1] Professor Terry's English texts for all Bach's vocal works had not appeared when this essay was written.

translator gives it. But the translation does not account for the
contorted movements of the bass; and what Bach meant by them
was '*Ob sie noch so brummen*'—i.e. 'though they roar never so'. I
regret that I have not been able to get a singable translation for
this drastic chorale-variation, which shall realize accurately the
apocalyptic figures which Bach's naïve text gave him. It is
not 'death' he defies, but 'the old serpent'. The first word is
'*Trotz*' ('despite')—for which there is an excellent monosyllable
in English, but public opinion is not ripe for its use by choral
societies. The other points I have adjusted as well as I could,
after consulting with friends better qualified to deal with poetic
problems.

Ex. 1 (above) shows in its lower stave how this chorus follows
the chorale-tune phrase by phrase. With the text I give in Roman
figures the corresponding clauses of the tune (a 'clause' being, of
course, the two bars between each pause).

> I. Death, I do not fear thee,
> Though thou standest (II) near me,
> Grave, I calmly spurn thee
> Though to dust thou (III) turn me!
> Strong in hope and faith.
> I. Rising up and singing,
> I shall, heavenward winging
> II. Soar [rising and singing]—
>
> (*Here the translation irremediably fails to
> follow the structure of the chorale.*)
>
> III. Soar and vanquish Death:
> (*Coda*) And with the blest
> Shall for ever rest.
> V. He that reigns
> Will rend my chains.
> VI. Earth and Tophet shall be silenced
> Though they rage exceeding.

The main bulk of the next chorus is a fugue in another key (G
major) on normal lines with a florid, yet formal subject given out
by the tenor. The text of the whole chorus is the ninth verse of
the eighth chapter of the Epistle to the Romans; the text of the
fugue is the first sentence, of which the first clause is the main
subject (Ex. 3), while the second clause, just as its words are a
condition connected with the first by an 'if', is a second subject
derived from the first by the figure marked (*a*).

> (Ex. 2) Ye are not of the flesh, but of the Spirit
> (Ex. 4) If in your hearts the Spirit abideth.
> If Jesu's Spirit be not yours, ye are not His.

Ye are not of the flesh

If in your hearts the Spirit

The fugue brings the two subjects into combination and comes to a close. The remaining sentence ('If Jesu's Spirit be not yours, ye are not His') is treated in massive harmony with a broad new melody first given by the soprano and then taken up by the bass. Just because the change of style is impressive, there is the less reason (as there is no authority) for the pause and the radical change of tempo which early editions (followed by most conductors) make at this point. Bach has shown in dozens of parallel cases that he values the effect of a passage that begins by sounding like a central episode to be followed by a return to the opening, but leads instead to a new movement and so shows that completeness is not to be looked for until the whole work is finished. Here this impressive corollary to the fugue leads to B minor, the dominant of the main key; and the next chorale (in four parts, without expansion, but with a great deal of movement below the melody) points the moral.

> Hence with earthly treasure!
> Thou art all my pleasure,
> Jesu, all my choice.
> Hence, thou empty glory!
> Nought to me thy story
> Told with tempting voice:
> Pain, or loss, or shame, or cross
> Shall not from my Saviour move me,
> Since He deigns to love me.

As the work reaches its middle point its range of key and style expands; and the next verse from the Epistle (ch. viii. 10) is in C major, 12/8 time, for alto, tenor, and bass.

If therefore Christ abide in you, then is the body dead because of transgression; but the Spirit liveth because of righteousness.

Its first clause is set in a flowing vein of melody, which the three voices share, taking up each other's phrases without breaking up the harmony or the rhythmic periods. With the second clause ('but the Spirit liveth') the style appropriately becomes that of a florid double fugue. This comes to a half-close on the dominant of A minor, so that the movement is not complete in itself but leads to the next.

The ninth movement, the fifth verse of the chorale, is one of Bach's great choral variations; not, this time, in the free declamatory style that so effectually disguises the structure of the third verse, but in a stupendously complete and clear form which only Bach has achieved, though his examples of it are so numerous that they are believed to be normal specimens of academic music. (The first chorus of the *Matthew Passion* is one.) The essence of this form is that, while one voice or part sings the chorale phrase by phrase, with pauses so long between each as to stretch the whole out to the length of a long movement, the other parts execute a complete design which may or may not have some connexion with the melody of the chorale, but which in any case would remain a perfectly solid whole if the chorale were taken away. This is a very different thing from the affair of shreds and patches that is taught in schools: we may confidently say that before Bach it was hardly known, and that it has never been attempted since. I have tried the experiment of playing this ninth movement through, leaving out the chorale-melody except for a few unemphasized notes to complete the mere harmony. The effect is not noticeably less solid and natural than that of the foregoing trio, No. 8. Of course this does not mean that the chorale is not essential to the whole: a work of art may remain surprisingly intelligible after being deprived of many essential elements. I even think that Bach has shown by about a hundred parallel cases (this figure is not rhetorical; I said 'dozens' when I meant dozens) that he wishes the chorale to be sung by the full chorus-part of altos, while the surrounding independent trio is either a literal trio or a semi-chorus. As the absence of a soprano in the eighth movement left the ensemble with a tone of sweet gravity, here the absence of a bass leaves it poetically aloof from the world. The naïve poem which Bach set gives a pathetic irony which the translation misses. ('*Gute Nacht*'—'Good night'—is a finer reproach than 'Fare thee well'.)

> Fare thee well that errest,
> Thou that earth preferrest,
> Thou wilt tempt in vain.
> Fare thee well, transgression,
> Hence, abhorred possession!
> Come not forth again.
> Past your hour, O pride and power:
> Worldly life, thy bonds I sever.
> Fare thee well for ever.

And now the wheel swings full circle. The conclusion of the

argument is set to the same music as the beginning. Bach's tenth movement is a compressed version of his second, the two statements of its contrasted themes being fused into one, with weightier climaxes. The first two clauses are set to the massive opening melody; and the conclusion ('by His Spirit that dwelleth within you') is set to the 'masked fugue' (Ex. 2).

If by His Spirit God, that upraised Jesus from the dead, dwell in you, He that raised Christ up from the dead, shall also quicken your mortal bodies, by His Spirit that dwelleth within you.

The great work then ends with the music of the first plain chorale:

> Hence all fears and sadness!
> For the Lord of gladness,
> Jesus, enters in;
> They who love the Father,
> Though the storms may gather,
> Still have peace within.
> Yea, whate'er I here must bear,
> Still in Thee lies purest pleasure,
> Jesu, priceless treasure.

HANDEL

CCV. 'ISRAEL IN EGYPT'

A Selection

Some effrontery is needed to present my selection from *Israel in Egypt* as comprising the 'authentic portions' of that monumental work. What is published as *Israel in Egypt* exists throughout in Handel's autograph, and was produced by him on the 4th of April 1739. It contained too many choruses and not enough arias for the public taste, and was, in fact, a work of a kind that had never been heard in London before. Subsequent performances were few, and at them a half-hearted attempt was made to lighten the work by inserting a few more arias adapted from Handel's operas, a procedure quite exceptional in his oratorios. Largely as Handel's works support themselves by taking in each other's washing, his operas and oratorios have practically no dealings with each other. The operas gave no scope for choruses, and the Italian singers did not sing English. The borrowed opera arias did not help matters much, and performances of *Israel in Egypt* remained rare in Handel's lifetime, and did not become commoner until the public learned that choral music was greater than solo arias.

As a whole, then, *Israel in Egypt* suffered less alteration than most of Handel's oratorios during his lifetime; yet it has since been found to be perhaps one of the most composite and heterogeneous works of art in the history of music; and the discovery of its patch-work construction has caused a real distress, ranging, according to one's temper, from cynical contempt to moral indignation, and producing pathetic efforts to explain away a situation shocking when presented crudely to the sensibility of the naïve music-lover.

I propose to deal with each detail of the situation as it arises. This is a much shorter method than that of discussing the general principles first; since most of these general principles can then appear as *obiter dicta*, whereas their more systematic discussion can only give an audience the impression of rising temperature in a hall full of earnest persons, holders of pious opinions, and iconoclasts, all set at loggerheads by technical experts. Two general principles only will I mention as of paramount importance: first, that in the eighteenth century an oratorio, even more than an opera, was only in the rarest instances a single composition, and was always an entertainment filling several hours. The author was neither anonymous like the master-builder of a medieval cathedral, nor multiple like the authors and composers of a modern revue, who are pro-verbially supposed to outnumber the stage crowd. But, as the provider of some four hours' musical entertainment he had the right to insert acknowledged favourite arias, to invite contributions from pupils, and, in course of time, to neglect the formula of acknowledgement. Two volumes of Mozart's arias, including trios and quartets, were written by him as insertions in operas by for-gotten composers; and passages from Handel's works more im-portant than any which Handel borrowed have become incorporated into the structure of some of Mozart's greatest choral music, not because Mozart is a plagiarist, conscious or unconscious, but be-cause such choral music is like architecture in being often con-structed of extensive procedures and elements that are common property.

The other general principle which must be laid down is that Handel, like Bach and other great masters, differs from his pre-decessors and contemporaries in that he is a composer, as most of them are not. This is a very important principle, which is less understood in English musical orthodoxy than almost any other fact in art. The fourth volume of the *Oxford History of Music* is entitled 'The Age of Bach and Handel'. It contains great wealth of information about the contemporaries of those composers, and shows, more by accident than design, a kind of historical sense inasmuch as it fails to make Bach and Handel more prominent otherwise than by bulk than they were to their contemporaries. This leaves the naïve reader at a loss to understand why two com-posers so indistinguishable from the common run should nowadays be selected for the title of their age. But the author of the volume shows, without admitting it, that he himself is equally at a loss on this matter. He sums up the fullest pontifical ineptitude of British nineteenth-century musical criticism in the following paragraph:

'In Theodora's first song, the slow crotchets on which she sings the word "Angels" have nothing to do with the more rapid phrase to "ever bright and fair".... The continuation of a subject from the germ contained in its opening notes was never a very strong point with Handel, and in "Sweet rose and lily" we have an opportunity of comparing his methods in this respect with those of his quondam rival Bononcini, who hit upon nearly the same melodic idea in his best-known song "Per la gloria".

(a) HANDEL:

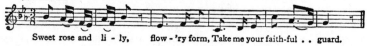

Sweet rose and li - ly,   flow - 'ry form, Take me your faith-ful . . guard.

(b) BONONCINI transcribed to same key and time.

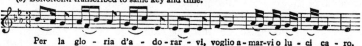

Per la glo - ria d'a - do - rar - vi, voglio a - mar-vi o lu - ci ca - ro.

It will strike every reader that the melodic germ of the subject, which is the figure in the second bar of each, is left by Handel quite undeveloped, while Bononcini carries it on in a delightful addition of two bars, and alludes to it again in the last bar but one, giving the whole strain a more obviously flowing character.'

Let us try some literary criticism on these methods.

Milton begins *L'Allegro* thus:

> Hence loathèd Melancholy
>   Of Cerberus and blackest midnight born
> In Stygian Cave forlorn
>   'Mongst horrid shapes, and shrieks, and sights unholy!

Compare this disjointed sense and irregular rhythm, held together only by the imperfect rhyme of 'Melancholy' and 'unholy', with the symmetry of Shakespeare at the end of *A Midsummer-Night's Dream*:

> Hence away;
> Make no stay;
> Meet me all by break of day.

It will strike every reader that the intellectual germ of both passages, which is the word 'hence', is left by Milton quite undeveloped, while Shakespeare carries it throughout the whole passage, with a delightful and logical inversion in the word 'meet'. (It is unnecessary to point out that Shakespeare wrote 'trip' instead of 'hence'; for the Oxford historian remarks in a footnote that 'it is unnecessary to point out that the key and time-values in Bononcini's song have been changed in order to facilitate comparison'.)

It was unfortunate for the doyen of English musical critics, as well as for criticism itself, that, for those who like that kind of thing, music can be enjoyed in the series of mere tastes of 'sugar piled upon honey' which was all that Charles Lamb made of the art in his *Essay on Ears*. This one comparison of Bononcini and Handel sheds far more light on our British standardized ignorance of composition than upon Handel's ultimate victory over his rival. The composer of a witty symmetrical tune like *Per la gloria* may or may not be able to carry it out on a larger scale than is revealed by its self-contained symmetry. The composer who gets as far as the first twelve bars of *Sweet rose and lily* must be intending to go much farther, and shows every sign of being able to do so.

This quality of composition is not the only condition of greatness in music or art; and it is compatible with childish immaturity and with insolent rubbish. A composition ascribed to Handel cannot be proved spurious on the ground that it is rubbish, nor can it be proved spurious because, whether otherwise good or bad, it is extremely careless in style; but, if a thing ascribed to Handel or extant in his writing has not at all events 'the gift of the gab', then you may be quite certain that he did not himself compose it at any period of infancy, youth or age. The six oboe duets which he wrote at the age of twelve differ from his later work chiefly in two facts: that there is much more in them line for line, and that there is much less evidence that they might not go on for ever.

At all periods of Handel's life his musical form is too improvisatorial to be amenable to any specially musical rules. He must be judged as a rhetorician, exactly as we would judge of a master of prose or a speaker. His work at the age of twelve has occasional defects, mostly in the nature of redundancies or tautologies, which do not occur in his mature works. When he was confronted with these juvenile sonatas at the height of his fame in London, he was quite unsentimentally amused, and laughed, saying: 'I wrote like the devil in those days, and chiefly for the oboe, which was my favourite instrument.' A sympathetic reader or hearer of these oboe sonatas might almost have expected Handel to show some signs of regret that his later compositions did not always maintain his early enthusiasm; but, on the contrary, Handel was capable of tempting a friend, while promenading in Vauxhall Gardens, to comment on the stuff that was being played by the band, and of replying: 'You are quite right, sir; it is very poor stuff, and I thought so myself when I wrote it.' But whether Handel was writing cynically poor stuff or recording his most sublime inspirations, he never wrote a page that halted. He did not always write at a tearing pace; and, though his average time for the first half of a three-act oratorio was a week of continuous writing, he would sometimes revise a single aria several times, or make a great many alterations in drafting a single version of it. Sometimes the results of such labour were what we regard as inspired, like the intensely pathetic 'Waft her, angels, to the skies' in *Jephtha*. Sometimes it is impossible to guess why Handel was so scrupulous, as in the case of the aria *Thou art gone up on high* in the *Messiah*, to which the most pious editors append the footnote: '*This air is generally omitted*'. The reasons for the omission are obvious. What is mysterious is, not only that there are six extant versions of the aria, but that there is no means of telling why any of them should be considered better than the others. As a whole the score of *The Messiah* was written in twenty-one days. Some of the six versions of its dullest aria were probably transpositions for the benefit of various singers at various performances; but I doubt whether any general principle will emerge from the study of Handel's revisions of his own work, such as can be shown in every detail of Beethoven's sketches. What is quite certain is that Handel could neither copy nor invent a paragraph of music without making it fluent. To this subject I must return each time that we come upon adaptations of earlier or foreign works in the course of *Israel in Egypt*. Let us now begin the point-to-point analysis of the selection which I produce as containing the 'authentic essence' of this mighty work within the compass of a little more than an hour.

As published, *Israel in Egypt* has no overture, but begins abruptly with a narrative recitative introducing the story of the plagues of Egypt and the exodus as told in Psalms lxxviii, cv, and cvi. Chrysander has restored Handel's own titles to the main sections of his work. The first part is called *Exodus*, and the second part *Moses's Song*. We are spared the duty of keeping our tempers and restraining our guffaws at the well-meaning absurdities of Handel's librettists, because in *Israel in Egypt*, as in *The Messiah*, Handel's words are entirely Biblical; and in the case of *Israel* there is no record that he did not select them himself. *Moses's Song*, which is considerably the larger part of the work, was written first, and occupied Handel from the 1st to the 11th of October 1738. The first part, or *Exodus*, was then written between the 15th and 28th of the same month. The reason why it begins so abruptly was that Handel prefaced it by his already-written Funeral Anthem for Queen Caroline, *The Ways of Zion do Mourn*, which he adapted under the title of *The Lamentation of the Israelites over the Death of Joseph*. This more than thoroughly explains the present opening of *Israel*; but the gain in a further volume of Handel's greatest choral music is outweighed by the fact that the Funeral Anthem is not well contrasted with what is to follow, and keeps us for half an hour with only Handel's new title to tell us that it has anything to do with either Israel or Egypt. After much thought, I have come to the conclusion that an ideal and very short way to introduce the oratorio and indicate the situation Handel has in mind is to use the Dead March in *Saul* as an overture.

After this plain indication of mourning, we see the point of the first sentence of the opening recitative.

I. RECITATIVE

Now there arose a new king over Egypt, which knew not Joseph; and he set over Israel task-masters to afflict them with burdens; and they made them serve with rigour.

Then follows an 8-part chorus in Handel's noblest style.

II. CHORUS

Ex. 1. And the children of Israel sighed by reason of the bondage:
Ex. 2. And their cry came up unto God.
They oppress'd them with burdens, and made them serve with rigour.

An alto solo delivers the first clause in one of Handel's finest examples of perfect melody and perfect illustration, the orchestra contributing to the realization of the word 'sighed'.

And . . the chil - dren of Is - ra - el sigh'd, sighed,

Then the orchestra develops an energetic theme, over which the sopranos and altos of an 8-part chorus sing a solemn *canto fermo* suggestive of modal harmony. The meaning of the energetic theme appears when the chorus takes it up, and the combination is shown in Ex. 2.

Ex. 2.
And . . . . their cry came
[They op-press'd them with bur-dens, and made them serve]
up un - to God. &c.

Thus Handel has stated his whole material with his maturest simplicity and breadth. This chorus would repay such an analysis as I have attempted to give of Beethoven's *Weihe des Hauses* Overture; but the analysis would be quite as difficult to write as to read. Meanwhile, it is easier to listen and enjoy the chorus, which is true Handel of the highest order. Apart from time-limits, that is one reason against adopting Handel's plan of using the great Funeral Anthem as a first part to *Israel in Egypt*. This chorus must be allowed to make its full impression without being forestalled by half an hour's music of the same quality and tone. A detailed analysis of it would soon show its difference from the second-hand parts of *Israel in Egypt*, if these also were thoroughly analysed; but as I am not producing the second-hand stuff, we can spare ourselves the trouble. We must not lump together as second-hand all the stuff where Handel borrows themes, or even whole passages, from other works. Originality lies in the whole. Nobody would be surprised if the *canto fermo* in Ex. 2 should prove to be liturgical: indeed, I should be surprised if it were not. Nor have I the slightest interest in the possibility that the other two themes of this chorus have been found elsewhere. They are, rather, such as it might be difficult to avoid in the musical language of the seventeenth and eighteenth centuries. All that matters is their perfect fitness for their text, and the grandeur of the form into which they are built. The chorus is in eight parts, but, although written for convenience as a double chorus, is hardly, if at all, antiphonal.

III. RECITATIVE

Ex. 3. Then sent He Moses, His servant, and Aaron, whom He had
    chosen: these shew'd His signs among them, and wonders in the
    land of Ham.
    He turned their waters into blood.

Handel's recitatives are written with the same secretarial efficiency as his other work. I hear rumours that the profounder Italian scholars can detect that his Italian recitatives are not quite the genuine article as supplied by the direct apostolic successors of the Neapolitan School. The evidence is doubtless as cogent as the evidence that Handel was not an Englishman. Recitative is a technical term meaning solo vocal music in which the composer's only purpose is to 'stylise' in musical notes the natural rise and fall and rhythm of spoken words, excluding all symmetries and ornamentations that might distract attention from this purpose. As this art was first developed in Italy, its recognized classical formulas naturally suit the Italian language. And we have no better reason to expect them to suit other languages than to translate *Qu'est-ce-que c'est que ça?* by *What is this that this is that that?* Nevertheless, already in the eighteenth century it was orthodox to comment upon Purcell's sturdy independence of foreign culture, that 'he did not adopt the art of recitative as recently developed in Italy'. Why should he? Purcell's declamation is English; and the only way in which his recitative deviates from what is universal in the Italian art is that he cannot resist the temptation to break into illustrative coloratura. In the same, but in a simpler, way Handel transcends the realism of recitative, and marks his intention of doing so by a renewed time-signature and key-signature, in what has always been rightly admired as one of his greatest strokes of musical rhetoric.

Ex. 3.

He turn-ed their wa-ters in - to blood.

As a rule, tenors do not like to expose the weakness of their low notes; but no tenor has ever failed to enjoy convincing the listener of the gruesomeness of his low D on the word 'blood'.

IV. CHORUS
Ex. 4. They loathed to drink of the river:
He turned their waters into blood.

Ex. 4.

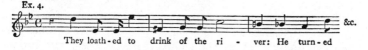

They loath-ed to drink of the ri - ver: He turn-ed

This is an excellent Handelian fugue, slightly above Handel's usual standard of solidity, and expressive of the words by reason of two points: its chromatic harmony, and the fact that its theme takes the extreme form of what is otherwise a matter of common property. The theme must have come into existence as soon as a solid minor scale had ousted the ecclesiastical modes. Its essential feature is the diminished seventh on the syllables 'to drink'. In its mildest form the first interval is a third, as in *And with his stripes we are healed*, and in Bach's A minor Fugue in the second book of the Forty-eight. The intermediate form begins with a fifth, as in the fugue of Haydn's F minor Quartet Op. 20, No. 4. I cannot off-hand say how many instances might be found of Handel's major seventh, but it is obviously selected here for expressive purposes, and chorus singers will perhaps pardon my remarking that, unless they are very experienced, they 'loathe' being caught by it unawares; which, of course, with experience they never are.

V. ARIA

It is highly undesirable nowadays that performances of *Israel in Egypt* should appeal, intentionally or otherwise, to one's sense of humour. I have no doubt that Handel enjoyed allowing his string-band to hop in a pretty pattern through the shocking tale of the frogs that infested even the king's chambers, and possibly (since the pattern prevails throughout the aria) had some causal connexion with the blotches and blains that broke forth on man and beast. Except for this pattern and its relation to the text, the aria might just as well be sung to some edifying moral; and it is certainly the more agonizingly funny the more beautifully it is sung. Only once have I heard it given with an accurate sense of the situation. That versatile artist, Marie Brema, instead of using the full fog-horn powers of the British contralto, presented it with the tremulous horror of a *Hofdame* clinging to the faint hope that the mess might be cleared up before Pharaoh could discover it.

VI. CHORUS

Ex. 5. HE spake the word: And there came all manner of flies and lice in all their quarters.
HE spake: and the locusts came without number and devour'd the fruits of the land.

We now come to what is really important in Handel's borrowings. Handel has represented for all time the rhythm and the solemn implications of the statement: 'HE spake the word.' With trombones and with echoes from antiphonal groups of orchestra and chorus, nothing can be simpler or more exclusive of other possibilities. As for the flies, the violins represent them with furious efficiency, and are joined by the basses in heavier flight when the locusts come without number. The whole conception shows Handel at his utmost efficiency, and is too grand to be comic. This being so, one of the greatest mysteries in the history of music is the fact that Handel took the trouble to copy the whole of an instrumental *sinfonia* from a Serenata by Stradella (1645–82), comprising twenty-six bars of the whole of forty-one of which this number consists. It saved him no trouble. Stradella was an interesting historical figure, the facts of whose real life were early in the eighteenth century completely obliterated beneath a romantic story which is now far better known than any of his music. The pathos of his style is said to have been such that the assassins who were commissioned to slay him for having eloped with the mistress of a Venetian nobleman desisted from their purpose on hearing his aria *Pietà signore* sung in church, and warned the lovers of their danger. The aria is supposed to have come down to us in unquestionably beautiful terms that certainly never took shape until early in the nineteenth century. In power of composition Stradella's genuine work shows a definite advance on what had been achieved by the middle of the seventeenth century, and the twenty-six bars which

Handel transferred to the present chorus show neither strength
nor weakness of form, but do contain at the outset quite interesting
modulations—

Ex. 5.

to which Handel gives proper weight by having established his
key in eight previous bars. These eight bars and a final ritornello
account for the difference between Stradella's twenty-six bars and
Handel's forty-one. For the rest, we may fairly say that Stradella
wrote this chorus first, with the exceptions that HE, the choral
writing, and the flies are omitted.

VII. CHORUS

Exx. 6–7. He gave them hailstones for rain;
Exx. 8a–8b. fire, mingled with the hail, ran along upon the ground.

We never know where we are with Handel. It is an absolute law
that his recitatives must lead correctly or effectively to what follows; and there are plenty of cases where the key-sequence of
complete movements is artistic. But there are plenty of cases where
it is quite crass. The great Funeral Anthem is firmly in and around
G minor, except for one number in the pointlessly incongruous key
of A minor; and *Israel in Egypt* has two examples of the same crass
indifference side by side with Handel's deepest harmonic thoughts.
The sequence of keys in ball-room dances is not more casual than
the C major of the famous Hailstone Chorus after the B flat of the
Chorus of Flies. But this is less mysterious than the fact that
Handel should have again troubled to draw upon the Stradella
Serenata for this famous chorus. Space obviously fails to go into
the intricacies of the case. By far the most able extant collection of
arguments on the matter is to be found in *Handel and his Orbit*,
by P. Robinson, who stoutly maintains that the main works in
question, the Stradella Serenata, the Erba *Magnificat*, and the Urio
Te Deum, are early works of Handel's own. Arguments based upon
minutiae of style are absolutely hopeless with Handel. The folios
and quartos of Shakespeare are not more careless than Handel's
autographs; and wherever Handel encountered any feature that
pleased him in any composer's style, he promptly imitated it, so
that you can almost date his settling in England by his adoption of
some pleasant archaisms in the style of Purcell. But, as I must still
insist, the one thing that I cannot find in any of Handel's earliest

works is an inability or indisposition to compose. 'Interminable cantatas of no great merit' is what his quarrelsome friend Matthe-son imputed to his nonage; but never until the fourth volume of the *Oxford History of Music* has any critic committed the ineptitude of mistaking the alternate abruptness and expansiveness of a Handelian exposition for shortness of breath. The first ten bars of the following extract are common to Stradella's Serenata and Handel's Hailstone Chorus, except that Handel begins with a bass note on the organ, and that his key is C instead of D. But at the twelfth bar Stradella stops and begins again on the dominant.

Ex. 6.

I am not clear what his overture represents. The initial rhythm may mean whatever 'Pip-pip' means, or it may mean knocking at a door. Far be it from me to be inattentive to its fitness for its own comic purpose; but, to borrow the admirable phrase sometimes heard in committees, what Opens a Serious Door is that neither here nor in the other two movements of his overture does Stradella even feebly begin to compose in any real sense of the term, whereas Handel's hailstones are beginning to fall thicker at the eleventh bar, and are soon coming down in spate, while he draws upon the last extant number of Stradella's Serenata to bring his twenty-one bars of introduction to a climax.

Ex. 7.

Basso 8..............: *loco.*   8........................

8........................: *loco.*   8

In Ex. 7 Stradella is illustrating the wrath of a presumably elderly
gentleman whose lady has tricked him. The shaking of his fists has
become the whiplash of Handel's hailstones; and one of his vocal
expressions has become the bass of Handel's most definite vocal
theme.

Ex. 8a.

sen - za l'ar - - mi del - lo sde - gno.

Ex. 8b.

min-gled with . . the hail ran a - long . . up - on the ground.

I flatly refuse to believe that the Serenata ascribed to Stradella is an
early work of Handel's. It has a certain number of pretty ideas
which attracted Handel, and a large number of equally pretty ideas
that were common currency. It has also, what is more material to
the Chorus of the Flies and the Hailstone Chorus than any number
of thematic borrowings, the idea of antiphonal groups of instruments, which Handel has gigantically supplemented by antiphonal
groups of chorus.

This raises the general question of the purpose of eight-part
writing. In the first chorus, *And the children of Israel sighed*, the
only use of antiphony is to enable the word 'sighed' to be detached
as a separate harmonic mass from the surrounding fugato; but in
the Chorus of Flies and the Hailstone Chorus antiphony is of the
essence of the contract. Handel had already written ostensibly
eight-part choruses in 1733 in the oratorios of *Deborah* and
Athalia. Only in one case, in *Deborah*, when the faithful Israelites
àre in altercation with the Baal-worshippers, are the voices grouped
in opposite masses for obvious dramatic reasons. In *Israel* the
reasons are purely musical. Genuine eight-part writing is a rich
fabric and laborious to calculate and write. Its technical difficulty

has always been overrated, even in the most classical times; and no
academic tradition is more infantile than that which still occasion-
ally survives in academic regulations ordaining five-part counterpoint for Bachelors of Music and eight-part for Doctors. I seriously
question whether any ten bars of Handel's eight-part writing would
satisfy an old-fashioned British examiner for a Mus.Doc. degree;
and, in fact, though his eight-part choruses, whether antiphonal or
not, require eight staves to set out the notes as Handel distributes
them, they contain a very small percentage of real eight-part
writing, and would lose much of their cumulative effect if they
contained more. Bach's eight-part writing is, like every aspect of
his forms, much more true to the terms of its contract than
Handel's, though an old-fashioned British examiner would again
have to learn Bach's aesthetic system from the rudiments upwards
before he was qualified to examine it. With *Israel in Egypt* Handel
evidently acquired an appetite for eight-part writing, and an insight into its true aesthetic principles. The richness of eight parts,
independent as such, very soon palls; but the opposition of complete masses of harmony is of elemental power. And when the
masses overlap, the eight-part harmony is a by-product, enjoyable
both for its own richness and for the way in which it happens. But
increase of power comes not from the multiplying of the parts,
but from their occasional or gradual fusion towards ordinary four-
part writing, and further, down to the thunderous unisons for
which Handel is famous, and fatally imitable by composers who
have developed the modern orchestra to an organization which no
chorus less than a football crowd can dominate. Ten years after
Israel in Egypt, Handel designed *Solomon* expressly for the purpose
of reviewing most of the subjects of Solomon's wisdom, sacred and
profane, in a series of descriptive choruses, mainly antiphonal. It
is interesting that only once should the motive of his antiphonal
writing have been dramatic, and that in *Deborah*, the earliest case
of all. The total bulk of Bach's eight-part choral writing is hardly
greater than that of Handel's. About half of it is contained in the
Matthew Passion, where the antiphony is mainly dramatic and is
implied by the text. The rest is comprised in four of the so-called
'unaccompanied'motets, two of the church cantatas, and the Hosanna
of the B minor Mass. As may be expected of Bach, the eight-part
writing is perfectly systematic; and so is the scheme by which Bach
makes his double choruses gradually coalesce into four-part harmony. He thus appears to miss the opportunity for the local
nuances Handel commands by doubling any voice as he chooses;
but the limitation is only apparent, for Bach's orchestra is often a
systematically independent chorus in itself, as in the multi-choral
Psalms of Schütz a century earlier, where the instruments, some-

times described merely as *vox instrumentalis* and always provided with the words, exactly like the voices, are grouped in a separate *capella* or two. If you have leisure to think of such things while you listen to a hailstorm as suggestive as Handel's, I can only wish you joy of your scholarship; and, as for Stradella, he extinguishes himself at the eleventh bar.

VIII. CHORUS

He sent a thick darkness over all the land, even darkness, which might be felt.

Handel's greatest power and depth are here manifest in every particular. And I do not see how any quotation, short of the whole chorus, can illustrate them. The chief difficulty in realizing his intentions nowadays comes from the fact that the modern orchestra provides a first and second bassoon to play the notes written for these instruments by Handel, but does not provide the twenty bassoons which seemed to him a reasonable number to balance his twenty oboes and his string-band of ordinary modern size. However, as the writer of the fourth volume of the *Oxford History of Music* remarks, our ancestors had no sense of proportion, any more than the composer of *Sweet rose and lily* had a sense of composition.

This raises the question of 'additional accompaniments', a matter far more difficult in the case of the improvisatorial Handel than in that of Bach, whose schematic accuracy compels us at all events to play exactly what he wrote, however we may be compelled to re-distribute it. The trouble with additional accompaniments began, as all the world knows, with Mozart, who certainly in the case of *The Messiah* was often distressingly out of touch with Handel's subject, but whose exquisite work on *Acis and Galatea* and the smaller *Ode for St. Cecilia's Day* results in a delicious compound style nowhere as incongruous as the elements which Handel has admitted into *Israel in Egypt*, and everywhere finished and imaginative where Handel is perfunctory to the extent of simply not condescending to write his music down at all so long as he was himself able to gag at the organ or harpsichord. Pious opinions have been the origin of dangerous heresies no less often, if not oftener, than they have attained the rank of orthodox doctrines. And of all pious opinions in music perhaps the most woolly-headed was the dictum of Rockstro in the first edition of *Grove's Dictionary* that all accompaniments added merely for the sake of noise are wholly indefensible. Here the word 'noise' is a crassly question-begging epithet for which the legitimate meaning is 'volume of sound', the offensive term being chosen to represent a sound which the writer does not like. The truth is that with the modern orchestra additions to increase the volume of sound are the only ones that can restore

Handel's balance of tone, and that the whole mischief of corruption that has obliterated Handel's style for a hundred and fifty years consists in the self-indulgence of composers and conductors who find the bare walls of Handel's edifices an admirable surface to scribble upon and to bedaub with the contents of more or less expensive paint-boxes. With ten or twelve oboes and ten or twelve bassoons to play the parts that Handel writes for them, we might recover something tolerably like Handel's orchestral colouring. Strange to say, modern developments of the orchestra have not helped us appreciably far towards this consummation. But we need not be very fastidious about the precise quality of tone that we may get by putting into unison all the wind instruments we have. Handel himself is evidently sometimes as vague as Schütz with his *vox instrumentalis*. In the whole of *Israel in Egypt* flutes are indicated in one passage in unison with the violins. Taken literally in terms of the modern orchestra, this would be repre- sented by solemnly engaging two gentlemen (or ladies) to sit for two hours in the orchestra for the purpose of doubling the violins in some twenty bars. We cannot suppose that this was Handel's intention. Probably most of his oboists could play the flute, and probably half of them were detailed to do so for any appropriate passages; while, no doubt, numbers of players were available whose main instrument was the flute. These would be encouraged to play for the very purpose so sternly reprobated by Rockstro. Handel set great store by the importation, or even the special manufacture, of a contrafagotto for use in his works. He never wrote a part for it; but he certainly used it to reinforce his basses whenever he could get it.

As to the quality of tone produced by twenty oboes, nothing like it has been heard in modern music, not even in Mahler's Eighth Symphony, a work which is known as the 'Symphony of a Thou- sand', because an orchestra and chorus of seven hundred and fifty is its minimum necessity and a thousand is what it needs for comfort. But what does appear from the disciplined and experienced hand- ling of such vast combinations is that the resulting tone-colours are neither so varied nor so vivid as those of music on a smaller scale. We may be certain that the general unison of all the wind instruments of the modern orchestra that can play at the same pitch will produce a tone fairly capable of replacing that unknown quantity, the tone of a dozen Handelian oboes. It is mere pedantry to say that the associations and sound of clarinets, or even of saxo- phones, are so foreign to Handelian aesthetics that their mixture with oboe tone is an outrage. So long as the players play in tune and the really Handelian opposition between brass and wood-wind and the rest of the orchestra is not obliterated, it does not matter two hoots of a saxophone what sort of soprano or alto wind instrument we use to impart to our orchestra something like the reediness which must almost have overwhelmed Handel's violins. I have not the slightest doubt that two clarinets, two cors anglais, and four muted horns, in unison with Handel's two bassoon parts, will approximate closely enough to his representation of darkness for all genuine aesthetic purposes; and I am equally certain that he would have thrown his wig at me if I had tried to fob him off with two bassoons alone.

The chorus becomes something like a choral recitative as the voices give up full harmony and grope their isolated ways through vastly remote keys; and when I speak of vastly remote keys I do not refer to that feeble-minded criterion which esteems all strokes of genius as 'remarkable for the time at which they were written'. The fact that our loud-speaker can give us an orchestral concert from the Antipodes before the sounds of the orchestra have travelled from the platform to the back of the hall, does not annul the record of a Channel swimmer. Handel's modulations are related, not to the time at which he wrote, but to the structure of his musical language. In the Chorus of Darkness they are as extensive as the modulations in Bach's Chromatic Fantasia, inasmuch as they traverse most of harmonic space. On the other hand, they differ profoundly from the Chromatic Fantasia, and from Handel's own Passion recitatives in *The Messiah*, because they are not enharmonic —that is to say, each step is known as far as it goes, but there is no general aim and the end of the groping is incalculably remote. (Handel's declamation is subtle to the extent of making distinctions between 'over all the land' and 'o'er all the land'; 'e'en darkness' and 'even darkness'. These should not be corrected. On the other hand, he puts an intolerable strain on the indefinite article when he makes it come, not only on an accented beat, '*A* thick darkness', but on the highest note of the four. So long as the notes are level, it would be pedantic to make any change; but in this last case I feel justified in reading 'Darkness sent He', especially as Handel continues by shortening the words into 'A darkness'.)

IX. CHORUS

Ex. 9. He smote all the first-born of Egypt, the chief of all their strength.

Daylight follows with drastic effect, which Handel enjoys as fiercely as the Psalmist. His twenty oboes and twenty bassoons double the voices, while the trombones and the violins put a very literal interpretation on the word 'smote'. Towards the end of this double fugue, the chorus does its own smiting with great zest, before bringing the fugue tersely to an admirable climax. Not less

admirable is the anticlimax of the seven bars of final orchestral
ritornello.

X. CHORUS

Ex. 10. But as for His people,
Ex. 11. He led them forth like sheep.
Ex. 13. He brought them out with silver and gold: there was not one
feeble person among their tribes.

One of the most perfect transitions, both in mood and harmony, in
all music is that effected by the first chords of this wonderful
chorus. After the close in A minor, the impact of the dominant of
G major perfectly represents the blessed change of mood from the
malicious joy at the smiting of the enemy to the deep gratitude for
God's care of his people.

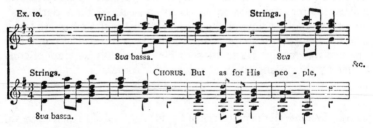

These simple-seeming opening bars might have been written by
anybody, but could never have been placed where they are by any
but a very great composer; and, as far as intrinsic beauty can be
conveyed in a theme of four bars and accumulated in echoes and
sequences for another thirty or forty, Handel continues to give us
his very own at its very best.

Ex. 11.

The orchestral colouring, even with a poor couple of oboes and
couple of bassoons, is beautiful according to the most exacting
modern orchestral criteria; and the theme is surely one of the most
beautiful that Handel ever *wrote*. Therefore it now behoves us to
follow the pious advice given to the young man who asked for
authoritative counsel how to deal with the arguments that assailed
his orthodoxy: 'Look them boldly in the face and pass them by.
This wonderful theme fills several more or less lively pages of the
Stradella Serenata, where its text, *Io pur seguirò*, inspires its canonic
imitations. Stradella's treatment of it becomes faster and faster,
until it reaches a presto; upon which the gentleman furiously
answers: *Seguir non voglio più* in the terms afterwards used by
Handel in the Hailstone Chorus, as shown in Exx. 7, 8a, and 8b.
I am as ready as any one to respect Stradella on his own merits as
an interesting historical figure, or even as something more; but the
rightful owner of an idea is the person who understands it, and
Stradella is the rightful owner of the comic chase-me-Charlie affair
that he makes of this theme. His own continuation of it at once

relegates it to its native seventeenth-century limbo of shreds, patches, and frustrations.

Ex. 12.

It is also quite sufficient to dispose of any theory that the Serenata can have been an early work of Handel's own. But the potential beauty of those first four bars explains all the rest. After turning Stradella's theme into a sublime vocal pastoral symphony, Handel repeats his introduction (Ex. 10), and continues with a setting of the words 'He brought them out with silver and gold' in a solid and appropriately broad fugue, which lasts for some sixty-four bars.

Ex. 13.
He   brought   them   out   with   sil - ver   and   gold . . . .

He   brought   them   out

He then summarily recapitulates his three sentences with their three themes, and ends in overwhelming triumph with neither themes nor polyphony, to the text: 'There was not one, not one feeble person among their tribes.' (The repetition of 'not one' is a glorious stroke of rhetoric and rhythm.) It is a popular opinion that Handel has an unmistakable style. The many difficulties in this proposition begin with the questions of what is a style, and how much of Handel's works are by Handel. But this chorus could have been designed, invented, composed, and compiled by no one but Handel. It is a pity that the word 'poet' has no verb in English, so that we cannot translate Beethoven's admirable epigram: 'Gedichtet, oder wie man sagt, componirt.' The least understood and most Handelian feature of this chorus is the two extra bars in which the orchestra quietly remarks—

Ex. 14.

And   that   is   that.

Orthodox theologians and gastronomes tell us that, though it were impious to doubt that the Almighty could have created a better fruit than the strawberry, the fact remains that he never did.

XI. CHORUS

Egypt was glad when they departed, for the fear of them fell upon them.

In a complete performance of *Israel in Egypt* it would be a mistake to omit the note-for-note transcription of an organ canzona by Kaspar Kerll (1627–93) which Handel adapts to the text: *Egypt was glad when they departed, for the fear of them fell upon them.* Hawkins, who, with all his unclubbability, sometimes knew a good thing when he saw it, gives the whole of Kerll's organ piece in his *History of Music*, without showing the slightest consciousness that Handel had used it. Mr. Robinson in *Handel and his Orbit* argues that the piece was the kind of thing that was highly esteemed by the promoters of the Concerts of Antient Music; and that, like Handel's other plagiarisms of whole pieces, its inclusion in such a four-hours' entertainment as an oratorio or an opera would be a compliment to the taste of his more learned patrons, and would require no acknowledgement. Certainly Handel was bitterly aware that his enemies were on the prowl for any opportunity of discrediting him; and certainly in the matter of plagiarisms his behaviour shows, not so much that he had no fear of detection, as that he had no reason to fear its consequences. The counterpoint of Kerll's double fugue in contrary motion is much more solid than any that is habitual with Handel. Kerll's canzona falls into two parts, which are repeated. The second part introduces the second theme, which Handel sets to the words: 'For the fear of them fell upon them.' Handel has taken considerable pains with the orchestration, although its sole function is to support the voices, which sing Kerll's canzona note for note. The first part is supported by the wind, the organ, and the basses. With the second part the strings and trombones enter, the strings doubling the voices in the higher octave, and thus attaining a powerful climax. The pitch is a tone higher than the original, so that Handel's version presents the appearance of a modernized Phrygian mode, which corresponds closely to the facts of its harmonic style. The whole thing perfectly expresses the glum relief of the Egyptians, and neither Bach nor Handel could have put anything better in its place. But it so happens that the next chorus, and the next topic, can follow 'But as for his people' just as effectively.

XII

We now come to the second and larger of the early sources of *Israel in Egypt*. Mr. Robinson is very anxious to prove that, Erba and Urio being the names of places at which Handel probably stayed during his Italian visit, the composers, the Rev. Don

Dionigi Erba and Padre Francesco Urio, may not have written them at all, and that ascriptions on Italian manuscripts often confuse the words *dal* and *del*. *Dal* simply means 'at the house (or place) of', while *del* means 'composed by'. Our view of the case will be obscured by the slightest anxiety to vindicate Handel's moral and artistic integrity, or even to consider them as involved in the question. Those who feel any such uneasiness ought to take courage from the fact that the fiercest champion of the author-hood of Stradella, Urio, Erba, and other *Händelquellen*, is Chrysander, who not only devoted his life to editing the works and writing the biography of Handel, but revered him so far on the further side of idolatry as to believe that music had done little but decline since Handel's death. Chrysander gives a reduced facsimile of two pages from Handel's autograph copy of the Erba *Magnificat*. Both of these show that when he made this manuscript he was not composing, but copying from a set of parts: a fact obvious at a glance to any one who knows how composers write and how they copy as distinguished from professional copyists. Chrysander does not tell us how he further deduces that the parts from which Handel copies must have been not only incomplete, but printed. The Erba *Magnificat*, says Chrysander, shows every sign of an Italian hand; and, moreover, one of the last decades of the seventeenth century. I do not myself feel confident that many pages of Handel do not show signs of an Italian hand, and even traces of the last decades of the seventeenth century; but poor Rockstro opined on pp. 221 ff. of his *Life of Handel* that this *Magnificat* might still be regarded as Handel's composition, for which Chrysander relegates him to the category of 'unauthorized persons who rummage now and then in Handel's manuscripts and get their opinions printed before they have acquired the capacity to form a judgement'. So we had better be careful.

The Erba *Magnificat* is alleged to have inspired Handel's setting of the following words:

> He rebuked the Red Sea, and it was dried up.

The setting of this has a considerable resemblance to the first four bars of the Erba setting of the text *Quia respexit humilitatem ancillae suae*. The resemblance is not nearly good enough to make the case interesting, and it would never have been noticed but for its occurrence in a work otherwise as full of quotations as *Hamlet*. The passage is so drastically simple that even a slight inaccuracy or addition to the quotation is as ruinous to the case as the evidence in favour of the court-martialled officer who wished to be wakened and called early, which would have exonerated him from the charge of riotous behaviour had not his faithful servant on further question-

ing added that he said he was to be the Queen of the May. To my
great loss 1 have never heard, and now never shall hear, a Handel
Festival at the Crystal Palace. Those great occasions were doubtless great mistakes; and very little has been said in their defence by
authoritative musicians. No music has ever been composed for
performance on so huge a scale. Even Berlioz directs that, if his
Requiem is to be performed by a really enormous chorus, only half
or a quarter of the chorus should be used normally, and the whole
mass reserved for the climaxes. The full mass is eight hundred
voices, with an orchestra in proportion. Our British ideas of the
balance between chorus and orchestra have always been inadequate
as regards the orchestra; but, in any case, Berlioz never imagined
that his *Requiem* would be performed by a quarter of the four
thousand singers and players of the Handel Festival of 1923, nor
has any composer made the slightest attempt to calculate for more
than the thousand performers that can comfortably produce
Mahler's Eighth Symphony. Even Berlioz's ideal scheme of what
Paris, with time and money, could achieve with an orchestra comprising, among other details, 32 pianofortes and 32 harps, amounts
to only 465 players and 360 singers. It is on record by an intelligent
critic that little contrast of tone or colour could be appreciated by
a well-placed listener to the vast forces of the Handel Festival; but
that an impressive exception was the effect of a contrast between
loud high chords and soft low chords in the case of *He rebuked the
Red Sea.* Here the *piano* at the words 'and it was dried up' came
out in clear contrast. In any performance the contrast ought to be
impressive, for two reasons: first, that these chords are the only
unaccompanied vocal chords in the whole work; second, that
they plunge into the dark key of E flat after the loud C major. The
whole conception is Handel's, and the traces of it in Erba omit
everything essential, and are suggested only by their surroundings.

XIII. CHORUS

Ex. 15. He led them through the deep as through a wilderness.

No two persons have the same sense of humour, and I have
been told that this chorus is one of Handel's funniest. To me the
only possible comic aspect must lie in difficulties of performance;

difficulties which ought to vanish in rehearsal, because it is a perfectly reasonable piece of choral writing, and, as far as I can understand music at all, a very impressive specimen of Handel's style at
its highest inventiveness. The fugue subject and its counterpoints
obviously illustrate the words; and the eye can easily perceive the
catch-as-catch-can appearance of the stretti to which the subjects
lend themselves. In rehearsal it may be legitimate or stimulating
to enjoy what fun is occasioned by the natural failure of sight-
singers to take exactly the right plunge on the word 'deep', but the
difficulties of rehearsals ought not to appear in performance.
Burney, commenting on what he believed to be the earliest specimen of recorded music, observed that, though it was not of such
excellence as to make us greatly regret the loss of things like it, the
disposition of those who were pleased with it may have been a great
blessing to them. I cannot emulate Burney's urbanity in my feelings towards those who find anything funny in Handel's setting of
He led them through the deep.

XIV. CHORUS

But the waters overwhelmed their enemies, there was not one of
them left.

Like all triumphs over enemies, this chorus is enjoyable in a less
solemn way. To all healthy-minded children, even in the days of
The Fairchild Family, the story of the plagues of Egypt has been so
enjoyable as hardly to fall within sabbatical limits. I, for my own
part, long misunderstood the exhortation at the beginning of our
Morning Prayer as telling us that the Scripture moveth us in 'Sunday' places; which places I naturally took to mean those which
should regulate our conduct, while other places, such as the story
of the Plagues and the Tower of Babel, were, with all due reverence, permissible sources of pleasure on week-days. The appearance of the orchestral accompaniment on paper is such that no
amount of zest on the part of chorus or orchestra will prevent profane persons and young children from remarking on the obvious
resemblance between this chorus and the act of splashing about in
a bath; but there is no reason why a young bath-spanker whose
favourite Bible lesson is the Plagues should not grow up into a
pious and heroic bishop or moderator. This would be much better
than that the child's natural pleasure in the vindictiveness of the
Psalmist should be unalloyed with the spirit of Handel and Haydn,
neither of whom could keep their cheerfulness within the bounds
of decorum when they thought of their Creator. No quotations
are needed: the chorus has no themes, but it declaims well and
leaves no doubt that 'there was not one of them left'. Handel
evidently expects the kettle-drums to enjoy themselves, and would

probably have been delighted to have two pairs, with two players. When he is in his best form the timing of his climaxes and contrasts is as magnificent as the ideas themselves. He now gives a great burst of slow eight-part harmony to the words:—

XV and XVI

And Israel saw that great work that the Lord did upon th' Egyptians; and the people feared the Lord.

He continues with a sober fugue to the words:

And believed the Lord and his servant Moses.

The subject of this fugue comes from the Stradella Serenata, much as the words 'And it came to pass' come from anywhere you please in the Bible. In a performance of the whole of *Israel in Egypt* this makes an adequate quiet end to Handel's first part; but the problem of selecting and arranging in an artistic order the great things, and none but the great, compels me to diverge at this point. Nothing important is lost by ignoring Handel's division between the narrative of the Exodus and the Song of Moses: certainly nothing so disastrous as Handel's own plan of preceding the first part by half an hour's funeral music to account for the statement that the reigning Pharaoh knew not Joseph. If we want a sublime contrast to the exultant shouts that 'there was not one of them left', we can obtain it, not only with decorum, but with the profoundest Handelian awe, in the short mysterious chorus, No. XXIV, *The depths have covered them, they sank into the bottom as a stone.* Handel has placed this chorus well on in the Song of Moses, between the famous duet, 'The Lord is a man of war', and not a very well declaimed rubadub to the words: 'Thy right hand, oh Lord, is *be*come glorious: thy right hand hath dashed in pieces the enemy', a chorus which contains nothing that Handel does not twice give with much greater force before and afterwards. In any case, Handel has placed *The depths have covered them* where it merely shows up the poverty of its surroundings and has no dramatic effect. I submit that where I propose to place it the dramatic effect is thoroughly Handelian, and the musical and harmonic values highly characteristic. It closes on the dominant of a foreign key, which leads quite naturally to the magnificent bright modulations with which Handel's orchestra introduces the Song of Moses.

XVII. CHORUS

Moses, and the children of Israel sung this song unto the Lord, and spake, saying:

I have called attention to Stradella's use of what the old theorists would have called an extraneous bright major mediant chord

(Ex. 5) and have suggested that, as with many passages in the Urio *Te Deum* and other bones from Handel's cache, this kind of bright modulation was what attracted him to various scrappy archaic composers. This introduction to the Song of Moses has not been traced to other sources, but consists essentially of such modulations. You will not find them in Bach, who is either orthodox or miraculous. They are not mysterious, they are bright flashes of colour, and the best-known early composer in whom you will find them is Domenico Scarlatti. The conception of this introduction is musically almost the archetype of Handelian grandeur, and its grandest literary aspect is the identifying of the act of singing with the words 'And spake, saying'.

XVIII

Then they spake and sang two interlocking fugues, not quite the same thing as a double fugue.

Exx. 16, 17, 18. I will sing unto the Lord, for he hath triumphed gloriously, the horse and his rider hath he thrown into the sea.

The first fugue is on one of the world's simplest and oldest canto fermos—

Ex. 16.
I   will   sing . . . . . .   un - to   the Lord,

which is delivered in alternation, but not combination, with the subject of the second fugue.

Ex. 17.
for he hath   tri-um-phed glo - - - - - - - - - - riously.

The business of the second fugue is obviously to display some coloratura singing. That of the first fugue is to go into double fugue with the galloping horse and his rider who are thrown into the sea.

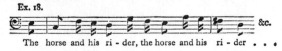

Ex. 18.
The   horse and his   ri - der, the horse and his   ri - der . . .

Both subjects of this double fugue can be sung in thirds, and could be so sung with pedantic accuracy if Handel had not the wisdom to diverge to more effective notes as occasion offered. The learned way of describing such counterpoint in added thirds is to point out that it is double counterpoint in the octave, tenth, and twelfth, and that

ninety-six permutations of it are possible: the presumption being
that the composer worked out each one of the ninety-six by trial
and error. In the same way, as is well known, the Forth Bridge
was designed from one rivet to the next. This chorus is a fine
specimen of Handel's triumphal rhetoric, and is also a reasonably
solid piece of counterpoint; but the pious habit of regarding it as
a learned effort is as naïve as the theology which imputes to the
Almighty the extraordinary power of throwing, not only a horse,
but his rider as well, into the sea.

At this point the wholesale borrowings from Erba begin. I do
not know why a duet for two sopranos should be pathetic when its
text is 'The Lord is my strength and my song, He is become my
salvation'; nor do I know why Erba, whoever he may be, should
have made an earlier and duller version of it to the second verse of
the *Magnificat*, '*Et exultavit spiritus meus, in Deo salutari meo*'.
Handel has made a longer, a better, and a more pathetic composition of it: why, I cannot think. Erba continues with the burst of
eight-part chorus which has been, as I think mistakenly, alleged
to have inspired Handel to *HE rebuked the Red Sea*. Erba
follows with the unimportant idea of *Thy right hand, O Lord,
is become glorious*, set perfunctorily and patchily to the words:
Ecce enim ex hoc beatam me dicut omnes generationes. Handel then
proceeds to transcribe the eight-part opening of Erba's *Magnificat*
to the words: 'HE is my God, and I will prepare Him an habita-
tion.' Erba's eight-part writing is muddy, though correct according to archaic standards. Why did Handel trouble to transcribe it?
He is obliged to add two bars to the words: 'My father's God.'
These look less orthodox, for they make the voices skip awkwardly,
but they would burst through Erba's fog like the sun through clouds;
and it is not as if Erba's fog had any great aesthetic qualities.

Then follows an archaic fugue, not unlike Erba, to the words:
'And I will exalt Him': a double fugue, though there is only one
text. This fugue is more solid than usual with Handel. But that
is not the only reason why I cannot believe that it is an original
composition of his; nor can I even rouse myself to much curiosity
as to its origin.

XXII

Some of us can remember Barnumesque announcements that in
such and such a performance of *Israel in Egypt*, not only in the
Crystal Palace, but in the Albert Hall, 'the duet, *The Lord is a man
of war*, will be sung by four hundred tenors and basses'. Under my
direction it will not be sung even by the two basses for which
Handel wrote it. The themes come from the Stradella Serenata,
and from any other places where such clichés may be found. Otherwise the composition is deplorably genuine. Handel can keep the

shouting and the piping and the fiddling going for 252 bars. Here
I certainly would apply Burney's urbane dictum that the disposition of those who are pleased with it may be a great blessing to
them. The seat of the scornful is a bad eminence; and its occupants
are liable to blaspheme masterpieces like *He led them through the
deep*. But people who have not outgrown the music of *The Lord is
a man of war* are in as bad a case as Christians who have not outgrown the theology of its text. And I have grave doubts whether
such naïve Handel-worshippers can appreciate the merits of the
next chorus, *The depths have covered them*: merits which I hope
will be obvious to every listener when that chorus is placed where
I have transferred it.

Handel follows the chorus, *Thy right hand, O Lord*, with another
fugue from the Erba *Magnificat*, *Thou sentest forth thy wrath, which
consumed them as stubble*. The original text was: *Fecit potentiam in
bracchio suo: dispersit superbos mente cordis sui*. If there is any
appropriateness in this borrowing, it may be held to lie in the word
'superbos', which when treated *staccato* can be transcribed as an
orchestral and choral representation of the words 'as stubble'.
This is hardly a sufficient reason for executing eighty-four bars of
mediocre seventeenth-century fugue, and it is still less reason for
transcribing it at all.

The great problem in performing the genuine essence of *Israel in
Egypt* is, not merely to get rid of Erba, but to arrange a coherent
whole of what remains of the Song of Moses.

Another long duet, *Thou in thy mercy hast led forth thy people*, &c.
(116 bars of larghetto), has been inflated by Handel from Erba's
Esurientes implevit bonis. We need not trouble about that, though
some of us may feel that the solo singers, already starved by Handel,
are being brutally treated in my selection. However, now comes
the occasion for amends. My problem is to find a way towards
No. XXVII (*And with the blast of thy nostrils*), one of Handel's most
picturesque choruses, which I cannot dream of omitting. Our way
has now been blocked ever since the horse and his rider were
thrown into the sea. But what could follow that triumph more
appropriately than the famous and spirited tenor aria, No. XXVIII?

XXVIII. TENOR ARIA

The enemy said: I will pursue, I will overtake, I will divide the spoil:
my lust shall be satisfied upon them: I will draw my sword: my hand
shall destroy them.

The declamation of this aria is not as faulty as it looks. It seems to
begin with a strong accent on '*The*', and this is not to be explained
away by Handel's double-sized bar in triple-time cadences. But,
besides the cadential ambiguity of ancient triple time (1, 2, 3, 4, 5, 6

versus 1, 2, 3, 4, 5, 6), there is a strong tendency, not yet extinct, though little recognized, for quick triple time to suggest the grouping 1, 2, 3, 1, 2, 3, rather than 1, 2, 3. Indeed, it is possible to maintain the view that this displaced accent, or amphibrachic lilt, is normal to the triple time of Palestrina and earlier music. Be this as it may, *The enemy said* is one of Handel's most spirited and Handelian bursts of jingoism, and deserves to be enjoyed with the utmost zest by singers and listeners.

XXIX

Handel follows it by one of the most picturesque and distinguished of his arias, wonderfully orchestrated and very difficult to perform. The organ, 'celli, bassoons, and violas keep up a perpetual flow, as a ground-bass. Two oboes, presumably soli, weave a tissue of various counterpoints and rhythms. Above and through this a soprano declaims the text, partly in sustained declamation, partly in coloratura.

Thou didst blow with the wind: the sea cover'd them, they sank as lead in the mighty waters.

XXX

Now comes another burst of eight-part harmony, declaiming the following words:

Who is like unto Thee, O Lord, among the Gods? who is like Thee, glorious in holiness, fearful in praises, doing wonders! Thou stretchest out thy right hand.

Handel modulates grandly, with an enharmonic change at the word 'holiness'. He follows these grand chords with the worst of all his borrowings: the most inappropriate in text, the clumsiest in music, and the least improved in transcribing.

Ex. 19.

The earth swal - - - - - - - - - low'd them.
Si - cut e - rat in prin - ci - pi - o et nunc et sem - per.

And here ends the deplorable mystery of Erba. Fortunately, it is possible and permissible to change the minor chord of 'right hand' into a major chord. This will enable us to pass to one of the most picturesque choruses in the whole work.

XXVII

Exx. 20, 21. And with the blast of thy nostrils the waters were gathered together, the floods stood upright as an heap, the depths were congealed in the heart of the sea.

The theme of *The waters were gathered together* comes from Erba's setting of the words *Deposuit potentes*; and Ex. 21 is, as the fifteen-

year-old Jane Austen might have said, 'gracefully purloined' from
Et exaltavit humiles.

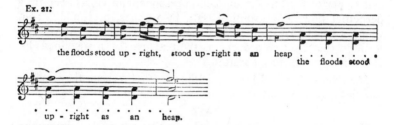

XXXIII

We can now pass on to the greatest of all Handel's choruses. The
choice of such an epithet is not only obviously unwise, but contrary to every one of my principles of criticism. But I make it
deliberately, for I think that it can provoke nothing less desirable
than the attention of every listener, whether he be an idolater, an
iconoclast, or a sensible person. And, after all, every great work of
art is a microcosm, and, therefore, for the time being, the greatest
thing in the world, inasmuch as it is the world so long as your
attention is within it. To my amazement I have found that in
selections from *Israel in Egypt* this chorus is generally omitted. It
was even omitted in my experience at a Leeds Festival at which
Joachim played and Stanford conducted. *Israel in Egypt* itself contains no mystery more surprising than that which has imposed
upon it the decree that the people shall *not* hear a chorus in which
all the noblest aspects of Handel's genius are concentrated and contrasted with a power unsurpassed and, I believe, unequalled, even
in *The Messiah*.

Exx. 22, 23. The people shall hear (*p*) and be afraid:
    (*f*) sorrow shall take hold on them:
    (*ff*) all th' inhabitants of Canaan (*p*) shall melt away (*f*) by
      the greatness of thy arm.

(*p*) They shall be as still as a stone,
    till thy people pass over, O Lord,
    till thy people pass over,
    which thou hast purchased.

Throughout more than half the chorus the orchestra accompanies in dotted-quaver rhythm, ♩ ♪♩ ♪ ♪♩ ♩♪, broken only at the first appearance of the theme: 'shall melt away'.

Ex. 22.

Chrysander traces this theme to the Stradella Serenata. I can just see the resemblance of five notes, since he points it out. The 'development of this small harmonic progression from Stradella's duet in so gigantic a chorus' does, indeed, as Chrysander remarks, surpass all expectation. It is almost as astonishing as the power of the electro-magnet with which Chrysander has extracted this needle from a haystack. The remarkable feature of the progression is not traceable in Stradella, but is so remarkable that Mendelssohn shows himself afraid of it in the excellent and much misunderstood organ-part which he wrote for the edition of the English Handel Society. It consists in the fact that, while the accent in the voices falls upon tonic harmony, the organ chords off the beat are dominant, as shown by the figuring of the bass, and are resolved only by the voices. Both Mendelssohn and Chrysander are afraid of this, and represent the chords by the bass only, in spite of the explicit sharp third provided for each note in the figuring of both organ and cembalo. The chords should, of course, be staccato; and Handel's intention is a picturesque illustration of the words. Handel's marks of expression are unusually clear. He has a sudden piano on repeating the words, 'and be afraid'; he bursts into forte at 'sorrow shall take hold on them', and his whole development of the text 'shall melt away' is piano. In fact, the scheme can be represented as I have given it in setting forth the words here, on the plan of a too copiously marked hymn-book. The modulations are unusually wide, ranging as far as C sharp minor, at the approach to which key mistakes have arisen in many editions from misreading Handel's notation of a double sharp.

The second part of the chorus follows naturally upon the outburst at 'By the greatness of thy arm'.

Ex. 23.

till thy peo - ple pass ov - er, O Lord,

They shall be as still as a stone . . . .

The bass lies still as a stone except when it rises a semitone, more
or less as we are told that the coast of Norway rises eleven feet in
a hundred years; and the people pass over for ever and ever, like
the generations in Bach's *Magnificat*, the only passage in choral
music which I can compare, *longo intervallo*, to this most moving
of all Handel's climaxes. As with all the great schematic things in
art, there are details not provided by the scheme; and of these the
subtlest is the moment where one of the scales becomes gratuitously
major, as I have foreshadowed by the sharp placed above the G in
my quotation. Berlioz once sent a letter to a friend consisting
simply of the melody of '*O malheureuse Iphigénie*' from Gluck's
Iphigénie en Tauride followed by four notes of exclamation. I wish
I might simply transcribe the whole of 'The people shall hear',
and use Berlioz's commentary.

Yet it is not often artistic to end a work with its finest number.
This chorus is best appreciated when followed, as Handel follows
it, refreshingly in contrast and worthily in substance. From this
point there is no more need to shorten the rest of the work, least of
all to omit repetitions which grandly appeal to our sense of form.

XXXV. ALTO ARIA

Thou shalt bring them in, and plant them in the mountain of thine
inheritance, in the place, O Lord, which thou hast made for thee to
dwell in, in the sanctuary, O Lord, which thy hands have established.

XXXIV. CHORUS

The Lord shall reign for ever and ever.

Recitative

For the horse of Pharaoh went in with his chariots and with his horse-
men into the sea, and the Lord brought again the waters of the sea upon
them: but the children of Israel went on dry land in the midst of the sea.

Chorus

The Lord shall reign for ever and ever.

Recitative

And Miriam the prophetess, the sister of Aaron, took a timbrel in her hand, and all the women went out after her with timbrels and with dances, and Miriam answered them:

Soprano solo

Sing ye to the Lord, for he hath triumphed gloriously!

Tutti

The Lord shall reign for ever and ever.

Soprano solo

The horse and his rider hath he thrown into the sea.

Tutti

The Lord shall reign for ever and ever: I will sing unto the Lord, for he hath triumphed gloriously, the horse and his rider hath he thrown into the sea.

In the tonic major of 'The people shall hear', an alto aria has expatiated on Zion and the Promised Land in a style and rhythm such as we know from other evidence to have been among the things Handel most enjoyed creating. It has no reason to be as pathetic as 'He was despised'. Nor is there behind it the tension of 'Comfort ye, my people'; but it has the same Handelian tenderness, and its direction, *largo e mezzopiano*, describes it well. It would be a crime to shorten the final group of choral outbursts and recitatives. The words 'The Lord shall reign for ever and ever' are set like a majestic *canto fermo*; and the solo of Miriam the prophetess is left unaccompanied. One of the brighter humours of our Handel Festivals was the observation that in the gigantic reverberations of the four thousand performers Handel's sublimest clash at the throwing of the horse and his rider was adequately represented by a single pair of cymbals. No doubt it was; but the inspiration was not Handel's, nor Urio's, nor Stradella's, nor Erba's, nor of any person before Sir Michael Costa. It is perhaps arguable that Handel might have tried at least to represent the timbrel which Miriam took in her hand, and the other timbrels of the women who went out after her. But we may as well be content to relegate the precise meaning of 'timbrels' to archaeologists, and enjoy the less trivial realism of Miriam's unaccompanied voice with its power to evoke the whole mass of chorus and orchestra. Upon which Handel ends the Song of Moses with a recapitulation of its opening chorus from Ex. 17 to the end.

HAYDN

CCVI. 'THE CREATION'

The time is ripe for a better understanding of Haydn's *Creation* than can be inculcated by fashion. The reasons why it was out of fashion at the end of the nineteenth century are both obvious and obsolete; but they are much the same as the reasons which may now bring it into fashion again. When fashions are in revolt against the sublime and the romantic, Haydn may become fashionable, like Mozart, for the wrong reasons: that is to say, he is only too likely to become patronized by people who see in him exactly what the Philistine of the 'eighties saw who wrote in the first edition of *Grove's Dictionary* that Haydn, in his *Creation*, 'represents Chaos by means of an exceedingly unchaotic fugue'. It is better to risk losing such patronage than to lose what Haydn's contemporaries appreciated in him; the elements of the sublime and the romantic. Haydn's representation of Chaos is not a fugue; but the Chaos he intends to represent is no mere state of disorder and confusion. He has a remarkably consistent notion of it, which harmonizes well enough with the Biblical account of the Creation; not less well with the classical notions of Chaos, whether in Hesiod or Ovid; but most closely with the Nebular Hypothesis of Kant and Laplace, which almost certainly attracted Haydn's attention. Kant's speculations on the subject had been already published in 1755, and Laplace's discussion of it was published in a readable and popular form in 1796, two years before Haydn's *Creation*. Haydn, who did a certain amount of dining-out in *fin-de-siècle* London, was as likely to have heard of the Nebular Hypothesis as a modern diner-out is likely to hear of Einstein and Relativity. Moreover, he visited Herschel at Slough, saw his famous forty-foot telescope and his less famous but more successful other telescopes, and doubtless had much conversation with Herschel in German on both music and astronomy, Herschel having been a musician before he made astronomy his main occupation. Moreover, on May 3rd, 1788, Herschel published in the *Star and Evening Advertiser* a poetic 'Address to the Star' welcoming Haydn to England in glowing astronomical terms. Be this as it may, the evolution of Cosmos from Chaos might be taken as the 'programme' of a large proportion of Haydn's symphonic introductions for many years before he achieved its grandest illustration with recognized and confessed purpose.

The text of the *Creation* is founded, at several removes, on *Paradise Lost*, and more especially on the account given to Adam by the 'affable archangel' in Book VII. Haydn is much more likely to

have heard of the Nebular Hypothesis than to have read Milton.
His librettist, the Baron Van Swieten, did not give him Milton's
phrase 'loud misrule of Chaos', and this is just as well, for the work
has nothing to do with the fiery ocean into which the rebel angels
fell, and Haydn's symphonic nebular hypothesis is much more
musical, as well as more universal. Being an artist, Haydn represent Chaos in a thinkable aspect; that is to say, he chooses a
moment at which the evolution of Cosmos begins. Here is your
infinite empty space.

Ex. 1.

Strictly speaking, this mighty unison is the most chaotic part of
the introduction. A significant chord would obviously be as futile
a symbol of Chaos as an armchair; and a violent and unexplained
discord would, even in modern music, be a mere phenomenon of
human petulance. Classical tonality is Haydn's musical Cosmos,
and modern atonality represents, as the modern composer is beginning to find out, a much narrower range of possibilities. So Haydn,
like Herschel, proceeds to explore the musical universe with higher
and higher powers of his telescope. And, while Herschel arrives
at remarkably sound conclusions as to the motion of the solar
system in space, Haydn is establishing his musical Cosmos in and
about C minor—

Ex. 2.

with ambiguities and boldnesses which show that he is fully aware
of the paradox inherent in any thinkable notion of Chaos. You
may think that Cosmos has already evolved to a prosaic order of
tonality when Haydn's third and fourth bars can clearly assert so
commonplace a phenomenon as the dominant. But four bars will
no more make a Chaos than they will make a Cosmos; and you
will get a much more vividly chaotic impression from statements
arousing expectations which are contradicted than from statements
which arouse no expectations at all. If the writer who described
Haydn's Chaos as an 'unchaotic fugue' had condescended to look
at its first four bars, he would probably have guessed that they

would lead straight back to the opening unison and then be repeated with a new harmonic outcome. Such, for instance, is Haydn's procedure in his ninth London Symphony in B flat, and such, on a much larger scale, is Beethoven's in his Fourth Symphony. But Haydn's fifth bar shows that the explorer of his musical Chaos will meet with the common experience of scientific explorers, the discovery that his theory was too small for the facts. The fifth bar does, indeed, match the first in being an outburst from the full orchestra; but instead of a unison it gives us the vague chord attained in the second bar; and the second bar of Wagner's *Tristan und Isolde* does not strike a more ambiguous note than that at the beginning of Haydn's sixth bar. This comparison is worth following out. Wagner's ambiguous chord proves to be typical of a special harmonic style consistently developed through an entire work. Haydn's remains isolated; and though his Chaos contains many similar effects, they remain independent of each other, explained away on the spot, and undeveloped into systematic features. In other words, they are admirably chaotic; they are not nonsensical, for their resolution is quite orthodox, though they occur as shocks for which their antecedents did not prepare us. Thus, like all the features of imperishable works of art, they are details which it is quite impertinent to praise as 'remarkable for the time at which they were written'. Such patronage is tolerable only with works that are otherwise not remarkable now. The details of the imperishable works remain always astonishing, because only a man of genius can present them in constantly true relation to a consistent style. Only a supreme artist could maintain such a style as that of Haydn's representation of Chaos.

The difficulties of achieving a sublime style for such a purpose were much greater for Haydn than they would have been for Bach, since Bach's musical language, even in its most rococo ornateness, is naturally ready to express the sublime, and the most characteristic features of its larger art-forms are cumulative; whereas the language of Haydn and Mozart is not only essentially dramatic, but mainly comedic, and in their art-forms greatness is always expressed in terms of symmetry. Fortunately, Haydn habitually achieves his symmetry in a paradoxical way. From one moment to the next he is always unexpected, and it is only at the end that we discover how perfect are his proportions. With Mozart the expectation of symmetry is present all the time, and its realization is delayed no longer than serves the purposes of wit rather than humour. Both composers are so great that in the last resort we shall find Mozart as free as Haydn and Haydn as perfect in form as Mozart; but the fact remains that Haydn's forms display their freedom before their symmetry, while Mozart's immediately display their symmetry, and reveal their freedom only to intimate knowledge. Wise critics do not prophesy what Mozart could not have done if he had lived. But it is evident that, as far as his and Haydn's methods differ, Haydn's are the more ready to produce a representation of Chaos that should give the listener pleasure by arousing the expectation and delaying the emergence of Cosmos.

In a slow tempo the dominant in the fourth bar has, as we have already seen, led us to one revelation that the universe is not going to show its symmetry to a first glance. The Wagnerian shock in the sixth bar explains itself away, and the music drifts towards E flat, the proper tonal region for its first modulation, but defined very slowly and vaguely. Observe that it would be far less chaotic to have modulated in an unorthodox direction, as if Chaos had after all been something from which any nonsense might emerge. Haydn's Chaos gravitates, and E flat is the direction in which his C minor would naturally gravitate. But his time-scale is larger than we could expect, and when the musical astronomer is reaching a decisive dominant of E flat in his nineteenth bar—

Ex. 3.

he does not 'restore the *status quo*', but violently contradicts the E flat theory by a perfectly clear D flat, of all keys the most subversive of E flat, though by no means inconsistent with C minor. In this disconcerting key an actual theme emerges.

Ex. 4.

In three sequential steps it leads us to a point from which after all the key of E flat can be, and is, triumphantly established. And for a while the theme, diminished to human proportions, can disport itself on a tonic and dominant with all the zest of a popular exponent of a scientific theory. One might even accept the brilliant clarinet accompaniment—

Ex. 5.

as symbolizing the adornment of popular exposition. I do not willingly introduce so frivolous a note into a review either of the universe or of Haydn's representation of it. But popular science is the only kind of science I can understand, and the profoundest science can do no more than enjoy with Haydnesque zest each discovery that enlarges our apprehension of Cosmos. The more effectively it does so, the more will it show the absurdity of regarding Chaos as a desert or morass from which science can reclaim any measurable area. Chaos will come again, not in poor Othello's sense, but in the sense that the universe will always remain a mystery rather than a mechanism. Nothing can be truer to art and to nature than the steps by which Haydn returns from his triumph in E flat to his original chaotic C minor. During each step, the thematic figure (*a*) appears in various regions of the orchestra, including a solo double-bass. Commentators have compared other features in the orchestration to meteors, distant thunder, raindrops, and the like. Be this as it may, the music makes a quite definite return to the opening, representing the initial C not by a sustained note, but by something like a peal of thunder. A fairly definite effect of recapitulation is given by the presence of figure (*a*) on a dominant pedal in C minor, culminating in an allusion to the close which led to Ex. 4. It is as if it represented some actual knowledge permanently gained.

The vision of Chaos ends in darkness with a sequence of the suspensions of Ex. 2, but their drift is now steadily downwards to a final close, and the figure (*a*) persists above them with wistful questions, which, to music-lovers whose minds are tangential, are prophetic of *Tristan und Isolde*.

The vision of Chaos is over, and Haydn makes no further allusion to it as soon as he begins to set the Biblical account of the Creation and Van Swieten's adaptation of Milton. Van Swieten,

by the way, is alleged to have translated his text from the English
of one Lidley, a name unknown even to the Post Office Directory.
But I do not know what difficulty there is in regarding the mysterious Lidley as a misprint for Linley, the name of a family of well-
known musicians, one of whom was a managerial musical factotum
at Drury Lane from 1774 till his death in 1795. If, as is rumoured,
the libretto had been offered to Handel and refused by him, the
elder Linley must have been young but not impossibly young
when it was drafted, for he was only 26 when Handel died in
1759. One of his sons was Thomas Linley, the remarkable boy
violinist, with whom another prodigious boy, Mozart by name,
struck up a great friendship in London; and the eldest of his three
beautiful daughters was Mrs. Richard Brinsley Sheridan. The
original edition of Haydn's score is thought to be the first that was
published in Germany with an English as well as a German text,
and there is reason to believe that Haydn himself attended to the
difficult changes of detail needed to fit the Biblical words to the
Authorized Version as well as to the German Bible. To persons
who have more faith than I in long-distance thematic references,
faint traces of figure (a) may be found in the interludes before and
after the clause 'and the earth was without form and void'. My
own opinion is that at the first words of the Bible Haydn has piously
closed his mind to any thoughts it may have harboured of Nebular
Hypotheses and the things he may have seen through Herschel's
telescopes, and is now concentrated wholly upon the Bible and
van-Swieten-Linley-Milton (I am sure that Lidley is only Linley
with a cold in his head).

The handling of recitative shows unmistakably how far a composer is the slave of convention. Recitative formulas were evolved
in Italy, and produced there in an enormous number of works
which established the universal language of classical music. But
the purport of recitative is to produce in musical form the natural
inflexions of speech. Great composers like Purcell and Bach
grapple with the problem in their own language, so that Purcell's
recitative is English and Bach's is German. Second-rate composers
may or may not have known the Italian language, but they used
the Italian recitative formulas whatever language they happened
to be setting. This does not do much harm, for Italian speech-
rhythms do not inflict any irremediable hardship on other languages.
There is a total defect of endings on an accented monosyllable,
but the composer can always slur the necessary appoggiatura or
omit it. With purely instrumental music, it is quite right that a
recitative formula, if used at all, should be Italian. It must in any
case be an allusion with a purport either sublime, like a Biblical
quotation, or mock-heroic; and such allusions are either classical

or unintelligible. By 1798 recitative was definitely an ancient language, except in comic Italian opera. Bach had not yet been discovered, or rediscovered; and Mozart had left only one important specimen of German recitative in the great scene between Tamino and the priest in *Die Zauberflöte*, his other great recitatives, such as 'Don Ottavio, son morta!' being Italian. For German opera preferred spoken dialogue, and all Mozart's other operas, except *Die Entführung*, are Italian. Haydn's achievement in the recitatives of *The Creation* is much more remarkable than it appears to be. Where the Bible is concerned, he is undoubtedly attending to two languages, neither of which can derive any benefit from Italian tradition. The subject is not dramatic, and, even in the description of the birds and beasts, is not meant to be comic. Hence, the virtues of Haydn's declamation are chiefly negative and can be discovered only by finding out the innumerable possibilities of going wrong. By these I do not mean slight faults of accentuation. The critics whose notions of declamation are confined to Wagner and Wolf are apt to betray a mere bell-metronome notion of rhythm and a far from poetic notion of prosody. Haydn never mastered English as thoroughly as did Handel. And, except when dealing with the words of the Authorized Version, to which he certainly gave his attention, he was not even dealing with an Englishman's English, for, as Messrs. Fox Strangways and Steuart Wilson point out, it is evident that the old English text of *The Creation* is a re-translation by a German from the German, not without refreshing details in the style of *English as She is Spoke*.

At the same time I respectfully and regretfully differ from the view of Haydn's recitative taken by the authors of the new translation. Their version of the choruses and arias is beyond cavil; but, like the distinguished authors of the new English versions of Bach's Passions, they seem to think that classical recitative formulas must be preserved note for note as if they were lyric or formal music; and that in that interest it does not matter how many notes go to a syllable, so long as they are the notes written by the composer. Now this is more superstitious than insisting on the syllabic Divine Inspiration of the translators of the Authorized Version; and it has not the excuse of the inconvenience of changing words that have acquired familiar and sacred associations. Nothing is more fatal to classical recitative than the putting of slurred notes to one syllable where the composer wrote a note to each syllable. To quote an example not from *The Creation*, a musical expression like—

Son   of   Man

is a monstrosity that no singer or composer ought to dream of tolerating. On the other hand, it seldom matters a fraction of a hoot whether a long note in recitative is divided into two or any number of notes that extra syllables may require; and the difference between such forms as—

is in most cases quite negligible. Another object of superstitious reverence is the accent on the first of the bar, for the preservation of which most modern translators will submit words and notes to the thumbscrew and the rack. Classical recitative is not Wagnerian declamation; it is musical speech-rhythm; it is not only vague as to whether the first of the bar has an accent, but habitually contradicts its own notation in almost every bar, and especially at the cadences. For instance, there is no need to alter Haydn's German accent on the last syllable of 'firmament' in recitative: the singer need not stress it, though it may come typographically on the first of the bar.

If you want to preserve Haydn's or Bach's exact notes in their recitatives you must sing them in German. Bach and Handel were ready enough to sacrifice originally good declamation in transcribing formal music to new texts; but they never transcribed a recitative to a new text. It was infinitely less trouble to compose a new recitative. And recitative that does not fall into the speech-rhythm of the language in which it is sung is neither speech nor language nor music. I shall doubtless be severely dealt with for altering the notes of Haydn's music; but, unlike the old Scotch lady who enjoyed learned sermons but 'wudna hae the presoomption to understand them', I presume to understand Haydn's recitatives. I claim to take no liberties; once alterations are admitted, notes may be altered in a wrong way as well as in a right way; but the modern proposition that recitative-formulas must not be altered at all in translations is no more scholarly than translating 'qu'est-ce que c'est que ça' by 'what is this that this is that that'.

This point being disposed of, let us continue our analysis. I will not pause to ventilate in detail my grievances against the critical *Gesammtausgabe* of Haydn's complete works, which, since the death of my beloved old friend Mandyczewski, has decided wrongly about the musical text of *The Creation* on at least five points on which I happen to know that Mandyczewski had decided rightly. The first of these is the fine and characteristic idea (perfectly unmistakable in the original edition of the score—which is our earliest source, the autograph being lost) that Gabriel sings with the chorus-basses at the words 'And the Spirit of God moved upon the face of the waters'.

From this point, that is to say, from the beginning of the vocal music, I shall give the words, not always as they will be sung, but according to the new Oxford text, with explanations of the points where I see reason to take my own line or even to return to the *disjecta membra* of the Linley-van-Swieten-English-as-She-is-Spoke confection.

Linley and the Baron van Swieten have between them devised an excellent arrangement for the distribution of the text. The words of the Bible are divided between three archangels, Raphael, Uriel, and Gabriel, and a chorus which, throughout the whole work, may be considered as that of the heavenly hosts. The list and description of created things is not distributed at haphazard among the three archangels: Uriel is distinctly the angel of the sun and of daylight; his is the tenor voice, and his is the description of Man. Raphael sings of the earth and the sea, of the beginning of all things. and (according to the unmistakable direction of the original edition of the score) of the Spirit of God moving upon the face of the waters. His also is the description of the beasts, the great whales, and 'every living creature that moveth'; and it is he who reports God's blessing, 'Be fruitful and multiply', in a measured passage which is one of the sublimest incidents in Haydn's recitatives. Gabriel, the soprano, leads the heavenly hosts and describes the vegetable kingdom and the world of bird life.

Lastly, Adam and Eve (Soprano and Bass) appear and fulfil the purpose announced by Raphael while as yet 'the end was not achieved; there wanted yet the master-work that should acknowledge all this good'. Or, as the first answer in the Shorter Catechism has it,

Q. What is the chief end of Man?
A. To glorify God and to enjoy Him for ever.

Asbestos is not in common use as material for writing or printing, and so I cannot express my opinion of the cuts sanctioned by tradition in performances of Haydn's *Creation*. That some cutting is advisable I do not deny; and if *The Creation* were the kind of work which (like many great things by Schubert) puts its finest material into its digressions, the task of cutting it would be difficult and painful. But Haydn is a supreme master of close-knit form; and it so happens that the subject of this oratorio is quite clearly and positively the Creation, up to and including Man's capacity to glorify God; and it is equally clearly not Paradise Lost, nor the conjugal felicity of Adam and Eve ('Graceful consort! Spouse adored', &c.). Hence, the beautiful terzet (No. 28) that interrupts the chorus at the end of Part II ('Achieved at last the glorious work') is untimely and intrusive when it introduces the thought, 'But if Thou turn away Thy face, with sudden terror are we struck: Thou tak'st our breath away; we turn again to dust.' The first exposition of the chorus and the whole of the terzet can therefore be cut out, with loss of some beautiful music, but with positive gain to the form of the whole. Only you must not begin No. 29, the resumption of the chorus, as it stands, but must remember that, instead of its allusive 2-bar opening, it needs to begin with the first seven bars of No. 27. Cuts inside a number are wholly Philistine, and nowhere more so than when they consist in skipping repetitions. We are not dealing with the cabalettas of Rossinian operas, but with symphonic forms on Beethoven's plane of thought. Some of our Bright Young Men (and even some Dull Old Men) are now beginning to cut the tuttis of Beethoven's Violin Concerto. I have fortunately not yet been present when this has been done; and, if it ever should happen in my presence, no consideration for the knees of my neighbours shall prevent me from instantly leaving the concert-hall with anybody and everybody else who thinks as I do about music.

Again, it is highly undesirable to spoil the Genesis-Milton-van-Swieten-Haydn scheme of Six Days of Creation, with the Heavenly Host singing in triumph after each. The fierceness of the Gothic Revival is abated, and we need no longer purge our cathedrals of every vestige of Grinling Gibbons. In musical affairs we feel towards Bach and Handel as we feel towards Gothic architecture; and our instinct is to confuse Haydn's irrepressibly cheerful worship of God (for which he himself hoped God would not be angry) with the naughtiest features of the masses Mozart wrote, in a hurry and a temper, for an Archbishop of Salzburg for whom nobody, Catholic or Protestant, has ever had a good word to say. But musical history is not as simple as our text-books would have it. Bach's spirit may be what we understand by Gothic, but the nearest architectural analogy to his musical language is rococo. As for Handel, if he had been an architect he would have been Palladian; and those people who sympathize with Burne-Jones's dislike of St. Paul's Cathedral have a musical consciousness of quite a different order from their other aesthetic sensibilities if they can enjoy Handel at all. This is quite possible; the wind bloweth where it listeth; and Bach's rococo language is not spiritually akin to an Austrian church decorated with wedding-cake cherubs. But the gulf between Haydn and Handel in choral writing is nothing like as great as we are apt to imagine; nor, except where Handel reaches his highest level, is the advantage of sublimity always—or, I will even say, often—with Handel. Moreover, to my unscrupulous

mind, Haydn's naughtiest brilliance, as in the solo coloraturas of
'The Lord is great, and great His might', is as glorious as Bach's,
though its symphonic foundations confine it to a much simpler
harmonic range.

Exaggerated ideas of the length of *The Creation* have, I believe,
been fostered by two disastrous misprints; the substitution of 4/4
instead of ₵ as time-signatures for 'The Heavens are telling' and
the aria 'On spreading wings'. (I do not myself see much amiss
with the old and faintly Miltonic 'mighty pens'.) The 4/4 signa-
ture, with Haydn's 'moderato' as tempo-mark, clips the eagle's
mighty pens to the capacity of the barn-door fowl, and accounts
for the tradition of omitting repetitions in the resulting tedium.
But, in a reasonable tempo, what sane person ever wished to prevent
a song-bird from repeating itself, since the time of the early English
saint who miraculously stopped a cock from crowing?

The case of 'The Heavens are telling' is far more disastrous. Like
most music-lovers of my age, I incurred in childhood the danger
not only of believing that where 'there is neither speech nor language' Haydn supplied the defect after this fashion—

but of the still more dangerous blasphemy of supposing that this
must be Good Music.

Besides the elimination of the terzet No. 28, with its redundant
introductory exposition of the chorus No. 27, my only other cut
in *The Creation* is the drastic one of ending with the greatest
design Haydn ever executed, and the sublimest number since the
Representation of Chaos, the duet of Adam and Eve with chorus of
angels, No. 30. Everything after that is not only an anticlimax but
involves the intrusion of the loss of Paradise ('Oh happy pair, and
happy still might be if not misled', &c., &c.). It is unfortunately
possible that Haydn might be shocked at the idea of ending without
another Palladian-Handelian double fugue; he probably thought

that such movements were intrinsically grander than those of the symphonic order in which he was supreme. But I prefer to imagine that he would, after some doubts, be glad to have due recognition of his real supremacy and would come to see that another Palladian double fugue in B flat, however grand, could add nothing but anti-climax to the symphonic and choral finality of the great Adagio and Allegretto which merge the praises of Adam and Eve in those of the Heavenly Hosts and establish the key of C major as the inevitable outcome of the C minor round which the first Chaos gravitated. Thus ended, the work is considerably shorter than Bach's B minor Mass,[1] and it falls into two parts; the two numbers (the E major representation of Morning, and the great duet and chorus) from Haydn's Third Part being only a few minutes longer than the two movements excised from his Second Part. The change from the B flat of 'Achieved at last the glorious work' to the indefinitely remote E major of the representation of Morning is a bold step to take without interposing an interval. But it is a Haydnesque step, and it differs from precisely the same juxta-position (D flat to G major) in the middle of Beethoven's Quartet in B flat, Op. 130, only in the Haydnesque particular that it remains a paradox whereas Beethoven's audacities of tonality are always rationalized.

Here, then, is the text of *The Creation* as I propose to perform it. I interpolate a few more comments where occasion arises. Haydn's (and Herschel's) Chaos we have already discussed.

THE FIRST DAY

Raphael sings:

RAPHAEL. In the beginning God created the heaven and the earth. And the earth was without form and void: and darkness was upon the face of the deep.

RAPHAEL *and Chorus.*

And the Spirit of God moved upon the face of the waters.
And God said, Let there be light: and there was light.

With effortless power the light bursts forth in music of a clear C major; the chorus on not at all a high note for any of the voices, but in simply a good average position for sonority, while the orchestra rises in vibrations that are slow enough to produce a maximum volume of tone.

Haydn's last appearance in public was at a performance of *The Creation* in Vienna. The old man was brought into the audi-

---

[1] The performance for which this essay was written began moderately punctually at 8 o'clock, and, with a ten-minute interval after Part I, was finished several minutes before 10.

torium in a chair. At the outburst 'and there was light' he pointed
a trembling hand upwards and was heard by those near him to
say, 'It came from thence'. He was evidently much moved, and
could not stay after the first part.

URIEL. And God saw the light, that it was good: and God divided the
light from the darkness (Gen. i. 1–4).

In the general history of music one of the greatest of Haydn's
achievements was his exhaustive exploration of remote key-rela-
tionships. He did not, like J. S. Bach, live in a harmonic world of
close key-relations liable to miraculous invasions from unknown
regions; nor did he, like Philipp Emanuel Bach, explain away his
remoter modulations by discursive rhetoric. But he also did not
achieve, or attempt to achieve, Beethoven's processes, by which the
whole scheme of remoter key-relations became as definite as New-
tonian astronomy. Haydn's paradoxes in tonality are always true,
and he is so sure of them that it would be impertinent to call them
experimental. But he does not explain them; and if they explain
themselves they do so only as things explain themselves to the
child who 'understands quite well, if only you wouldn't explain'.

Without any explanatory modulation the C major gives way to
A major, as (with due explanation) in the first movement of Beethoven's C major Quintet, Op. 29, or as in the G major-E major
schemes of his Trios, Op. 1, No. 2, and Op. 9, No. 1; or, again,
as in the B flat-G major schemes of his Trio, Op. 97, and his
Sonata, Op. 106. Some of Haydn's greatest symphonies, quartets,
and trios show the same or similar key-relations, with the same
brilliance of contrast. (By the way, the disastrous substitution of
4/4 for ¢ occurs here also.)

URIEL. Now vanish before the first command
The gloomy laws of ancient night,
And light doth rule the world.
Let chaos end, and order must prevail.

But suddenly our A major is brought into contrast with the C
minor of Chaos.

So Hell's black spirits seek the realms below,
Down they sink to deepest abyss where light cannot come.

CHORUS.
In cursing snarling terror they fall beyond our sight.

The symphonic balance of keys is restored in favour of A major;
and here is Haydn's notion of the new created world. I understand
that once upon a time people found this trivial; but Beethoven has
not indulged in the cruel sport of prig-sticking in vain, and I am

proud to ally myself with the company of persons who are as completely and shamelessly bowled over by it as by anything in Bach's B minor Mass.

Ex. 7.

The first of days ap – pears; the first of days ap – pears and

or – der reigns at God's com – mand.

At each recurrence this is differently harmonized. Hence I quote only the melody, which is the quintessence of Haydn in his most dangerous innocence.

THE SECOND DAY

Secco-Recitative.

RAPHAEL. And God made the firmament, and divided the waters which were under the firmament from the waters which were above the firmament: and it was so. (Gen. i. 7.)

Descriptive Recitative.

Now all the powers of the sky are released,
The winds blow the clouds like chaff in the air.
And dreaded lightning burns in the sky,
And thunder answers the leaping flame.
Now vapour from the flood ascends to form the cooling rain,
The harsh and stinging hail, and softest flakes of snow.

The classical rule for the musical illustration of words is that, unless, as at the words 'And there was Light', the music is itself the action at the moment, the illustration should come first and the words afterwards.

The observance of this rule has two advantages. First it compels the composer to make his illustration intelligible as pure music. Secondly, the intelligible music being thus secured, the critic who chooses to say of the illustration 'Not a bit like it' can always be met with the retort 'Who said it was? I am a musician and am enjoying myself in that capacity'. This retort is hardly possible if the music has followed the words with the evident purpose of illustrating them. With the classical method there is always a reasonable chance that the illustration may be apt enough to make the listener greet the words with the delighted recognition 'So *that's* what the music means'; and whether this happens or not, the listener will at all events have heard some good music without annoyance or distraction.

The high soprano of the archangel Gabriel is now heard for the first time, and is joined by all the heavenly hosts.

GABRIEL *and Chorus.*

The angels rank on rank arrayed
Behold amazed the marvels done,
And sing in silver trumpet voice
The praise of God and of the second day.

In plausibility the case for canonizing Haydn ranks midway between the cases for canonizing Pepys and Dr. Johnson. But the critic who can frown at the glorious cheerfulness of this choric song has not the remotest conception of real saintliness; he is in the state of Bunyan's Talkative whose notion of the first workings of Grace is that it begins by producing 'a great outcry against sin';[1] and he can know nothing of Christian's or Bunyan's feelings when his burden fell off, or of Haydn's when, as he tells us, 'Never was I so pious as when composing *The Creation*; I knelt down every day and prayed God to strengthen me for my work'.

THE THIRD DAY

Secco-Recitative.

RAPHAEL. And God said, Let the waters under the heaven be gathered together unto one place, and let the dry land appear: and it was so.

And God called the dry land Earth: and the gathering together of the waters called he Seas: and God saw that it was good. (Gen. i. 9–10.)

Aria (the first part in D minor).

See how the rolling waters
In boisterous play uplift their heads.
Mountains emerge from the plains,
Their heads with drifting clouds are crowned
And from their heights to depths look down.
Through open plains of fair extent
In winding courses rivers flow.

With characteristic freedom of form Haydn now finishes his aria with a second part in D major that has only a faint trace of thematic relation to the rest.

Softest music murmuring
Through silent vales glides on the brook.

Some small part of Haydn's inspiration may be derived from the most beautiful tone-picture in Gluck's *Armide*, Rinaldo's enraptured descriptions of Armida's garden: 'Plus je vois ces lieux, et plus je les admire.' This, in its turn, is said to be hardly finer that

[1] *O brave Talkative!* (Bunyan's marginal comment).

Lully's setting of the same passage in his *Armide* of ninety years earlier. But Haydn's inspiration is also in large measure his own, or the answer to his prayers; and it became the source of many things in the style of Schubert, besides many solemn calms in Beethoven. (By the way, Haydn gives no authority for a slower tempo here; he leaves to a later poet the suggestion to 'Bear me straight, meandering ocean, Where the stagnant torrents flow'.)

Secco-Recitative.

GABRIEL. And God said, Let the earth bring forth grass, the herb yield-ing seed, and the fruit tree yielding fruit after his kind, whose seed is in itself, upon the earth: and it was so. (Gen. i. 11.)

ARIA (hitherto known as 'With verdure clad'). The new Oxford text aims not only at singability but at introducing some genuine Miltonic epithets where the resemblance of the Linley-van-Swieten-English-as-She-is-Spoke complex can be traced back to Milton. I am not sure that the result is always worth the trouble; the Miltonic epithets sound un-Miltonic and often puzzling when transferred from blank verse to the ambling rhymes of the oratorio librettist; and I have encouraged our present artists to return, now and then, to use and wont in this matter.

> The fields are dressed in living green
> That soothes the heart and charms the eye,
> While flowers of every hue,
> Bedeck the meads in trim array.
> With perfume sweet the air is filled
> And plants to heal abound.
> The pampered boughs with ripening fruit are full
> And leafy trees invite with deepest shade.
> On mountain side majestic forests grow.

I am told by one of the truest of Haydn-lovers that this aria does not stand the strain of 7,459 consecutive performances at Competi-tion Festivals. Never having tried any such experiment, I am defenceless in still finding it as beautiful as anything else in Haydn, Schubert, Brahms, or any other master of lyric melody. Clearly there is need for a Society for the Prevention of Cruelty to Classics and Adjudicators. (Reverence dictates that we should put the Classics first.) Another brutal sport which I am ashamed to indulge is Mendelssohn-baiting. But here the occasion is too tempting; Mendelssohn is really asking us to show how neatly his uncon-scious misquotation displays the difference between a strong and a flaccid style. Among his *Lieder ohne Worte* the 'Duetto' is a very clever piece, though not one of the best; but the third and fourth bars of its melody (bars 4 and 5 of the piece) are a clinically perfect type of the weakness of his melodic constitution, which seldom has

enough stamina to get through its second clause without giving
at the ankles.

Ex. 8.

HAYDN. 'With verdure clad', bars 5-8.

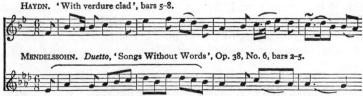

MENDELSSOHN. *Duetto*, 'Songs Without Words', Op. 38, No. 6, bars 2-5.

Another of Haydn's brilliant key-contrasts now follows; B flat
yielding abruptly to D major. The recitative does not *lead* from
B flat to the D major of the chorus; it asserts the D major at once.

Secco-Recitative.

URIEL. And the heavenly host proclaimed the third day, praising God
and saying:

Chorus.

Awake the harp, awake the lute,
Let all the world your song re-echo,
In praise of our God, the Creator of all,
Who hath invested with splendour
The earth and the sky and the sea.

This chorus, the first of what I call the Palladian architectural-
musical features of Haydn's *Creation*, is admirably terse and of a
brilliance and power that does not suffer by comparison with
Handel at his best. My beloved counterpoint-master, James
Higgs, had a keen nose for such game as Haydn's device of 'pro-
longing the first note backwards', as when the fugue-theme—

Ex. 9*a*.

Who hath in - ves - ted with splen - dour the earth and the sky.

produces the full majestic effect of an 'augmentation' with no more
loss of time than a single bar, by means of entries like this—

Ex. 9*b*.

and this

Ex. 9*c*.

(A complete augmentation would make the theme spread over four
bars and a half.)

THE FOURTH DAY

Secco-Recitative.

URIEL. And God said, Let there be lights in the firmament of heaven
to divide the day from the night, and to give light upon the earth,
and let them be for signs and for seasons and for days and for years.
He made the stars also. (Gen. i. 14–16.)

Descriptive Recitative.

The sun is up, and from his chamber comes to run his course,
A bridegroom in his youth, a giant in his strength,
      Through highest heaven.
      With softer beams and milder light
      Sails on the silver moon through silent night.
The infinite space of open sky is filled with stars beyond all human
count,
      And the Sons of God proclaimed the fourth day,
      And all the morning stars
         Together sang his praise.

Of all the comparisons the most odious in its unfairness is that
between *The Creation* and *The Seasons*. I live in hope of an opportunity of reverently and enthusiastically producing *The Seasons*
some day, or preferably some two days, so that few cuts may be
necessary and better justice be done to the work than was done to
it by Haydn himself, who undertook it under protest, and said
much harsher things about it than have been said by anybody since,
condemning its whole scheme as Philistine, and declaring that the
undertaking of it had killed him. Some part of this complaint is
justified. The most alarming and pathetic sign of failing power is
that the 'Palladian' choruses are, on the average, twice the size
of those in *The Creation*, and thus and in other ways betray an
anxiety lest they should be inadequate. But the work is full of
glorious things; and perhaps the most cruel item of all that it cost
Haydn is that it compelled him to do another picture of a sunrise,
the words of which are assigned to the Farmer's Daughter, Hanne
(*anglice*, Jane), and to which the appropriate comment is the English text of the subsequent chorus, 'Hail, O Sun, be hailed!'

The sunrise in *The Creation* is as perfect and as simple as the
Parthenon; and if its method is obvious, that of the moonrise is a
paradox of astonishing accuracy and boldness. What composer of
less than the greatest order would have thought of beginning his
moonlight in the deep bass and representing its culmination by the
string band alone on its lower strings?

If any part of *The Seasons* must be regretted, it is that in which
the libretto imposes, as it were, upon the architect of the Parthenon the responsibility for the Edinburgh Folly of Calton Hill

The creation of the material world is now finished, and the First Part of Haydn's work ends with the well-known chorus so often misrepresented because of a long-standing typographical blunder as to its tempo.

Trio and Chorus (GABRIEL, RAPHAEL, *and* URIEL).

The Heavens are telling the glory of God,
The firmament itself shews forth his handiwork.
For day unto day doth utter his speech
And night unto night her knowledge doth shew.
Their sound goes out through all the lands,
Neither speech nor language, yet their voice is ever heard.

(Adapted from Ps. 19.)

Ex. 10.

Of the main theme the figure (*b*) becomes that of the fugal climax, while (*a*) becomes the starting-point of the dangerously simple passages for the trio of archangels. The danger of these passages lies in what I believe to be Haydn's discovery of the charm of simple cadential chords held with indefinite pauses by solo voices. Doubtless there is some learned historical sense in which this is not Haydn's discovery; for a prevalent view of the history of art is that its chief aim is to show that the most famous strokes of genius have been anticipated by from six months to two centuries, either in some dead and misunderstood convention, or in some work preserved in the British Museum in a copy which has hitherto remained unique because nobody has been stupid enough to think of transcribing anything so dull. I cannot cultivate a historic erudition that eliminates the rare accident of genius from works of art; and I shall continue to ascribe the strokes of genius in *The Creation* to Haydn without inquiring whether earlier composers may have produced semblances of them without the genius. Moreover, I shall go further, and continue to recognize Haydn's strokes of genius in their echoes *as strokes of genius* by later composers. Mendelssohn's *Duetto* (cited in Ex. 8) suffers from its resemblance to 'With verdure clad', because it misses the point. The climax of the coda in the first movement of Beethoven's Second Symphony does not suffer from comparison with the end of 'The Heavens are telling', because Beethoven no more misses Haydn's point than Virgil misses the point when he translates

Homer; and Virgil's achievement in erecting a mass of Homeric and other lore into a monument to the glories of Rome is not essentially greater than Beethoven's in making a normal symphony capable of digesting a choral climax. And by this I do not mean the problem of the Ninth Symphony with its actual chorus, but the simpler and subtler questions of tonality and time-scale within the limits of absolute music.

Ex. 11 a.
HAYDN.

Beethoven's harmonic range is wider, and while the second chord here marked with an asterisk corresponds exactly with that marked in Ex. 11a, it is the remoter marked chord (a 6/4 in E flat minor or D sharp minor) that, together with the rising bass, is inspired by Haydn.

Ex. 11 b.
BEETHOVEN, Second Symphony.

Quite a long book might be written about the influence of Haydn's *Creation* on later music. The innocent solo-trio pauses have been a danger to later musicians and critics because nothing is easier than to live on the income of their natural effect. The prig who is proud of his artistic conscience is in the long run (which, however, the poor fellow never gets) less detestable than the more fashionable prig who is proud of having none. It is mere snobbishness to say that Haydn's juicy vocal pauses are mere Sullivan; the difference between Haydn and Sullivan is that Haydn's self-indulgence in this matter is a small and severely disciplined element of relaxation in some of the hardest work ever achieved by mortal man—whereas Sullivan—

il res - to nol   di - co.

PART II

With the Fifth Day of Creation Animal Life appears. Haydn has the acumen to refrain from any attempt to stress a miracle not less stupendous than that of Light; he treats the whole scheme as one, and begins the second part of his work with a recitative that starts on a chord in middle position as if to continue a narrative that has been punctuated rather than interrupted.

THE FIFTH DAY

GABRIEL. And God said, Let the waters bring forth abundantly the moving creature that hath life, and fowl that may fly above the earth in the open firmament of heaven. (Gen. i. 20.)

Aria (F major).
On spreading wings majestic soars the eagle aloft
And cleaves the air in swiftest flight to the blazing sun.
His welcome bids to morn the merry lark,
Enraptured coo and bill and tender doves,
From every bush and grove resound
The nightingale's delightful notes.
No grief affected yet her breast
Nor yet to mournful tale were turned
Her soft enchanting lays.

The aria, redeemed from the disastrous consequences of a 4/4 instead of Haydn's alla-breve time-signature, illustrates its text with more discretion than some critics seem to realize. The right tempo gives something of the power of the eagle's flight. Ravel can attain the actual pitch of the lark's trill with violin harmonics which Haydn's ear and taste would fail to discriminate from a gas-escape. I do not for a moment suggest that Haydn would be justified in condemning either Ravel or the real lark, though both habitually emit sounds that would be merely destructive to Haydn's music. But Haydn is certainly right, for his own purposes, in generalizing the lark's morning welcome as a 'merry' tune on the clarinet. The nightingale is in another position; its note, as we know it, is well within the best cantabile range of the wind instruments of Beethoven's Pastoral Symphony, and Beethoven's nightingale is realistic as well as musical. But before you receive Haydn's nightingale with the Producer's proverbial criticism 'Not a bit like it', please note that the text expressly forbids Haydn to let his nightingale say 'jug-jug' or 'Tereu! Tereu!' Thus Haydn has to invent a bird of the same name, but peculiar to Eden; and his invention no more failed him than it would have failed Lewis Carroll. And perfect music unites with perfect realism in the billing and cooing of Haydn's doves. Tennyson's 'moan of doves in immemorial elms' is not finer onomatopoeia than Haydn's combination of bassoons and violins in their fourth string.

Descriptive Recitative and Arioso (D minor).

RAPHAEL. And God created great whales and every living creature that moveth, and God blessed them, saying,

> Be fruitful all and multiply, and fill the seas.
> Yea, multiply ye fowl upon the earth,
> And in your God and Lord rejoice.
> (Adapted from Gen. i. 21-2.)

The arioso ('Be fruitful') is scored for divided violas and violoncellos with independent double-basses. It ought to be a *locus classicus* for such scoring, but perhaps the writers of text-books are afraid to quote a passage more than usually full of the kind of Haydnesque or Gluckesque inaccuracies which leave us in irresolvable doubt whether we are dealing with strokes of genius or blunders. Still, there is no excuse for the modern editing of the double-bass part which, because of a few outlying low notes such as occur in every classical bass-part before Wagner, puts almost the whole part an octave higher, and so confines God's blessing to creatures who could be safely invited to fill the Round Pond in Kensington Gardens.

Secco-Recitative.

RAPHAEL. And the angels struck their immortal harps and sang together the wonders of the fifth day.

Terzet (A major).

GABRIEL. The hills in order stand new clad in grassy green,
    In thanks they lift their heads.
    Their pebbled freshets sing with everflowing gift
    Of water clean and bright.
URIEL. The birds in wheeling flight are playing in the air
    And sing their hymn of praise,
    And in their ordered ranks their wings reflect the sun
    In rainbow coloured light.
RAPHAEL. Now fish in glistening shoals abound,
    And play in schools a thousand strong,
    While monstrous from the deep, mighty Leviathan
    Upheaves his bulk immense.
All Three. How manifold thy works, O God! Who may their number
    tell?

Haydn's glorious freedom of form is well displayed in the various phases of this tone-picture as delivered by the three archangels in turn. The three unite in a new theme which inspired Mendelssohn to the burden 'O blessed are they' in 'I waited for the Lord'; a fact disastrously evident on an occasion within my memory when his *Lobgesang* (without its three symphonic movements) was used as a substitute for the Third Part of *The Creation*.

The Terzet leads to the most brilliant of all Haydn's choruses. I refuse to concede any courtesy to the scruples of people who are shocked at the coloraturas of Gabriel and Uriel, which thrill me as much as anything in Bach or Handel, though they are confined to the cadential harmonies of an operatic cabaletta. Gothic revivals may have swept away Grinling Gibbons and the village crafts-man from our cathedrals with one hand while they built Albert Memorials with the other; but the monuments of music remain in print, and the 'restoring' of them need not be destructive.

Chorus (with the three Archangels).

The Lord is great and great His might, His glory lasts for ever.

THE SIXTH DAY

Secco-Recitative.

RAPHAEL. And God said, Let the earth bring forth the living creature after his kind, cattle, and creeping thing, and beast of the earth after his kind. (Gen. i. 24.)

Now comes the most dangerous, disputed, and in some ways the most delightful passage in the whole work. Beethoven deserves forgiveness for angrily laughing at it. He was occupied in the gigantic task of raising the language of music from the level of comedy of manners to something equally beyond the Gothic sublimities of Bach and the Michael-Angelesque sublimities of Handel. His range was Shakespearean, and his sense of humour was at once the foundation of his sense of tragedy and his defence against egoistic pessimism. An artist's business is to get on with his own work, and we have no right to annoy him with requests to take a large-minded critical view of tendencies the vogue of which thwarts him. On the other hand, nobody but the artist so thwarted has any right to take less than a large-minded critical view, except people whose responsibilities are confined to knowing what they like, or (what comes to much the same thing) liking what they know.

I give the text of Haydn's menagerie as it has been ingeniously revised in the new Oxford edition. But in actual practice I find that in some details the old text, or some other alteration of it, is necessary. Nor can I wholly agree with the conclusion of my old friends the Oxford editors that 'Much of the amusement past generations have had from the text of *The Creation* has been enjoyed under a misapprehension. There was no intention to amuse, but rather to edify.' In the first place, Haydn's mind notoriously failed to draw a sharp line between amusement and edification. There is abundant evidence that he was often scolded for this failure; and his assertion, quoted above, that he had never been so pious as when writing *The Creation*, shows every sign of being a defence against some such scolding; just as Bunyan, who endured fiendish tortures of remorse for his deadly sins of church-bell ringing and tip-cat, flared up at once at any suggestion that he ever led an immoral life. Again, it is not implied by the Puritan Milton that in the Earthly Paradise itself amusement was inadmissible without edification; at all events Milton does not tell us what serious lessons Adam and Eve were to learn from 'the unwieldy elephant' who—

> To make them mirth, used all his might, and wreathed
> His lithe proboscis.

Haydn is no unwieldy elephant, but why should he be forbidden to use at least some of his might to make us mirth in the Garden of Eden?

The Oxford edition represents Haydn's animals as follows. I will not trouble the reader with my poor makeshifts where its literary merit seems to me to have been achieved at the expense of the music, but will merely indicate the difficulties in question.

Descriptive Recitative.

RAPHAEL. Straight opening her fertile womb
The earth obeyed the word, and lo,
Creatures innumerous teemed at a birth
All fully grown.
The tawny lion pawing to get free,
And, breaking from his bonds, the tiger leaps out;
The antlered stag protrudes his branching head,
With flying mane and spurning hoof
Impatient neighs the fiery steed.
The cattle graze, some rare and solitary,
Some in herds are seen.
And o'er the ground like fleecy plants
Arose the gentle sheep.
At once came forth whatever creeps the ground,
Insect or worm.
In sinuous trace, they their long dimension draw.

This text restores the picture given by Milton and many an old illustrated Bible; according to which the animals are seen in the act of struggling out of the ground. Unfortunately this picture was not presented to Haydn either by Linley-Lidley or the Baron van Swieten; and I find it a fatal objection to the use here of the Miltonic 'pawing to get free' that if Haydn had been presented with any such idea he could not have failed to illustrate it unmistakably in his music. The same objection applies to the 'bonds' of the tiger and the 'protruding' head of the stag. What Haydn does illustrate is animals already freely active. The action of the lion is very Haydnesque, but it has the misfortune to have been obliterated by an ancient piece of editorial stupidity which infuriates me all the more by reappearing in an aggravated form in the new critical *Gesammtausgabe*, ostensibly under the name of my beloved and lamented friend, Mandyczewski, who, as I happen to know, emphatically agreed with me on this very detail at least thirty years ago. Haydn's recitative begins with a *forte* of all the strings, plus bassoons.

Ex. 12a.

After the words 'All fully grown' this phrase is resumed *piano*, with the following result—

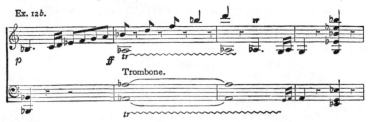

Ex. 12b.

Trombone.

The otherwise excellent Peters full score, published some sixty years ago, substituted a *forte* for the *piano*. The new critical edition seems to have been revised (I presume since Mandyczewski's death, or overruling his opinion) by some one who has had the intelligence to notice that the violins have no support from the basses, and who accordingly thinks *forte* insufficient and substitutes *fortissimo*. Swinburne would certainly have ascribed to 'the intelligence of a beetle' the capacity to see that the weakness of the unsupported first violins confirms the *piano* mark as correct. Haydn's lion is not 'pawing to get free'; all Haydn knows is that 'Vor Freude brüllend steht der Löwe da', and I cannot see much objection to the English text which he had before him; 'Cheerful roaring stands the tawny lion'. What Haydn represents is this: the Editor not having yet coiled himself round the Tree of Knowledge, some more harmless and necessary animal, such as a goose, is walking past the lion's ambush, whereupon that tawny animal, not being a beast of prey until after the Fall of Man, plays his obvious and Haydn-esque practical joke and says 'Bo!'

The listener will do well to remember the classical rule that the illustration comes first and the words afterwards throughout the recitative. To me the whole series is as delightful as the medieval cries of the animals on Christmas Day; the cock with his 'Christus natus est', the duck with 'Quando, quando?' the raven with 'In hac nocte', the cow with 'Ubi, ubi?' and the sheep with 'In Bethle-hem'. I am compelled to restore the line 'In long dimensions creeps with sinuous trace the worm'. It is not much more absurd than Milton's elephant; and the previous introduction of the worm into Haydn's illustration of the 'host of insects unnumbered as the sands' is a fatal mistake. In fact I cannot imagine how the Oxford editors allowed themselves to obliterate the whole meaning of Haydn's tremolo.

Aria (D major).

RAPHAEL. Now heaven in all her glory shone,
Earth in her pomp consummate smiled,
The vault of air by fowl is flown,
The water swum by frequent fish,
Behemoth's self doth walk the ground.
But yet the end was not achieved.
There wanted yet the master work
That should acknowledge all this good,
Adore and worship God supreme.

This is an entirely majestic composition, though Behemoth's self (a more particularized item than Haydn's 'heavy beasts' or 'schwerer Last der Tieren') breaks through in the person of the contrafagotto almost as subversively as cheerfulness broke into the philosophy of Dr. Johnson's friend Edwards.

Still, there is nothing here that need minimize the grandeur of the prophecy that Man was yet to be created in order to glorify God and enjoy Him for ever.

Secco-Recitative.

URIEL. So God created man in his own image, in the image of God created he him: male and female created he them. (Gen. i. 27.)
He breathed into his nostrils the breath of life, and man became a living soul. (Gen. ii. 2.)

Aria (C major).

In native worth and honour clad,
With beauty, courage, strength adorned,
His eyes to heaven turned upwards, stands a Man,
The lord and king of nature all.
His forehead broad and arching high,
Proclaims that knowledge dwells with him;
And through his eyes transparent
Shines the soul, the breath and image of his God.
While at his side his partner stands,
Made from his flesh for him,
A woman fair and full of grace.
Her glance of smiling innocence
As fair as blushing spring
Invites him to find there love and joy serene.

Here we have not only the quintessence of Haydn but the perfection of *bel canto*. We have also Haydn's freedom of form, shown in
his instant readiness to follow the lines suggested by his text. The
themes descriptive of Eve are only vaguely connected with those
descriptive of Adam; the aria is allowed to fall into two subtly contrasted portions and there is no thought of complicating matters
by a da capo. Another comparison with a later composition may
be excused for its unfairness because of its aptness in showing the
difference between a stroke of genius and an ambitious effort.
Schubert at the height of his power has no cause to fear comparison with the greatest things in any art; but Schubert, after
writing an ambitious exercise in his second-best style, would perhaps not be angry with us for using that exercise to measure the
power of his beloved Haydn. The song *Die Allmacht* is an ambitious effort. Its very title, to say nothing of its text, would forbid
us to blame Schubert for the contrast between its emphatic pon-
derosity and the heavenly lightness of Haydn's aria; but the two
compositions have at least one thought in common, the thought
that the Almighty's power is best felt in the heart of Man; or, as
our Oxford text of Haydn's aria has it, 'through his eyes transparent Shines the soul, the breath and image of his God'. Now
this climax Schubert represents with a beautiful purple patch in
A flat major, the tonic being, as with Haydn, C major. The purple
patch occurs twice, and the repetition is quite welcome and orthodox
in form. Haydn, on the other hand, first modulates to the ordinary
dominant, and it is at the moment of apparently repeating this
modulation that he diverts it to the remoter key of A flat. This is,
in its quiet way, as overwhelming as the outburst at 'and there was
Light'.

When Vienna was bombarded in 1809, Haydn had long been

bedridden; but when the first shot fell near to his house he called out to his servants, 'Children, don't be frightened; no harm can happen to you while Haydn is by'. His last visitor was a French officer who touched him greatly by his singing of 'In native worth'. Soon afterwards, at one o'clock in the morning of May 31st, Haydn died.

Secco-Recitative.

RAPHAEL. And God saw everything that he had made, and, behold it was very good. (Gen. i. 31.)

And the Sons of God saw all the days of creation ended, and shouted for joy.

The introductory statement of the angelic chorus is fine in itself, and contains a short fugato not used afterwards, besides a short postlude that significantly anticipates the double fugue to be developed later. The terzet of the three archangels is a beautiful slow movement (Poco adagio) which it is a pity to lose. But, as I have already pointed out, it introduces thoughts that are not clearly relevant either to the Six Days of Creation or to the Seventh Day, on which God rested but certainly did not turn away His face or strike us with sudden terror, take our breath away, and reduce us again to dust. And I do not find, in actual practice, that, when introduced by the right first seven bars, the last chorus of Haydn's Second Part loses more than it gains by standing alone. It may speak for itself, double fugue and all, without musical quotation. A very detailed analysis would be needed to explain the subtle elements of its grandeur, which is rendered the more astonishing by the fact that its cadential formulas are neither Bachian nor Handelian but purely symphonic, or, if you will, operatic, without the slightest excuse for a ritardando. Technically the most surprising thing in its orchestration is its almost completely modern treatment of the brass. The classical treatment of trombones is nowadays often misunderstood because of a failure to recognize that in the organ-galleries of vaulted churches they assimilate themselves closely with voices and have by no means the penetrating power that most writers on orchestration ascribe to them. But Haydn shows that he wrote *The Creation* for the concert-room rather than the church; and his brass ensemble, including such Beethovenish clashes as—

Ex. 13. Trombones.

is at once safer and bolder than anything we are accustomed to expect from Mozart, Beethoven, Schubert, or even Weber. By the way, Haydn does not seem to know the modern or late-Victorian rule that 'you must never use the bass trombone without the others'. His rule appears to be that you may do so by all means, but need neither presuppose that he will play like a pig nor compel him to play thus by writing so low as to give him constant rapid changes of his slide from the first position to the seventh. On the other hand, Haydn entrusts to him, or to the conductor, the dangerous task of simplifying the passages where a manifestly insane agility is the result of the directions (Trombone III col Contrafagotto) × (Contrafagotto col Basso) × (Basso col Violoncello).

Chorus.

Achieved at last the glorious work,
The praise of God shall be our song.

Double Fugue.

Glory be to God eternal. He reigns on high for evermore. Hallelujah.

Let us disregard the suggestion of an interval between Part II and Part III; and let us give its proper Beethovenish effect to Haydn's extreme contrast between B flat and E major (equivalent to Beethoven's contrast between the D flat Andante and G major Tedesca of his Quartet in B flat, Op. 130). Morning arises on God's Seventh Day of Rest.

Introduction and Descriptive Recitative.

URIEL. Now rosy-fingered, fresh awaked by music's sound,
            The dawn lights up the sky.
        And quiring angel companies sing purest harmony
            To earth below.
        See now the happy pair, how hand in hand they go,
        Their shining faces show the unspoken thanks they feel.
        Soon with expressive voice they sing the praise of God.
        Then let our voices ring, united with their song.

Haydn's delicious three flutes are, except in one passage, supported by strings with chords (sometimes, but not always, pizzicato) of which the bass doubles the third flute three octaves below. The sight of this in the score must set every musician's teeth on edge; and I can find no theory to explain the astonishing fact that the actual effect is not only excellent but that any correction of it merely makes the flutes sound out of tune. Trust Haydn's ear; he is one of the untidiest of artists; but, as he said to Prince Esterhazy, 'That, your Highness, is *my* business'.

Now comes the greatest thing in *The Creation* since the Chaos and the Light. I will not distract the listener's attention by further expressions of vexation at editors and cutters, except to express my gratification that my Oxford friends have refused to fall into the booby-trap into which a misprint in the original edition led the editors of the *Gesammtausgabe*. (Here again I cannot imagine how Mandyczewski's judgement came to be overruled.) The first long note of the oboe was misprinted as a minim in the middle of the bar. The editor of the Peters score, though he fell into the booby-trap of the cheerful tawny lion, here had the gumption to see that, as semibreves in the old score were always printed in the middle of the bar, it was much more likely that the minim was a misprint for a semibreve than that an initial rest had been omitted. A semibreve produces the *messa di voce* characteristic of all vocal or sustained openings of this kind; whereas an entry at the half-bar is a mere grammatical possibility with no discoverable meaning. But it has been faithfully put into the band-parts.

Analysis of this grand pair of movements would be futile unless it were an exhaustive précis. I merely indicate the key-sequence in the Allegretto, the wanderings of which are as spacious as the review of the heavens and earth by Adam and Eve, who anticipate the Song of the Three Children in Nebuchadnezzar's burning fiery furnace ('O all ye works of the Lord').

Adagio (C major).

ADAM *and* EVE.	Thy bounteous care, O Lord and God, Fills heaven and earth with good. This world so great, so wonderful, Thy mighty Hand has made.
Chorus of Angels: (pianissimo)	We know the mighty power of God. We praise His name for evermore.

Allegretto (F major).

ADAM.	Of stars the brightest, Shine thou on, fair harbinger of day. Shine on, thou too, O sun on high, Thou universal flame.
Chorus: (forte) EVE.	Proclaim in music of the spheres The mighty God and praise His name. And thou, the solace of our nights, And ye, O starry host, In all your galaxies declare His praise While constellations sing.
ADAM. (B flat major) (Drift towards A flat)	And ye, O elements, By whose work new shapes and forms are made, Ye, O clouds and lightnings, Whom the winds assemble and disperse,
With Chorus:	We bid you magnify the Lord: Great is His name and great His might.

EVE.   O singing streams, acclaim your fount,
(A flat)   Bow down your heads, O trees,
                   And show your fragrance, plants and herbs,
                   For all sweet smells are His.

ADAM.   Ye who on mountain heights do dwell,
(Drift through   And ye of lowly ground,
E flat minor   Ye who in flight cleave upper air,
and beyond)   And ye who swim below.

With Chorus: All creatures magnify the Lord,
(Dominant of G)   Praise Him all ye works of His.

ADAM *and* EVE.   Ye shady wood, ye hills and dales,
(G major; destroying Be witness of our thanks:
the initial effect of Re-echoing from morn till night
F major and firmly Our grateful hymns of praise.
establishing C major)

Final Section in C major.

Chorus: (piano) Hail, bounteous Lord! Creator, hail!
                   For by Thy word the world was made.
(forte, in fugato) Both heaven and earth Thy power adore,
                   We praise Thee now and evermore.

But the best way to raise the reader's expectation to the height of
Haydn's great argument is to quote Milton's version of this song,
which is dimly but unmistakably traceable throughout the Linley-
Lidley-van-Swieten-Fox-Strangways-Steuart-Wilson evolution.

> These are thy glorious works Parent of good,
> Almighty, thine this universal frame,
> Thus wondrous fair; thyself how wondrous then!
> Unspeakable, who sitt'st above these Heavens
> To us invisible or dimly seen
> In these thy lowest works, yet these declare
> Thy goodness beyond thought, and Power Divine:
> Speak ye who best can tell, ye Sons of light,
> Angels, for ye behold him, and with songs
> And choral symphonies, Day without Night,
> Circle his Throne rejoicing; ye in Heav'n.
> On Earth join all ye Creatures to extol
> Him first, him last, him midst, and without end.
> Fairest of Stars, last in the train of Night,
> If better thou belong not to the dawn,
> Sure pledge of day, that crown'st the smiling Morn
> With thy bright Circlet, praise him in thy Sphere,
> While day arises, that sweet hour of Prime:
> Thou Sun, of this great world both eye and soul,
> Acknowledge him thy Greater, sound his praise
> In thy eternal course, both when thou climb'st,
> And when high noon hast gain'd and when thou fall'st.

Moon, that now meet'st the orient Sun, now fly'st,
With the fix'd Stars, fix'd in their Orb that flies,
And ye five other wandering Fires that move
In mystic Dance not without Song, resound
His praise, who out of Darkness call'd up Light.
Air, and ye Elements the eldest birth
Of Nature's Womb, that in quaternion run
Perpetual Circle, multiform; and mix
And nourish all things, let your ceaseless change
Vary to our great Maker still new praise.
Ye Mists and Exhalations, that now rise
From Hill or steaming Lake, dusky or grey,
Till the Sun paint your fleecy skirts with Gold,
In honour to the World's great Author rise;
Whether to deck with Clouds the uncolour'd sky,
Or wet the thirsty Earth with falling showers,
Rising or falling still advance his praise.
His praise ye Winds, that from four Quarters blow,
Breathe soft or loud; and wave your tops, ye Pines,
With every Plant, in sign of Worship wave.
Fountains and ye, that warble, as ye flow,
Melodious murmurs, warbling tune his praise.
Join voices all ye living Souls: ye Birds,
That singing up to Heaven Gate ascend,
Bear on your wings and in your notes his praise.
Ye that in Waters glide, and ye that walk
The Earth, and stately tread, or lowly creep;
Witness if I be silent, Morn or Even,
To Hill, or Valley, Fountain, or fresh shade
Made vocal by my Song, and taught his praise.
Hail universal Lord, be bounteous still
To give us only good; and if the night
Have gathered aught of evil or conceal'd,
Disperse it, as now light dispels the dark.

The last three lines are, of course, relevant only to the subject of
Paradise Lost', referring, as they do, to the disquieting dream sent
as a warning to Eve. But it would be a pity to cut Milton's paean
short of its appointed end.

On the other hand, the more I study *The Creation*, the better I
am satisfied to end it here. The love-duet between Adam and Eve
I dearly want to hear, and without cuts; but on some other occasion.
And another Palladian chorus would need to be even finer than the
end of Haydn's Part II if it were to command our attention after
what I believe to be the greatest movement, or pair of movements,
that he ever wrote, whether vocal or instrumental. Haydn's actual
last chorus 'Praise the Lord all ye his creatures' is good, but does
not, like the last chorus of *The Seasons*, achieve another opening

of the gates of Heaven. The sublimest note is undoubtedly that
of Haydn's innocent symphonic style when the human voices of
Adam and Eve in the Garden of Eden lead the choirs of angels.

CCVII. 'THE SEASONS'

Haydn's *Seasons* (*Die Jahreszeiten*) has suffered from the hard
things he was the first to say about it. He began it in 1799,
immediately after he had finished *The Creation*, but yielded with
reluctance to the persuasions of his librettist, the Baron van
Swieten, saying in the first place that he was old and his powers
were failing, and in the second place, in terms diplomatically
modified for van Swieten, but more direct to other friends, that
the whole scheme of musical illustrations to common objects of the
countryside was Philistine. Afterwards, when the success of
the work was hardly, if at all, less than that of *The Creation*, he
resented being praised for his imitations of the croakings of frogs
and the bleatings of sheep, saying 'dieser französische Quark ist mir
aufgedrungen' (this Frenchified trash was forced upon me). He
also often complained that '*The Seasons* gave me my finishing
stroke'. We have exaggerated ideas as to the length of Haydn's
career and even as to the volume of his work. Verdi was 80 when
he wrote *Falstaff*; but Haydn was 77 when he died in 1809, and
after *The Seasons* was performed in 1801, he wrote only some vocal
quartets, a fragment of a string quartet, and some accompaniments
for Scottish, Welsh, and Irish airs for an Edinburgh publisher.

During the composition of *The Creation* Haydn had already
feared that he might have a stroke, and his pessimism about
The Seasons no doubt had its physical causes. It is the more
unfortunate for the reputation of a great work that his self-criticism
should amount exactly to what any fool can say beforehand. It is
much more true that the obvious defects are the most negligible
aspects of Haydn's qualities. The *französischer Quark* was forced
upon him largely in consequence of the success of what it is now
becoming priggish to condemn in the word-painting and animal-
painting of *The Creation*. It is an automatic function of his sense
of humour, which, as is now proverbially known, was never so
irrepressible as when he rejoiced in the goodness of God.

I have refrained from announcing *The Seasons* as an oratorio,
because only a small part of the work has any pretensions to be
sacred music at all. And I dislike the alternative title 'cantata'
because, except in the case of Bach, it has become associated with
a kind of village harvest festival music: an association which is
the more unfortunate because it derives some details of its style
from Haydn's *Seasons*. The best way to rid oneself of prejudices is

to take advantage of the fact that hardly anybody nowadays has ever heard a performance of *The Seasons* in its integrity, and to treat such a performance as that of a new discovery of a work *sui generis*.

Thomson has suffered almost as much as Haydn from the Baron van Swieten's acknowledgement of indebtedness. I have read Thomson's *Seasons* in the critical edition of Dr. Otto Zippel, 'a reproduction of the original texts, with all the various readings of the later editions, historically arranged', and have failed to find in it more resemblance to Haydn's text than *Paradise Lost* shows to the text of *The Creation*. As in my analysis of *The Creation* I quoted Milton in preference to the obligatory Mongrelian of the English libretto, so here I shall quote Thomson wherever I can substitute him for a lingo that has not yet had the advantage of drastic re-writing by musical editors in the Oxford University Press.

As a matter of fact, the Baron van Swieten is guilty of the grossest slander in coupling his name with Thomson's at all. The indebtedness of *The Creation* to Milton is by no means as obvious as its indebtedness to the Bible, and Milton could almost as well afford to be indebted to the Bible as he could afford to be faintly recognizable here and there in the Mongrelian language of the committee of translators and adaptors of Haydn's libretto. But poor Thomson cannot afford to be misrepresented. To the incurious his name recalls the exclamation from his *Tragedy of Sophonisba*: 'O Sophonisba, Sophonisba O'; because of the critic's retort 'O Jimmy Thomson, Jimmy Thomson O'! In Thomson's (but not in Haydn's) *Spring* you will find a much more famous line, 'To teach the young idea how to shoot'; but this does not provoke critics to call attention to its authorship. More famous still is 'Rule Britannia', which even Tennyson and Palgrave allowed to appear in *The Golden Treasury* with the feeble indicative 'Britannia rules the waves' instead of the authentic imperative 'Britannia rule the waves'. To either version Carlyle's pencilled comment was 'Cockadoodle doo!' A revival of Haydn's *Seasons* will incidentally revive a few other lines from the opening of Thomson's *Spring* in a chorus which has never lost its popularity; and this is unfortunate, because it will create in most listeners, as it created in me, the expectation that the rest of Haydn's libretto is equally indebted to Thomson. It would be really scandalous to perpetuate such a libel on the *magnum opus* of an English poet who, as Dr. Johnson said, 'has as much of the poet about him as most writers. Everything appeared to him through the medium of his favourite pursuit. He could not have viewed those two candles burning but with a poetical eye.' Haydn's most depised *Tonmalerei* has precisely this Thomsonian quality. I don't know how you would express two burning candles musically, but Haydn could

no more help hearing the bleating of sheep and the croaking of
frogs than the goodness of God with a musical ear. As to the
libretto, not only has every vestige of poetry vanished from it, but
Thomson's attitude towards at least two of the principal things he
describes has been flatly contradicted and replaced by vulgar conceptions which we need not even recognize as specially English.
Great Britain is not a wine-growing country, unless you count
whisky, but one of the finest things Haydn ever wrote is the chorus
in praise of wine at the end of *Autumn*. Beer is not mentioned,
though Thomson has his vivid word for the 'brown October'; and,
while Haydn's dancing to pipe and tabor and some kind of bag-
pipes is entirely delightful, we must not ascribe to Thomson the
leading words of the chorus, 'Revel, riot'. This, however, is not
because Thomson has a more sympathetic view of alehouse
festivities. On the contrary, here is part of his account of what
happens when

> . . . the dry divan
> Close in firm circle; and set, ardent, in
> For serious drinking. Nor evasion sly,
> Nor sober shift is to the puking wretch
> Indulg'd askew; but earnest, brimming bowls
> Lave every soul, the table floating round,
> And pavement, faithless to the fuddled foot.

The real Thomson is gloriously quotable; but if van Swieten
had allowed Haydn to get a glimpse of him, there would have been
less wonder that Haydn thought the scheme unmusical. My own
belief is that his quarrel with van Swieten would have become
serious, and that he would have developed an interest in a real
English poet of kindred spirit. We should have lost a great choral
work which Haydn himself underrated; and I am not sure that
the few more symphonies and string quartets that we might have
gained would have overtaxed Haydn less than the composition
of *The Seasons*. The more I study the technique of Haydn's middle
and later works, the more I am impressed with his own conviction
that he was neither a facile nor a quick writer, and that his mature
handling of musical form needed immense reserves of energy used
in procedures which were individual for each work. It is significant that that most pathetic of fragments, his last quartet, consists
of the two middle movements, the andante and minuet, and that
there are no traces of the first movement or the finale.

In *The Seasons* I do not find any abatement of power as compared with *The Creation*. Except in the last chorus, the whole
subject is of a lower order, and its appropriate treatment represents
Haydn at his best. There is more that can be cut out than in
The Creation, but cuts within an individual number are quite as

unpermissible. I used to think that the greater length of what I
call the Palladian choruses was a sign of old age, representing a
nervous fear lest their size should be inadequate, but on rehearsal
I find them terse and their choral power as great as that of any
choral music. The time is ripe for us to recognize in Haydn and
Mozart choral writers of the calibre of Handel. The rediscovery
of Bach, who, as Schweitzer very truly says, is Gothic, has blinded
us to the merits of other styles of musical architecture; but the
choral art of Mozart and Haydn has yet the power to rise out of
all the squalor in which their patrons tried to keep it.

SPRING

With the orchestral introduction and first numbers of *Spring*,
Thomson is not worse misrepresented than can be expected
in the circumstances of an eighteenth-century musical libretto.
Haydn begins with a glorious symphonic orchestral representation
of winter weather.

Ex. 1.

I learn from the article on Haydn in the first edition of *Grove's
Dictionary of Music and Musicians*, written in the 'seventies, that
opinions are divided as to the relative merits of *The Creation* and
The Seasons. The solemn goose-step tempo ($\downarrow = 138$) given for
the vivace in the vocal scores is one of the traditional ineptitudes
that make it a miracle that the work should ever have had any
popularity at all, and the hired orchestral material nowadays available shows alarming signs that such traditions have been quite
recently followed. Haydn, like Bach, is notoriously inconsistent
in his use of the C and ₵ time-signatures; but this should not
prevent even classical music from being played as music. Haydn
is always splendid when his temper is blustering. His representation of winter gains both in realism and musical power from its
concession to sonata form when Haydn modulates to the orthodox
complementary key and gives us a brief glimpse of snowdrops.

Ex. 2.

The wintry storms return and develop. A symphonic return

is made to a full recapitulation and expansion of Ex. 1; and the stormy material is only further developed, with no trace of Ex. 2, until the voices of Simon and Lucas (*alias* the Baron van Swieten distantly translating from Thomson) explain that all this blustering is merely winter's Parthian shot. Where I can quote Thomson I shall spare the reader our efforts to adjust to music the traditional mistranslations of van Swieten's rhymed prose. Thomson says:

> And see where surly Winter passes off,
> Far to the North, and calls his ruffian Blasts;
> His Blasts obey, and quit the howling Hill,
> The shatter'd Forest, and the ravag'd Vale:
> While softer Gales succeed, at whose kind Touch,
> Dissolving Snows in sudden Torrents lost,
> The Mountains lift their green Heads to the Sky.

These seven lines go a little further than what Haydn had before him, but they give all the better idea of Haydn's music.

Now follows the best-known item in all Haydn's *Seasons*. Van Swieten has meticulously omitted every detail that could possibly catch a poetic eye or distract an incorrigibly illustrative composer; so the listener need not know the bittern's time, nor trouble about the wild notes of the plovers.

> Come, gentle Spring, Æthereal Mildness, come,
> And from the Bosom of yon dropping Cloud,
> While Music wakes around, veil'd in a Shower
> Of shadowing Roses, on our Plains descend.
>
> As yet the trembling Year is unconfirmed,
> And Winter oft at Eve resumes the Breeze,
> Chills the pale Moon, and bids his diving Sleets
> Deform the Day delightless; so that scarce
> The Bittern knows his Time, with Bill ingulpht
> To shake the sounding Marsh; or from the Shore
> The Plovers theirs, to scatter o'er the Heath,
> And sing their wild Notes to the listening Waste.

The Baron and the Translator then inform us through the mouth of that typical British farmer, Simon, that

> Now in his course the sun has reach'd the winter-butting Ram.

This is ingenious; but perhaps Thomson's reference to the signs of the Zodiac is a little more clear, so let us see the matter through Thomson's poetic eye.

> At last from Aries rolls the bounteous Sun,
> And the bright Bull receives Him. Then no more
> Th'expansive Atmosphere is cramp'd with Cold,
> But full of Life, and vivifying Soul,
> Lifts the light Clouds sublime, and spreads them thin,
> Fleecy, and white, o'er All-surrounding Heaven.

Then comes the other of the two most famous numbers of
Haydn's *Seasons*. Let us again listen to Haydn's music with the
aid of Thomson's poetic eye.

> Joyous th'impatient Husbandman perceives
> Relenting Nature, and his lusty Steers
> Drives from their Stalls, to where the well-us'd Plow
> Lies in the Furrow loosen'd from the Frost.
> There, unrefusing to the harness'd yoke,
> They lend their Shoulder, and begin their Toil,
> Chear'd by the simple Song, and soaring Lark.
> Mean-while incumbent o'er the shining share
> The Master leans, removes th'obstructing Clay,
> Winds the whole Work, and side-long lays the Glebe.
>
> White thro' the neighbring Fields the Sower stalks,
> With measur'd Step, and liberal throws the Grain
> Into the faithful Bosom of the Earth,
> The Harrow follows harsh, and shuts the Scene.

In this splendid aria perhaps the most remarkable fact is that in
representing the husbandman's 'wonted lay' by the famous tune
borrowed from the 'Surprise' Symphony, Haydn has chosen a
melody which for all its extreme rusticity can be neither whistled
nor sung. (The Baron's 'flötend nach' is truer to the original
than the Translator's 'wonted lay'). Try it, and however brilliant
you may be at whistling you will be surprised at your inefficiency as
a piccolo in this instance.

Ex. 3.

So Haydn gives the singer counterpoints.

Ex. 4.

SIMON :

In   lan-gen Fur-chen schrei - tet er dem Pflu-ge flö-tend nach

In a short further recitative the British farmer is praised for
having done all that can be expected of him, and the prayers of
the poet and the composer now rise in one of Haydn's finest
movements.

The slow movement of Haydn's Symphony in B flat No. 98,
with its unmistakable reminiscence of that of the 'Jupiter'

Symphony, has always seemed to me a kind of requiem for Mozart. It also closely resembles the following trio and chorus:

Ex. 5.

Sei   nur   gnä-dig,   mil-der   Him-mel!

but the fugue with which it ends is hardly less than a direct allusion to the 'quam olim Abrahae' of Mozart's Requiem.

Ex. 6.

Uns sprie-sset Ue-ber-fluss und dei-ner Güte

&c.

Ex. 7.

&c.

quam o-lim A-bra-hae   pro-mis-is-ti

The fugue subject is, of course, an inevitable tag; but the figures of the orchestral accompaniment, though equally conventional, make a combination the resemblance of which is beyond coincidence. Also, the beautiful hush towards the end seems to ask for Mozart's blessing upon this work of Haydn's old age.

In the next recitative, Jane, the farmer's daughter, comments favourably upon the weather in terms which it were an irksome task to discover in Thomson. The ideas have, as a matter of fact, been entangled in the previous recitative and chorus. Perhaps the following quotation may cover the ground:

> Be gracious, Heaven! for now laborious Man
> Has done his Due. Ye fostering Breezes blow!
> Ye softening Dew, ye tender Showers descend!
> And temper all, thou influential Sun,
> Into the perfect Year!

Then follows a delightful trio with occasional outbreaks of chorus. For all I know, the Baron may have appreciated the surroundings of his country estate, but he does not commit himself

to more than a townsman's vagueness in enumerating the common
objects of the country. To quote the Translator, Jane remarks,

'Oh what num'rous charms unfolding shows the country now!
Come, ye virgins, let us wander on th'enamell'd fields';

to which Lucas answers, substituting 'gay fellows' for 'ye virgins'.
Further particulars are

Lilies, roses and the flowers all;
Groves, meadows and the landscape all;
Land's surface, waters and the lucid air;

the frisking and capering of 'the lamkins'; the flouncing and
tumbling of the fishes; the swarming and rambling of bees; and
the fretting and fluttering of birds. (The listener need not listen
for *these* words when I produce *The Seasons*, but I shall not trouble
him with my makeshifts.) What Haydn's musical ear catches is
the precise difference between the bleat of a lambkin and that of
a sheep, and the glitter of sunlight upon the wings of bees. Incidentally, he breaks the otherwise inviolable classical rule that the
musical illustrations should precede and not follow the words; but
the dominating sentiment is that expressed in all Haydn's music
by his own confession and here clearly aimed at as the conclusion
to which this movement is to lead. The music pauses on the
dominant of an unorthodox key, and then the praise of the Almighty
is inaugurated with the full power of the orchestra. Here is
Thomson's summing-up of the whole matter:

What is this mighty Breath, ye Curious, say,
Which, in a Language rather felt than heard,
Instructs the Fowls of Heaven; and thro' their Breasts
These Arts of Love diffuses? . . . What? but God!
Inspiring God! who boundless Spirit all,
And unremitting Energy, pervades,
Subsists, adjusts, and agitates the Whole.

After a majestic formal introduction Haydn's vocal trio sings a
lyric song of gratitude in a short poco adagio punctuated with
doxologies from the chorus. Then the song of spring is concluded
with a majestic fugue—

Ex. 8.

Eh - re, Lob und Preis sei dir

which is a masterpiece in its terseness and the variety of means by
which contrast and climax are achieved. Great power emanates
from the partial augmentation of the first two notes of the subject—
a device already effective in the choruses of *The Creation*. These

two notes underlie the coda, in which symphonic formal elements are allowed to relieve the polyphonic style.

It is perhaps not without practical grounds that *Spring* is the best-known part of Haydn's *Seasons*. But I cannot go so far as to admit that it has any marked superiority over the rest, except in this, that it is the only part in which the text has any but the most negligible traces of that genuine poet, Thomson. The improvers of the first translator have tried to increase the percentage of Thomson; mostly with the obviously disastrous result of misfitting the music of Haydn.

SUMMER

Haydn's *Summer* begins with a recitative describing the approach of dawn. The Baron's mythical and un-Thomsonian creatures— Lucas the young countryman, Simon the farmer, and his daughter Jane—take it in turns to describe in flat German and inflated English the approach of dawn, the retirement of the night-birds, and the awakening of the shepherd by 'the crested harbinger of day'. The last-named bird is brilliantly represented by one of Haydn's most famous oboe solos. The only possible matter for doubt is whether the oboe, rather than heralding the dawn, has not laid an egg.

Haydn's shepherd is not a little boy, nor are we told that his garments are blue, but he blows his horn as characteristically as Siegfried in an aria which, together with Jane's following recitative, fortunately describes the sunrise efficiently enough to enable us to omit the following chorus, which, though brilliant in its way, suffers sadly by comparison with the magnificent and simple sunrise and moonrise in *The Creation*. As I have already said, cuts within any of Haydn's movements are as criminal as cuts in Beethoven, but *The Seasons* is unquestionably too long for complete performance in less than two evenings. And I confess to a great sense of relief on finding that the recitatives will join together without traceable scar if we omit one of the most difficult and at the same time most conventional of Haydn's choruses. So let us say with the first English translator: 'Hail, O Sun, be hailed, in shouting praise resounds thy name through Nature all'; and let us proceed to Haydn's description of noonday heat in a wonderful recitative and cavatina, in which the tenor voice, muted strings, an oboe, and a flute express Haydn's full power and breadth of rhythm in a slow tempo.

Jane, the soprano, follows with a recitative describing welcome woodland shades and the refreshing coolness of a rivulet. The Baron has not allowed the composer any opportunity for Thomson's charming episode of the virtuous countryman chivalrously refraining from taking Actaeon's advantage of his Diana and seeing that no other profane eye shall approach the pool in which she is bathing. You can trust the Baron to present the composer with no pictures whatever; but the countryman's rustic pipe is allowed speech in one of the most beautiful of coloratura duets for oboe and soprano.

I approached the production and discussion of Haydn's *Seasons* in the conviction that my experience with *The Creation* had familiarized me with all the conceivable mistakes of our oratorial traditions. I was right, but what I had not foreseen is that these would be far outnumbered by the inconceivable ones that have been added to them. The original, or shall we say the aboriginal, English translation is often ridiculous, but in the following recitative, and in several other places, I have found it not impossibly ridiculous, and do not think the desire to restore Thomson a sufficient excuse for texts which make Haydn interpolate a five-bars' rest between a verb and its object; which speak of the rising sun where the music is describing the flight of hares; which mention lightning flashes that the music has no opportunity of noticing; and which twice cause Haydn's drum-rolls of distant thunder to come in the wrong place. Few things in descriptive music are more accurate than the recitative in which the three country folk describe the approach of a thunderstorm. To trace the Baron's indebtedness to Thomson is to look for needles in haystacks. Thomson has described the storms and earthquakes of every known earthly climate, and the Baron has merely generalized the result with as few particulars as possible, and has never dreamt of venturing upon Thomson's tragic detail of the English countryman who has seen his beloved struck by lightning. But, as Haydn's recovery to fine weather is distinctly European, if not English, we may take it that we are not dealing with the destruction of Pompeii, although we are told that the 'deep foundations of earth itself are moved'; and it is surprising to find even the later English translations making the chorus translate 'Weh' uns' by 'O God!' 'Woe's me' is quite adequate for the situation. Anything stronger rests upon the misapprehension of Mark Twain's German friend who said, 'The two languages are so alike: how pleasant that is; when we say "Ach Gott", you say "Goddam"'.

Ex. 10.   Weh   uns!

Er - schüt - tert wankt die Er - de bis in des Meeres Grund.

When the storm has died away a delightful allegretto describes
the clearing of the evening sky. There is also a charming collection
of Haydn's *französischer Quark*: the return of the cattle to their
stalls with lowings admirably imitated by Haydn and completely
missed by the improvers of the English translation; the call of the
quail to her mate, a sound less known to the British than to the
Germans, who proverbially represent the bird as saying *Lobet Gott*;
and realistic, with Straussian dissonance, the chirp of the cricket;

Ex. 11.

the frogs in the pond, again represented by Haydn with a sweetness
much more true to nature than our libellous word 'croak'; and,
lastly, the toll of the curfew. Then the summer's day closes in peace
with a description of the evening star and the country folk virtuously
going home to bed at the command of the curfew. From the first
edition onwards the translators have been misled by the word
'winkt' (*Von oben winkt der helle Stern*). *Winken* does not mean
wink, but beckon or make a sign, and the 'clear star' is not the
host of glittering stars, which in any case do not appear all at once
in evenings with a long twilight; and a planet does not twinkle.
Von oben, 'from above', is, of course, the Baron's mistake, for
Venus can never be very high up in the sky either as evening or
morning star. Be this as it may, Haydn's picture is correct, and
we do not want it set to obvious mis-statements.

AUTUMN

I neither expect nor desire complete assent to the omissions I
have to make in order to bring *The Seasons* within the compass of
an evening's performance; and in defence of my drastic reduction
of Haydn's *Autumn* I can plead only that I have omitted a large
tract where I have always found my attention apt to wander, and
where I am reminded chiefly of things which Haydn has treated
more impressively elsewhere. Probably, if I had once begun
rehearsing my omissions, nothing would have induced me to part
with them, but nothing should prevent the audience from enjoying
the whole of Haydn's *Winter*, which is to me as moving as anything
in *The Creation*.

The *Autumn* begins with a movement expressive of sentiments
proverbially unknown to the British farmer, viz. the husbandman's satisfaction at the abundant harvest. In real life we know
that, even if all records for more useful crops had been broken,
it must have been 'a main poor year for mushrooms!' I do not

say that this is an excuse for my omitting the trio and chorus in praise of industry: 'From thee, O Industry, springs every good'. The text has faint traces of Thomson, and the music represents Haydn better than the chorus in praise of the sun. The country folk then proceed to gather nuts (in May?), in the course of which occupation Jane and Lucas sing a love duet which I am very sorry to omit. In the middle and towards the end it glows with real warmth, but in the first part the Baron has imposed upon Haydn and the lovers a needless preoccupation with the spuriousness of townsfolk and the superiority of real complexions over lipstick. No doubt Jane is quite right in saying: 'Ye vain and silly fops, keep of! (*sic*) keep of! here wily tricks and cheats are lost and glozing tales employ'd in vain; to them we listen not'; but Haydn, too, is not inclined to listen or to rouse his humour to more than a perfunctory playfulness; though I am sorry to miss the glow of the passages in which the lovers have forgotten their superiority to the towns-folk.

Having reluctantly skipped the harvest and the love-making, we will let Haydn's recitative tell us how 'Anon the sportsman's voice is heard', and we will listen to an aria describing with admirable music and realism the pointer in full pursuit until he makes his point and the huntsman fires his fatal shot. Haydn has timed the gunshot accurately with the words, which is more than can be said for the translators.

Then comes a hunting scene which seems to owe more to continental ideas of a *battue* than to any traditions of British sport. Still, that is no reason why the translators should represent the rounding-up and panic of hares by phrases about the orient sun and the assembling of huntsmen to the meet.

The following hunting chorus is a delightful movement showing Haydn's utmost freedom of form. But the merest justice to the reputation of Thomson compels us to protest against associating his name with its sentiments. His own feelings towards sport were substantially those of the Member for Burbleton, the Lady Topsy Haddock, *née* Trout; and his description of a stag at bay is of high pathos, of which the Baron allows Haydn no nearer hint than will illustrate a cheerful soprano episode in the subdominant, expressive of the British huntswoman's faith that the quarry enjoys the chase. The range of country covered by the huntsmen is well symbolized by Haydn in the fact that his chorus begins in D but eventually settles in E flat. As the Baron has given us no evidence that the country is British, or anywhere in particular, I see no reason for altering the French hunting cry *Hallali* used by Haydn, especially as Haydn associates with it the ancient French horn tunes used by Méhul in his overture to *La Chasse du Jeune Henri*, a very pretty

piece which was once popular and may as well become popular
again.

Ex. 12.

Great Britain does not claim to be a wine country, but neither
Haydn's music nor the translators have been able to avoid the
associations of the Rhine and the Moselle; nor is it possible to
adapt the ensuing glorious bacchanale to any particular place.
The translation of the original edition will not do. No choir-
master can ask a British chorus to sing: 'Now let our joy break
out, and heyday, heyday, hey, in loudest strains resound.' We are
told that 'the bulky tuns are filled'. From the music it would rather
appear that they were being emptied and that some other pinguid
bodies were being filled. I have already pointed out with quotations
that Thomson is not weakly optimistic about the festivities in a
British alehouse; but, while the listener may neglect our feeble
efforts to provide singable English for one of Haydn's greatest
movements, there is no reason why we should not enjoy the music.
The first section, in quick common time, modulates widely and
wildly, only to settle in a quite orthodox dominant. Then the dance
begins. Skirling pipes, rolling drums, scraping fiddles, and snarling
drones are duly catalogued and illustrated. The chorus is ejaculatory
and spasmodic, but the music is gloriously continuous in a way
which possibly inspired Mahler in one of his best movements, the
Scherzo of his Second Symphony. At last the orchestra becomes
learned and works out a quite solid fugue on the following subject:

Ex. 13.

It is some time before this theme penetrates the intellect of the
chorus; but at last the whole chorus, having been helped into the
home tonic, joins *en masse* to an extempore accompaniment of
triangle, and tambourine. Thus ends the *Autumn*, with a display
of Haydn's highest symphonic powers.

WINTER

Thomson's *Winter* appeared as a separate poem before the other
Seasons. I believe that it was always considered the finest part of

the work, and I find Haydn's setting of the Baron's alleged extracts from it an inviolable self-contained masterpiece.

'The overture paints the thick fogs at the beginning of winter' in a beautifully orchestrated Adagio; after which Simon explains the wintry details. What is now known more scientifically as a 'depression from Iceland' is illustrated by an admirably startling and shrill chord of A major, which Jane explains as 'rough winter stepping forward from Lapland's vaults'. She then sings a cavatina which is a wintry twin brother to that in which Lucas described the height of summer. Lucas now describes the frozen lake and the snowbound landscape. Then, in an admirable aria, he describes the traveller lost in a blizzard. Haydn's presto, not being alla breve, implies a tempo which is able to deal both with the wayfarer's efforts to press on and his sinking courage and the danger of abandoning effort. Suddenly he sees a cottage light. And all is well if editors and conductors will realize that, in spite of the anomalous time-signature, the ensuing allegro in E major is allabreve, and not slower, but faster, than the presto.

Ex. 14,

The traveller reaches the hospitable cottage and finds in a large warm room a gathering of country folk occupied in conversation, basketmaking, netmending, and spinning.

The spinning song is in D minor, and its rustic modulations to C major and E minor foreshadow in mere picturesqueness the most heartbreaking features of Schubert's *Gretchen am Spinnrade*.

Ex. 15.

When the spinning song is over, Jane entertains the company with a tale akin to the rhyme of 'Where are you going to, my pretty maid?'

Ex. 16.

In spite of his protests, the young Lord's intentions are presumably not honourable, and the company is slightly shocked and greatly puzzled by the Young Person's apparent readiness to listen to his suggestions. The more modern translators seem to be shocked also, for they make her display virtuous scruples, which would entirely spoil her plan of getting his lordship to look over the hedge to see if her brother is in sight. As soon as his lordship's back is turned she jumps upon his nag and rides away, leaving him all agape; a less drastic remedy than Randolph Caldecott's reading of 'Sir, she said', according to which the pretty milkmaid's companions took up the unfortunate man and set him on the back of a lively bull-calf. At all events, the chorus is quite satisfied with the capacity of the Young Person to take care of herself; and, as for his lordship, 'Ha, ha, ha, ha, and serve him right!'

Now comes the solemn end of Haydn's last great work. The text owes something to Thomson and more to the 15th Psalm. First, Simon, after describing the conquest of the year by winter, sings a solemn aria comparing the winter of the year to that of man's old age. *Où sont les neiges d'antan?* The Baron reduces Thomson's noble climax to platitudes; but Haydn's music more than reinstates the poet, who concludes:

> —And see!
> 'Tis come, the glorious Morn! the second Birth
> Of Heaven, and Earth! Awakening Nature hears
> The new-creating Word, and starts to Life,
> In every heighten'd Form, from Pain and Death
> For ever free.

The final trio and chorus is as moving as anything in *The Creation*. The squalors of any practicable vocal score give no idea of the heavenly boldness and radiance of the orchestral opening, which, owing to a timely birthday present from an aunt, I had the advantage as a boy of knowing from the full score before I knew that anything worse could be made of it. For which, as Bunyan would say, 'The trumpets sounded for her on the other side'.

Ex. 17.

After joining in dialogue with the trio in some lines suggested by the 15th Psalm ('Lord, who shall dwell in Thy tabernacle?'), the chorus settles down to a fugue.

Ex. 18.

Uns lei - te dei - ne Hand, O Gott! ver - leih uns Stärk' und Mut

To which Haydn answers *Amen*, in strict time, with one of the most overwhelmingly energetic closes I have ever heard.

Ex. 19.

Chorus.

Orch.

A - - men. Orch.

Chorus.

A - - men.

BEETHOVEN

CCVIII. MISSA SOLEMNIS, FOR CHORUS AND ORCHESTRA (OP. 123)

I

English Prayer-book version.

Kyrie eleison [Ex. 1, 2].　Lord, have mercy upon us.
Christe eleison [Ex. 3].　Christ, have mercy upon us.
Kyrie eleison [Ex. 1, 2].　Lord, have mercy upon us.

II

Gloria in excelsis Deo [Ex. 4]. Et in terra pax hominibus bonae voluntatis.

Laudamus te [Ex. 4], benedicimus te, adoramus te, glorificamus te; gratias agimus tibi propter magnam gloriam tuam [Ex. 5]; Domine Deus [Ex. 4], Rex coelestis, Deus pater omnipotens.

Domine fili unigenite [Ex. 4 *transformed*] Jesu Christe; Domine Deus agnus Dei, filius Patris;

Glory be to God on high, and in earth peace, good will towards men.[1] We praise thee, we bless thee, we worship thee, we glorify thee, we give thanks to thee for thy great glory, O Lord God, heavenly King, God the Father Almighty.

O Lord, the only-begotten Son Jesu Christ; O Lord God, Lamb of God, Son of the Father, that takest away the sins of the world, have mercy upon us. Thou that

[1] The Latin reading means, of course, 'peace to men of good will'.

Qui tollis peccata mundi, miserere nobis [Ex. 6]. Qui tollis peccata mundi suscipe deprecationem nostram. Qui sedes ad dexteram Patris, miserere nobis;

Quoniam tu solus sanctus [Ex. 7], tu solus Dominus, tu solus altissimus Jesu Christe, cum sancto spiritu in gloria Dei Patris. Amen [Ex. 8, 9].

takest away the sins of the world, have mercy upon us. Thou that takest away the sins of the world, receive our prayer. Thou that sittest at the right hand of God the Father, have mercy upon us.

For thou only art holy; thou only art the Lord; thou only, O Christ, with the Holy Ghost, art most high in the glory of God the Father. Amen.

III

Credo [Ex. 10] in unum Deum, Patrem omnipotentem, factorem coeli et terrae, visibilium omnium et invisibilium;

Et in unum Dominum Jesum Christum, filium Dei unigenitum, et ex patre natum ante omnia saecula, Deum de Deo, lumen de lumine, Deum verum de Deo vero, genitum, non factum, consubstantialem Patris per quem omnia facta sunt;

Qui propter nos homines et propter nostram salutem descendit de coelis,

Et incarnatus est de Spiritu Sancto ex Maria Virgine [Ex. 11], et homo factus est [Ex. 12];

Crucifixus etiam pro nobis [Ex. 13], sub Pontio Pilato passus [Ex. 14] et sepultus est;

Et resurrexit tertia die secundum Scripturas;

Et ascendit in coelum; sedet ad dexteram Patris [Ex. 15], et iterum venturus est cum gloria judicare vivos et mortuos, cujus regni non erit finis;

Et in Sanctum Spiritum [Ex. 10] Dominum et vivificatatem, qui ex patre filioque procedit, qui cum patre et filio simul adoratur et conglorificatur, qui locutus est per Prophetas, Et in unam sanctam

I believe in one God the Father Almighty, Maker of heaven and earth, And of all things visible and invisible:

And in one Lord Jesus Christ, the only-begotten Son of God, Begotten of his Father before all worlds, God of God, Light of Light, Very God of very God, Begotten, not made, Being of one substance with the Father, By whom all things were made: Who for us men, and for our salvation came down from heaven, And was incarnate by the Holy Ghost of the Virgin Mary, And was made man, And was crucified also for us under Pontius Pilate. He suffered and was buried,[1] And the third day he rose again according to the Scriptures, And ascended into heaven, And sitteth on the right hand of the Father. And he shall come again with glory to judge both the quick and the dead: Whose kingdom shall have no end.

And I believe in the Holy Ghost, The Lord and Giver of life, Who proceedeth from the Father and the Son, Who with the Father and the Son together is worshipped and glorified, Who spake by the Prophets. And I believe one Catholick and Aposto-

[1] The punctuation of the Latin text gives 'He suffered under Pontius Pilate, and was buried'. This is very clearly brought out by Beethoven.

catholicam et apostolicam ecclesiam, Confiteor unum baptisma in
remissionem peccatorum, et exspecto resurrectionem mortuorum,
Et vitam venturi saeculi. Amen
[Ex. 16, 17, 18, 19].

lick Church. I acknowledge one
Baptism for the remission of sins.
And I look for the Resurrection
of the dead, And the life of the
world to come. Amen.

IV

Sanctus, sanctus, sanctus, Do-
minus Deus Sabaoth [Ex. 20].
Pleni sunt coeli et terra gloria tua;
Osanna in excelsis [Ex. 21, 22].
Benedictus qui venit in nomine
Domini [Ex. 23, 24, 25, 26, 27].
Osanna in excelsis [Ex. 25].

Holy, holy, holy, Lord God of
hosts, heaven and earth are full of
thy glory. Hosanna in the highest.
Blessed is he that cometh in the
name of the Lord.
Hosanna in the highest.

V

Agnus Dei qui tollis peccata
mundi, miserere nobis [Ex. 28].
Agnus Dei qui tollis peccata
mundi,
Dona nobis pacem [Ex. 29, 30,
31, 32, 33].

O Lamb of God, who takest
away the sins of the world, have
mercy upon us.
O Lamb of God, who takest
away the sins of the world, give us
peace.

The Mass in D occupied Beethoven from the years 1819 to 1823.
It was written with the intention of having it ready in time for the
installation of Beethoven's beloved friend and patron, the Archduke
Rudolph, at Cologne, as Archbishop of Olmütz, but it was not
finished until two years too late for that occasion. Nevertheless, it
is unique in the history of music as being a Mass actually designed
for a certain liturgy of exceptional pomp and magnificence, and
written at a time when music with the aid of the symphonic
orchestra was compelled to take whatever text it had to illustrate in
a much more dramatic sense than any liturgical music requires.
Thus it is only the exceptional pomp of the installation of a Royal
Archduke as Archbishop that has rendered the large scale of the
music possible or conceivable for an actual service. This dis-
tinguishes Beethoven's Mass from such works as the Mass in B
Minor of Bach, which is practically an oratorio on a text which
happens to be that of the Catholic Mass. It is therefore a mistake
to regard Beethoven as composing his text in any agnostic spirit
of art for art's sake. He achieves art which maintains itself as purely
artistic, by really inspiring himself with the definite needs of the
occasion; and whether we agree with his treatment of the text or
not, we are compelled, the more we study it, to realize that Beethoven's insight into its meaning is, from a certain point of view,
profound. The point of view is not that of Palestrina, nor indeed
of any one, whether Protestant or Roman, who is in touch with

ecclesiastical traditions. But nothing could be more misleading than to say with Rubinstein that Beethoven treats the text in a disputatious or criticizing mood.

Another subject on which we must clear our minds from prejudice is Beethoven's choral writing. Its difficulties are appalling, and even Bach seems easy in comparison. Yet it is not unlike Bach in its rewards for those choirs that grapple with it. Everybody can see that Beethoven puts a terrible strain upon the voices. This is evident when they are singing prolonged high notes, and still more so when they are trying to articulate many syllables on these high notes. We do not notice the equally serious difficulties arising from Beethoven's reckless use of low notes; because the passages which lie too low simply fail to be heard. However, these defects, for such they are, must not be imputed to a lack of choral imagination. Beethoven does many things which he and lesser musicians ought not to have done, and so his choral style is not a 'good model'. But he leaves nothing undone which he ought to have done. There is no genuine choral possibility undeveloped by Beethoven in the Mass in D. His high notes may be too high, but he has not failed to imagine their resonance. He does not inadvertently write high; he merely over-estimates the capacity of voices to sing so high with comfort. Again, though the low passages certainly are not well heard on the voices, they are very well supported in the orchestra. A case can be made out for saying that Beethoven gives his voices relief by these low passages. That, I fear, was not his motive. The same characteristic happens constantly in the choral writing of Bach, and is there mainly accounted for by much the same methods of supporting those passages by the orchestra. The only other respect in which Beethoven's choral writing is abnormal, is that he seems to think that voices can determine rhythms with the same kind of percussion as instruments. One of the leading features of Beethoven's polyphony is the use of rhythmic figures that could be recognized if merely drummed upon a table. Voices do not express those rhythmic figures nearly so well as instruments, especially when they are to be declaimed on one note to a word like 'kyrie', where the middle consonant is a liquid, and two of the syllables are successive vowels. The singer is at the mercy of his words in these matters, and requires to be taught a somewhat artificial staccato before the rhythms will come out as Beethoven intended them. Lastly, it must be confessed that when Beethoven is writing a contrapuntal scheme or combination of themes, he has no facility in handling his accessory parts. Any chorus that tries to sing a big choral work of Bach will find that, immensely difficult as much of the music is, there is hardly any

passage which does not remain in the memory. Even the parts
that are merely filling in, and not contributing actual themes to the
design, have some inherent sense. This is very rarely the case
with any of Beethoven's accessory counterpoints. It is possible for
the pianoforte player to memorize a Beethoven fugue, because he
has the whole design in his two hands. But it is difficult to see
how any choral singer can get one of Beethoven's inner parts into
his head except where he comes upon one of the main themes.

These reservations then cover a wide ground; but the positive
fact nevertheless remains, that Beethoven's choral writing contains
everything that a chorus can do. It neglects no opportunities.
Not even Bach or Handel can show a greater sense of space and of
sonority. There is no earlier choral writing that comes so near to
recovering some of the lost secrets of the style of Palestrina. There
is no choral and no orchestral writing, earlier or later, that shows
a more thrilling sense of the individual colour of every chord,
every position, and every doubled third or discord. I well remember, a good many years ago, Sir George Henschel, happening to
glance at the score of the D major Mass, open at its first page,
putting his finger upon the first chord and saying, 'Isn't it extraordinary how you can recognize any single common chord scored
by Beethoven?'

Let us now turn to the themes and structure of the composition
as a whole. The form of the Mass in D is as perfect as the form of
any symphony, or, in other words, of any purely abstract music.
This is not in spite of but because of the fact that it is in every
detail suggested by the text. The forms of purely instrumental
music are not suggested by any text or any external programme,
but they are acquired by a profound experience and a profound
conviction of the meaning of music. They are developed by the
material of the music, and when many works arrive at the same
form, they arrive at that form through development from within,
exactly as do living creatures. The form of this Mass will not
therefore be the form of a symphony, nor will it be the form of any
other Mass. It could not have been written except by a man to
whom the prayer for peace with which every Mass concludes was,
as Beethoven calls it, a 'prayer for outward as well as inward peace'.
It could not have been written except by a composer to whom
instrumental and orchestral music had attained a dramatic power
fiercer and more concentrated than any that finds expression on
the stage; and it could not have been written for a smaller occasion
than that which we know to have called it forth. The way to grasp
the form of this Mass is therefore to treat it exactly as we would
treat a Motet by Palestrina. That is to say, we take each clause of
the text and find out to what themes that clause is set. Where we

find these themes recur, we shall find either that the composer has returned to the words associated with them, or that he has some more than merely conventional reason for reminding us of those words. It is through analysis on these lines that we are enabled to come to certain general conclusions as to how Beethoven treats his text; and I will begin with these general conclusions.

In the first place we find that, unlike many contemporary composers who were quite familiar, perhaps more familiar, with the service of the Mass, Beethoven has taken great pains to inquire into the meaning of the text. He did actually consult people who knew something about it, not having much confidence in his own recollections of the small Latin he learned as a boy; and he arrived at perfectly definite notions as to what doctrinal aspects of the text he would bring out. First then, he brings out an overwhelming and overwhelmed sense of the Divine glory, with which he invariably and immediately contrasts the nothingness of man. The very first notes of the Kyrie, as stated in the orchestral introduction, assert the two conceptions, with the great massive chords and rhythm on the word *Kyrie*, followed by the pleading of the solo wind instruments, afterwards to become solo voices.

Ex. 1.

Then the prayer rises, passing from one harmony and one position of the key to another on the word *eleison*. This word has a new theme, adorned by a more florid version in the wind instruments.

Ex. 2.

At the appeal *Christe eleison* comes the expression of the idea that Christ is the mediator for our prayers. The movement becomes more agitated, and the pair of themes with which the solo voices build up their polyphonic texture—

Ex. 3.

develops in one of Beethoven's characteristic fugue passages in which the sound recedes into vast distances and then grows with

almost threatening power, only to recede suddenly again. The
Christe eleison dies away on an incomplete minor chord which,
by Beethoven's favourite method of modulation, becomes part of
the original major tonic chord of the Kyrie. The rest of the
design is a recapitulation, altering the order of the keys and ending in the tonic with one of Beethoven's most beautiful quiet
codas. Throughout the Kyrie the choral writing must be granted
to be quite normal, and nobody would ever have suggested a
moment's doubt, on the evidence of this piece alone, as to Beethoven's being a choral writer with imaginative power at least equal
to that of Bach or Handel.

With the Gloria we may expect the difficulties to begin. The
first clause, *Gloria in excelsis Deo*, is a blaze of triumph in which
the whole orchestra and the voices work out this theme—

Ex. 4.

Glo - ri - a in ex - cel - sis De - - - o

accompanied by the strings in a long passage which is like the
ringing of all the bells in Christendom. As is natural, the words
et in terra pax bring a dramatic contrast—the first such feature we
have as yet encountered in the Mass. The moment of this contrast
is impressive, and, like most of the impressive things in this Mass,
extreme; but nothing could more thoroughly justify such extremities
than the pious beauty and calm of the harmonies which follow.
The blaze of glory, with the opening theme, is resumed with
Laudamus te. The words *benedicimus te, adoramus te*, and
glorificamus te are declaimed to short fresh points, for the simple
reason that their rhythm does not fit the original theme; and
there is the characteristic sudden hush at the words *adoramus te*.
Here then, as everywhere, we see Beethoven enraptured at the
thought of the Divine Glory, but immediately prostrated by the
sudden consciousness of the nothingness of man. With the text
Gratias agimus tibi propter magnam gloriam tuam, the notion of
'thanksgiving' suggests to Beethoven a happy and quiet mood; and
there is a radical change of key to B flat with a new theme in a
somewhat slower tempo.

Ex. 5.

Gra - - ti - as a - - gi - mus ti - bi prop - ter

mag - nam glo - ri - am tu - am

Then at the *Domine Deus* the original Gloria theme returns (in
the instruments, not in the voices, because here again new themes
are required by the rhythm of the text); and the words *Pater
omnipotens* call forth the full power of the orchestra, the first
entry of the trombones, the first use of the full organ with pedals,
and one of the mightiest modulations Beethoven ever wrote.
Then with *Domine fili unigenite* comes the thought of the Godhead becoming human. This thought is not yet defined. The
definition is reserved for the Credo; but the actual theme of the
Gloria is transformed into pleading and touching tones, in order
to suggest the contrast that is already in Beethoven's mind between
the inaccessible Divine glory and the incarnation. But as the
Domine Deus is resumed, to culminate in the address *filius
Patris*, the blaze of glory mounts again to a climax. As in all
orthodox and liturgical settings of the Mass, the words *filius Patris*
mark the end of a section. The choral harmony at the extreme top
of the voices dies away in the sustained and spacious manner so
characteristic of Beethoven's last works. Clarinets are discovered
leading down from a high note to the slow movement to which
Beethoven sets the prayer *Qui tollis peccata mundi*. This is
worked out in a manner that brings out clearly the idea of a
threefold prayer, the main theme being given out by the wind
instruments and re-stated by the voices thrice, each time with
a different continuation in different keys, F, D, and B flat.

Here is the first vocal statement:

Ex. 6.

As the text changes, so does the prayer increase in intensity.
The most dramatic expression of the contrast between the Divine
glory and the nothingness of humanity is reached in the great cry
Qui sedes ad dexteram Patris, followed as it is by the most awe-
struck prostration, before the voices, now in the dark and distant
key of D flat, resume their pleading *miserere nobis*. The pleading
rises now to its climax,[1] this time a climax of human prayer, and

---

[1] Beethoven goes so far as to add an interjection 'ah, miserere nobis!'
(corrected in later editions to 'o'). This is for him a measure hardly to be
distinguished from such points as the astonished stammering of the word

at last dies away in the same spacious manner as the visions of Divine Glory. With a sound like distant thunder, a new movement (allegro maestoso) begins with the text *Quoniam tu solus sanctus.*

Ex. 7.

The word *sanctus* is almost whispered in the midst of the solemn shouts of praise, and this allegro maestoso, which maintains a clearly introductory character, expands with great pomp, indulging in solemn flourishes of trumpets. At last, with characteristic swelling and receding and swelling out again, the chorus leads into the final fugue *In gloria Dei Patris. Amen.* This begins on normal lines with a subject of what we would call Handelian majesty if we had not learned to call it Beethovenish.

Ex. 8.

The fugue takes its leisure in covering its ground, and is evidently going to be on a gigantic scale. Unlike most of Beethoven's fugues, it has started with full volume of tone. What it has in reserve is, not any increase of power, but a strange event that occurs when we feel that we have just got well into the swing of its development. Suddenly the chorus recedes into distance. The solo voices enter, while the choral tenors and basses declaim to a solemn canto fermo the words *Cum sancto spiritu.* The question in the listener's mind is, What new developments are going to happen? Certainly something great is in prospect. But the practical question is how the fugue can be carried out on this scale at all. A more guileless composer would have tried to work it out normally, and would not have got through it in twenty minutes. What happens with Beethoven is that within the compass of six bars he contrives

'et' in many passages of the Credo. These procedures are very unliturgical; but so is the notion of using Beethoven's symphonic orchestra in church. The liturgy is too reticent for oh's and ah's, if it is to receive a purely choral setting of its text. But reticence is relative to the whole (unless we are to confuse it with comfortable inefficiency); and the reticence of voices in a dramatically orchestral ensemble suffers little from an interjection necessitated by the broad rhythm of a beautiful new melody introduced after the final climax of the prayer.

to give a sense that this passage has gone round the universe. While the tenors and basses are twice quietly declaiming *Cum sancto spiritu*, as if they were singing two phrases of a slow recitative, the solo voices are just as quietly climbing in an adumbration of a stretto. Meanwhile the harmonies are rising through a series of six modulations, each a tone higher than the last. The result is that the listener, although the sequence of harmonies is quite simple, entirely loses his sense of key. He knows only that he is being whirled through a vast distance, but loses all consciousness of time. The whole of this process is shown in the following illustration:

The chorus then re-enters for one line and a half of stretto; and the result is that within thirty bars the whole middle and peroration of the fugue are accomplished. Majesty and breadth are given to the short choral stretto which finishes this astonishing passage, by the fact that the subject is treated in 'augmentation' (i.e. in notes twice as slow as before). Then follows a coda in nearly double the tempo, in which Beethoven is no longer preoccupied with the old-world architectures of the fugue style, but is able to expand in symphonic forms. The solo voices enter, while the chorus in awe-struck whispers, repeats *Cum sancto spiritu* as in a prayer; until suddenly the chorus bursts out in full speed with *in gloria Dei Patris*, and brings the scheme to an end with tonic and dominant passages somewhat in the style of Handel's Hallelujahs. The whole edifice is crowned with a return to the text *Gloria in excelsis Deo* in the final *presto*; and the actual last chord is the word *Gloria* thrown into the air by the chorus after the orchestra has finished.

In the Credo Beethoven has the longest text to illustrate, and this means, as it meant to the sixteenth-century composer, that he is compelled to develop the tersest and most concentrated resources of his style. He at once begins by asserting a key that is dark in contrast with the Gloria, though the first chord is a semitone higher than that last heard. The opening chords define the key of B flat through the chord of E flat, and the basses declaim the word *Credo* to a mighty musical motto, the pregnancy of which carries Beethoven through all the most difficult and musically thankless parts of his text.

Ex. 10.

But there is no difficulty for Beethoven in building up a sublime structure for the opening clauses. Such ideas as 'Maker of all things, visible and invisible', inspire him to moments of awed pro-stration, from which the praises of 'God of God, Light of Light', arise with renewed vigour. There is no contrast between the clause *Credo in unum Deum* and that of the belief in Christ. The topic here is the Godhead of Christ in inaccessible glory. The change of tone, and the change to a darker key, comes where we ought to expect it, at *Qui propter nos homines et propter nostram salu-tem descendit de coelis.* The word *descendit* is set with naïve symbolism, as it has always been in every setting of the Mass since polyphony began. And now comes the great mystery. Here Beethoven suddenly changes his tempo and goes for the first time in this Mass unmistakably into modal harmony. Such harmony had not been heard since the time of Palestrina, except in a modernized form in certain works of Bach which Beethoven did not know, and in academic exercises by persons who themselves regarded such modes as archaic. Beethoven was enormously in advance of his time in recognizing that they are nothing of the sort; and until we begin to share his culture in this matter, we have no more qualifications for appreciating the aesthetics of choral music than an eighteenth-century dandy, fresh from his Grand Tour, would have had for appreciating the Elgin Marbles. The Incarnatus is set to mysterious and devout strains in purest Dorian tonality (pure, that is, from Palestrina's point of view). We may notice here, what will have already aroused attention in the setting of earlier clauses, that the word *Et* is treated by Beethoven extremely dramatically. It bursts forth from the lips of the singers, both choral and solo, almost with a stammer; being nearly always followed by quite a long pause, and then repeated before the sentence is continued.

Ex. 11.

In the original edition, and in some modern editions, this theme is announced by the solo tenor; but it is possible that Beethoven's intention was to announce it by the choral tenors, and for the solo quartet to take it up in the following harmonized passage. The result is certainly both more mysterious and more beautiful. As the solo quartet develops its harmony, supported by throbbing chords from soft wind instruments, a flute is heard mysteriously warbling in the heights. There is no reasonable doubt that the picture in Beethoven's mind is that of the Holy Ghost hovering in the likeness of a dove. Perhaps one of the most touching notes in the whole Mass is the sunshine and warmth of the change into D major in triple time, when the tenor, with his excited repeated *Et*, comes to the consummation *et homo factus est.*

Ex. 12.

The joy lasts for a short time before it is broken in by the terrible sorrow and mystery of the Crucifixus.

The profoundly impressive voice parts of the solo quartet, supported by solemn sustained notes in the chorus, are heightened by the orchestra that has its own more elastic means of expression. Thus it may be claimed that the main theme of the Crucifixus is on the violins as an expression of the word *passus*.

We expect some dramatic contrast when we come to the Resurrexit. Beethoven's Crucifixus has ended in a darkness and a modulation not unlike the end of the Crucifixus of Bach's B minor Mass, a movement which we know Beethoven had studied. Bach's Resurrexit is one of his most glorious and highly developed choruses, and starts with a splendid formal melody. Beethoven's contrast is not less startling, but much more unexpected. He does not develop this text at all. He simply has an excited outburst of unaccompanied chorus led by the tenors with their feverish detached *et*; and the sentence is given in four bars of pure Mixolydian harmony, pure, that is to say, as Palestrina would conceive it, with the B flattened in order that it may bear an effective triad. This is the only unaccompanied choral passage in any Mass of the period. The descriptive music comes with all the greater *naïveté* with *et ascendit*. Beethoven has been ridiculed for illustrating the word *ascendit* by an ascending scale. But it was really less trouble to do what every composer up to Beethoven's time had done automatically, than to go and look for some more out-of-the-way illustration, or to avoid illustrating. We may dispute whether the terms 'high' and 'low' have the same meaning in music as they have in space. But we cannot deny that to sing high notes on the voice is to raise one's voice, or at all events to make an effort undoubtedly suggestive of raising something; and it cannot be said that there is anything inherently absurd in Beethoven's using a rising scale for symbolizing one of the central miracles of Christianity. In any case, the theme of the text *et ascendit* is not a cardinal theme in the piece, but a mere local descriptive touch. The real theme of the whole of this movement is again in the orchestra, the voices having nothing to do but to declaim each

sentence of the text in their simplest natural rhythm, while the
strings are busy with this theme—

Ex. 15.

which they carry through a wide range of well contrasted keys.
And so we come to the statement, *et iterum venturus est cum
gloria.* How is this tremendous text to be illustrated? Berlioz in
his *Requiem*, under the provocation of a text which deals in three
impressive lines of verse with the trumpet that 'scatters a wondrous
sound through the regions of death', tries to illustrate the Last
Trump by four brass bands placed at the four corners of the
concert-room. No doubt he achieves some impressiveness by this
material outlay. Beethoven ventures to allude to the Judgement
Day by an unexpected note upon a solitary trombone. The point
is not that it can make a great noise, but that the harmony is
unexpected and unsupported. Beethoven took an infinity of pains
over this passage, of which there are many sketches. The whole of
his effort is devoted simply to getting subtlety into his rhythm and
distinction into his modulations. The conception is as spiritual
and as immaterial as if he was writing for a string quartet. The
words *vivos et mortuos* suggest again one of those startling
contrasts, with a sudden pianissimo, with which Beethoven contrives to punctuate his designs and at the same time to keep in
touch with the text. This contrast would perhaps not have occurred
to anybody else at that particular place, but it would be a mistake
to suppose that it does not serve its purely musical purpose as well
as its characteristically naïve illustration of the text.

And now, after the words *cujus regni non erit finis*, we come
to the most difficult part of the composer's task, a long series
of doctrines which do not lend themselves to illustration. *Et in
spiritum sanctum* might very well have served as the text of
an independently inspired movement of the utmost mystery and
devotion, but the note required there has already been sounded in
the Incarnatus. What Beethoven here has to do is to provide
a bridge from the mention of the Day of Judgement to the final
clause about 'the life of the world to come'; and this very passage,
which with so many composers is a source of weakness in the
composition, becomes for Beethoven the key-stone of his design.
He contrives to give relief from the purely dramatic aspects of his
text by achieving here a not less conspicuous beauty of form.
The whole of the next six clauses are dealt with in a recapitulation of the opening movement of the Credo, and all difficulty

in illustrating their individual meaning is evaded, as it ought
to be evaded in a musical setting. Unless you are writing purely
formal music, and unless you can, like Bach, make an aria upon
any text whatever, and rely upon intrinsic beauty of design without illustrating it at all, it is impossible to do anything but cover
the whole design with a general theme. One of the things that
Beethoven hereby brings out is the grammar of the whole text. We
may not be able to hear the individual words of the clauses, but
we do hear now, and are reminded thoroughly, that the whole
text from beginning to end is one sentence, the object of the verb
credo. Thus by purely musical means a master of musical form
can hold a sentence together across an unlimited interval of time.
Bach in his *Magnificat* takes advantage of the fact that in Latin
the subject will come at the end of the sentence, instead of at the
beginning; and so he is able to unroll the tale of *Omnes generationes* to sublime lengths. And Parry is able to hold together
fifteen lines of Milton's *At a Solemn Music* with a musical punctuation exactly analogous to that of Milton's enormous verse-paragraph.
These examples are not more wonderful than Beethoven's achievement here. The whole procession of doctrinal clauses marches to
its climax, to the tune of the word *credo*, with its conclusion in
et expecto resurrectionem mortuorum; and so leads into the final
fugue *et vitam venturi saeculi*. This starts with an orchestral
introduction in which Beethoven strikes one of his irresistible
tender notes, anticipating the main rhythmic figure, 3/2 ♩|♩ ♩ .
Here is the calm opening pair of themes of the double fugue *et
vitam venturi saeculi*, with the second subject to the word *Amen*.

Ex. 16.

The orchestration maintains a note of devout peace. There are no
violins; the voices are supported by exceptionally low flutes and
clarinets, and no higher octave is sounded. The pair of themes
becomes inverted as the fugue develops.

Ex. 17.

In spite of the calm tone of the whole, Beethoven is ruthless in ascribing to the sopranos the power to sing the theme at the top of their voices, articulating the syllables on the high B flat; and this is one of the few places where a note is forced before Beethoven really intends to make a climax. But by the time the fugue has reached what is evidently its middle development, he rises to a genuine climax and seems to be closing in his main key, when suddenly the violins burst in with a new modulation. The time quickens, the orchestra whispers a preliminary announcement of the theme 'diminished' (i.e. stated in notes of twice the pace), with results rhythmically new, besides a hint of a third subject.

Suddenly the chorus bursts out with perhaps the most difficult choral passage ever written.

This 'diminished' fugue soon reaches a tremendous climax on the dominant, and the two versions of the main subject are combined (i.e. the treble of Ex. 16 is sung simultaneously with the lower voice of Ex. 19).

Now comes a much misunderstood feature of classical choral music. When a chorus finds itself singing a long series of final chords, the singers of the highest notes naturally imagine themselves to be the main object of attention. But when we look at such passages in, say, Handel's autographs, we shall find disconcerting signs that the only thing Handel wrote first, in blocking out, was the bass, that he usually filled in all those top parts afterwards, and that he does not care what they sing, so long as they sing the right notes for the harmony. Yet I have seen the parts of the Beethoven Mass edited by a famous choral conductor in Germany, who altered the orchestral parts in order to support the voices better,

and who took particular pains to get the trumpets to support the
sopranos in their climax. Now, as a matter of fact, the trumpets
are wanted by Beethoven for a very different purpose, and the
sopranos are a mere accessory. What is meant to dominate the
whole peroration of this fugue is the figure of the first bar of Ex. 19
on the brass instruments, and we cannot spare the trumpets for
any other purpose.

This peroration rises once more to its climax, which is just the
same as the climax before the original fugue broke off; but it
is now in quite a slow tempo. The grand cadence dies away with
Beethoven's favourite choral effect of suddenly receding into the
depths of the universe. And then the heavens open.

Ex. 20.

We now come to the central part of the Mass. Here Beethoven,
for the first time since Palestrina, reconciles the needs of an actual
liturgy with the needs of the highest order of music. To the
sixteenth-century composer a voluminous text was a restriction
upon the scale of his work, rather than a stimulus to his invention. The medium of unaccompanied choral music is not dramatic; it is purely rhetorical; and though the chorus can give
dramatic outcries, it is quite incapable, without instrumental
accompaniment, of providing any background for them. The
sixteenth-century composer therefore treats the Gloria and Credo
of his Mass in a much simpler style than the rest. He sets the words
in a not elaborately polyphonic way, and hardly repeats a clause
more than once. It is just in the Sanctus and Benedictus, where
the words are few and where the moment in the liturgy is supreme,
that the sixteenth-century composer is able to unfold a broad
musical design, and he accordingly uses his opportunity.

We have seen how Beethoven's eminently dramatic genius
responded naturally to the possibilities of a chorus supported by
an orchestra that had for more than a generation been accustomed
to express itself dramatically; and how in the Gloria and Credo
the multiplicity of words gives Beethoven occasion to produce
some of his most gigantic symphonic designs. I say 'symphonic'
in full view of the fact that the forms thus produced are in no way
a priori, but are dictated at every point by the course of the words.

But now Beethoven, who had no models for these special choral-

N

symphonic designs, transcends them all, and comes, like Palestrina, into his full heritage where symbols and forms transcend all words. The forms he now develops are easily identifiable with certain types of sonata and concerto form; and until we have better notions of musical forms than we shall find in the text-books, this may mislead us. The great creative artists have an idea of form which is so free that it becomes a matter of unconsciousness to them whether the form they have in hand has been classified or not; the right thing will enter in the right place, and no naïve listener will be able to tell from its manner whether it happens to be a subversive paradox or the most familiar convention of its epoch. In art there is no fundamental distinction between form and matter; but every work of art is created under practical conditions which the artist regards as his data. These conditions are given and cannot be altered. The tendency will be to call these data the 'form', and everything else in the work the 'treatment'. In the last resort a correct analysis will break down the distinction between form and treatment. The portrait-painter, if he has retained his interest in his art as a thing in itself, regards his sitters as among the data from which he makes works of art. The relatives of the sitter regard all the artists' technique as among the data to which they may ascribe his failure to realize their idea of the sitter. In the last resort we may suppose that everybody is satisfied; in other words, that form and matter become one and inseparable. The musical student who has been trained to think that the sonata forms are rigid, and that to do without them is to be 'free', naturally thinks that in the Gloria and Credo Beethoven is handling 'free' forms. There is no textbook which tells him that you start a Gloria in a certain key, that you make this or that section of it 'the recapitulation' of this or that other section, and that you assign a certain portion of the text for 'the development'. And so it will appear that Beethoven is 'free' in his Gloria and Credo, and 'strict' when in the Benedictus he writes one of his most profound symphonic slow movements in a form readily recognizable as a type of concerto-aria or concertante-sonata movement. But Beethoven was always free; and never more perfectly free than in this Benedictus, one of the most simply beautiful and easiest of all his slow movements. Nor is he less free in the *Dona nobis pacem*, one of the most difficult and elaborate designs he ever achieved.

And so from this point onwards in the Mass Beethoven is free to produce forms much more like the symphonic music he had been producing all his life. For that reason, and because he had to write for a special ceremony which was sure to be of abnormal length, we have the unique phenomenon of a Mass really written for a liturgy, but of such proportions that, in spite of full indul-

gence in the resources of a dramatic orchestra, the weight of
the music is concentrated where the liturgy requires it to be most
impressive. Now if Beethoven had ever seen the Sanctus of
Bach's B minor Mass (which we do not know to be the case),
it would be very significant that he did not allow himself to be
influenced by it. Bach was not writing for the Roman liturgy.
He was merely setting the text, and he was at liberty to make the
sound of the seraphim blowing their loud uplifted angel trumpets,
to let his rhythms represent the swinging of censers before the
starry throne, and generally to portray in sounds a vision of Divine
glory. But that is quite inappropriate to a liturgical Sanctus during
which everybody present is absorbed in the most awe-inspired act
of worship. With no nearer classical models than the negative
asceticism of Cherubini, Beethoven instantly achieves the right
contrast here. His distant vision of the life of the world to come
has vanished into the heavens; and we are on earth, kneeling before
the altar.

Ex. 21.

This quotation gives the voice-parts, but the voices do not enter
until the orchestra has completed an introduction on the theme
represented in the lower stave. After the close of the Credo in B flat,
it would be impossible to select three opening notes which more
mysteriously and radically change the key and arouse solemn
expectation. After that first awe-struck moment, the harmony
unfolds itself on broad and clear lines, until solemn chords on
the trombones, closing into the entry of the voices, bring the
balance of key round to that of the main design. The Sanctus is
sung by the solo quartet, and is a short intensely devout movement,
ending with a note of the kind of fear that would be cast out by
perfect love. The next clause (*pleni sunt coeli et terra gloria tua*)
is a brilliant fugato (Ex. 22) accompanied by the organ and full
orchestra, even the trombones entering towards the end. In
all editions, and presumably in the autograph, the voice parts
are assigned to the solo quartet, and this is also the case with
the Osanna. Nobody has been able to explain how Beethoven
came to let these two movements be printed on the solo staves

Ex. 22.

The accompaniment makes the supposition of solo singing so impossible, that one would be surprised to hear that in any performance it had ever been attempted without the full chorus. The Osanna is another short fugue—

Ex. 23.

hardly more than an exposition of the four voices; and it comes rapidly to a climax and finishes abruptly with a very unexpected cadence.

So far, we see no sign that Beethoven has any intention of expanding. These three movements are no longer than the corresponding settings in a short Mass by Mozart. They are, of course, intensely dramatic, and expressive of the fiery excitement that pervades the whole Mass; but it is evidently no part of their purpose to make a broad design in themselves. The three short movements are designed to throw into the greatest possible relief the breadth of what is to follow.

Now comes the elevation of the Host, accompanied by a piece of solemn instrumental music called by Beethoven *Praeludium*. The lower strings and the flutes translate into living tones the devout harmonies of quiet organ music over the miraculous depth of one of those 32-foot pedal notes which only the organ itself can produce. Over this immense darkness there suddenly breaks a ray of light. The entry of a solo violin, supported by two flutes, is one of those completely simple strokes of genius which, once accomplished, seem to have been in the world since time began, and which can never be repeated. Certainly there has been no composition for the Church or for any form of religious music, in which the idea of accomplishing a miracle, the descent of something divine, has been more simply and convincingly expressed. As the solo violin comes down, the basses of the chorus are heard softly intoning the words *Benedictus qui venit in nomine Domini.*

Ex. 24.

Ben - e - dic - tus   qui   ve - nit in no - mi - ne Do - mi - ni,

The violin settles down into a broad melody, the phrases and interludes of which are going evidently to be the main themes of a kind of aria-concerto of violin, voices, and orchestra. The interludes of the wind instruments lay the foundations for the new Osanna.

Ex. 25.

Ex. 26.

The brass instruments accompany the violin in solemn chords which, as far as rhythm and musical idea are concerned, are repeating the word *Benedictus.* (These chords, among the most solemn inspirations in Beethoven's works or in any church music, were those which Sir Michael Costa angrily struck out of the score, because they impressed his gigmanity as resembling, on paper, the chords of dance music.) The melody, which the violin delivers to that solemn accompaniment, becomes a remarkably expressive canon when the solo voices take it up. (In Ex. 25 it is given in that form.) A contrapuntal device does not lose expressive power by being quotable in text-books. It so happens that canons in the upper second or in the lower seventh have a special accent of pleading, because the second voice repeats the phrases of the first a step higher in the scale; so that, unless the composer mishandles his resources, the answer can hardly fail to out-vie the original subject in its intensity. We shall find that the canon in the upper second or in the lower seventh has always had this effect wherever

it has been used (e.g. the *Recordare* of Mozart's *Requiem*).
Beethoven, immediately after finishing the Mass, used this very
same device in one of the variations in his C sharp minor Quartet.
The second of the phrases which the violin announced—

Ex. 27.

develops into a regular second subject in the dominant. When
the design comes to its close in the dominant, the words *in
nomine Domini* break out from the chorus as if to make a formal
cadence; but the harmony diverges, and happening to light upon
a subdominant chord, surprises us by leading to a new episodic
theme.

Ex. 28.

This episode does duty for development, and turns round into C
major. The choral writing is of bold simplicity, consisting of a
mere bass sung by all the chorus in octaves while the solo violin
is bringing out the first theme in C major. From this point
onwards, the chorus plays the same role that was so wonderfully
played by the brass instruments at the beginning of the movement
before the voices had entered. The solo voices bring the music
back to the main key and resume the theme which we have learned
to regard as the second subject (Ex. 27). Now we have a regular
sonata-like recapitulation in the tonic, leading to the same close
as we had at the end of the exposition, and the same pause on
the subdominant. And so the coda begins with the new theme
(Ex. 28) and works it out with great breadth, until at last the chorus
takes up the unassuming instrumental interlude for the wind
instruments that separated the phrases of the violin melody (Ex. 26).
The chorus turns this instrumental interlude into a short fugue
on the text *Osanna in excelsis*, which rises to a powerful climax,
culminating in a pause. Then the violin resumes the second subject (Ex. 27), which the chorus accompanies with extraordinarily
impressive octaves in monotone, till the tenors and other voices
break through once more with the Osanna; and so in a few more
bars the Benedictus dies away in quiet glory.

The Agnus Dei, in the key of B minor (which for some obscure
reason Beethoven regarded as extremely dark), begins with a cry

de profundis. Its broad melody is harmonized in sombre colour, and given to a deep bass voice.

Ex. 29.

The low tenors and basses of the chorus answer it; and, in a structure realizing the ancient conception of the Agnus Dei as a threefold prayer, we have this theme exposed in three stages, rising among the voices until it fills the chorus. This design is laid out very broadly, and is completely rounded off. Having eventually died away in the key of B minor in which it began, it turns in a new direction with a quiet modulation like an approaching dawn. Then the *Dona nobis pacem*, entitled by Beethoven 'Prayer for inward and outward peace', enters softly with an introductory theme—

Ex. 30.

leading to a calm pair of subjects in double fugue—

Ex. 31.

which is exposed systematically in all the four voices, culminating in one of the most striking and haunting phrases in the whole Mass.

Ex. 32.

This gives rise to a short, dignified fugato, which modulates in symphonic style to the dominant. Now we have one of those second groups, typical of Beethoven's finales at all periods of his work, and especially characteristic of his last period. The type consists of a number of short themes, depending on sharp contrasts

of colour and rhythm. First there is the following simple antiphonal piece of vocal euphony—

Ex. 33.

pa - - - - - - - cem,   pa - - - - cem

accompanied by the instruments in delicate staccato scales.

It is answered by a paragraph of variously contrasted phrases,
ending in a burst of triumph, that asserts with great confidence
the chords of the key in a formal cadential manner. Suddenly
the triumph dies away, and there are sounds as of distant war. The
voices, both solo and chorus, renew with expressions of terror the
prayer, *Agnus Dei, qui tollis peccata mundi,* and the threatening
sounds draw nearer. Quotation is unnecessary: no listener can miss
the meaning of those drums and trumpets.

But the danger passes away, and the peaceful current of the
Dona nobis pacem is resumed in a variety of modulations, till we
come to a quite regular recapitulation of our second group (Ex. 32
and its sequels) in the tonic. This ends, as before, in triumph. But
now the triumph breaks away in a very strange instrumental fugued
passage, in which one of the subjects is evidently derived from the
double-fugue theme.

Ex. 34.

It is permissible to interpret this as the change from prosperity to
arrogance followed by its Nemesis. At all events there is no doubt
that the chorus has ended in triumph, and that this first outbreak of
independent energy in the orchestra is not in itself agitated, but
rather exultant. But this fugue passage becomes alarmingly rough
and wild, and it is scattered in a strangely excited and headlong
way over the various groups in the orchestra.

Suddenly the trumpets and drums return with terrible power.
The prayer of the chorus is mightier, and peace returns with
a deeper mystery. The end is one of Beethoven's most touching
and subtle codas. All the themes of peace are there, resounding
close at hand and dying away in heights and depths. There is the
calm principal theme of the second group (Ex. 33); above all there
is the haunting climax of the first group (Ex. 32), which is the
actual last word of the chorus. It is twice answered by faint echoes
of the war—broken rhythms on the drum, entirely unaccompanied,
in their distant key. The chorus ends in peace, and the orchestra
abruptly closes the mighty work with chords of innocent triumph.

CCIX. DUNGEON SCENE FROM 'FIDELIO'

Some day *Fidelio* will become to English music-lovers what it is in Germany, the opera to which every right-thinking married couple goes on the anniversary of their wedding. One step towards this consummation is already nearly accomplished: it is now no longer excruciatingly funny to be a right-thinking married couple, so long as one does not interfere with couples whose mental co-ordinates are Gaussian. The other step still remains to be taken. We are in the throes of the discovery that opera is an interest of national importance; and therefore it behoves us to pay attention to the orthodoxies of the old-stager critics whose grandparents learnt from Wagner that *Fidelio*, besides having an impossibly bourgeois subject, is not a good model for students in operatic technique. These old stagers might be very funny if they were not as mischievous as they are pathetic. In 1902 I was surprised to learn, when I wrote the programme notes for the Meiningen Concerts, that it showed 'paralysis of mind' to speak of *Fidelio* as if it were a good opera. My surprise was caused by no doubts as to the defects of *Fidelio*, which had been as obvious to me as to any intelligent child of my age when I first heard it in Berlin in 1888. And, lest I should miss them or be misled by them then, they were explicitly pointed out to me by certain spiritual pastors who worshipped every note of the music and almost every word of the text. What surprised me was that, even in 1902, anybody should still be so unused to the defects of *Fidelio* as to suppose that they mattered. We know that *Paradise Lost* conspicuously fails in its purpose to 'justify the ways of God to man'. That failure is a defect, just as many features in the music and libretto of *Fidelio* are defects. But we also know that blank verse will not rhyme, that heroic couplets will not make Miltonic verse-paragraphs, and that the first irruption of spoken dialogue into music produces a disagreeable shock if you do not expect it. The old-stager school of critics does not always show that it can distinguish the working hypotheses of art-forms from defects of execution.

Perhaps the listener, after being warned against the shock of the first irruption of spoken dialogue, may come to agree with Macfarren (who wrote an admirable and fearlessly critical analysis of *Fidelio* in the 'seventies) that the effect of the spoken words after the trumpet-call is one of the greatest 'thrills' ever achieved on the stage. The fact is that after Beethoven transformed the *Leonora* of 1804–6 into the *Fidelio* of 1814, all the remaining defects of the work were confined to the first part of the first act, which no amount of revision could make quite clear. The second act (originally the third) comprises the dungeon scene and the finale.

The dungeon scene is, in its now extant version, from first to last, 'one of the greatest thrillers to be seen on any stage'. That expression is as out of date as Pizarro's thirst for 'crrimson blood and the hour of my rrevenge':—but 1814 is pretty near to the actual date of that expression. Thus, even the humble literary values of the libretto are those of an original and not of an imitation. And they are faithfully translated into the music of Beethoven. Some day I hope, with suitable though belated acknowledgement to the much-abused Macfarren, to produce a complete and historical analysis of *Fidelio*. Meanwhile my account of the two great *Leonora* overtures must suffice, together with a few remaining *obiter dicta* on the present scene. The elements of operatic convention in it are clear enough to justify themselves, and they actually bulk much smaller in reality than in common report. Moreover, as we are dealing with first-rate melodramatic thrills, it is only fair to compare them with parallel phenomena in the cinema during the few years in which that modern art shall still give us opportunity to observe such phenomena.

For instance, it has been remarked, and justified as a good operatic convention, that Pizarro would in real life have a dozen chances of still killing Florestan while the music of the great quartet is pursuing its torrential course. I rather doubt this; few dramatic critics, and even fewer modern composers, know how short the apparently formal processes of classical music really are. The Wagnerite apostle Hueffer accused Mozart of 'keeping Fate, in the person of the Count, with a drawn sword, at bay while Susanna and Cherubino sing an excellent duet' before Cherubino jumps out of the window. In actual stage-timing Mozart gives Cherubino none too much time to make up his mind to risk a breakneck fall, and certainly only just enough time for the Count to come back with the crow-bar he had fetched in order to force the Countess's locked door. However, supposing that Beethoven's quartet does stretch the action beyond realistic limits in order to achieve a musical purpose, that musical purpose fully occupies the listener's mind here and now, and only increases the dramatic tension; whereas in the cinema the only reason why the hero is tied to a barrel of gunpowder and left there to await the burning down of a six-inch candle is because common sense on the part of the assassins would make it impossible to announce that another episode of this hair-raising drama will be given next week. Professor Dent's new English translation of *Fidelio* respects the essentials of the original without a mistaken piety towards the details, many of which are naïve beyond the limits of recognizable convention.

An orchestral introduction gives an impression of darkness and of echoing vaults. At first there are no themes, but time is slowly measured out with sounds that build up rhythm, while the harmony firmly asserts its dark key from the outset. An articulate theme is heard on the dominant—

Ex. 1.

Mysterious drum-notes deepen the darkness—

Ex. 2.

A gleam of consolation appears in a new key—

Ex. 3.

but the darkness returns like the black waves that drown the after-images in tired eyes.

The curtain rises. Florestan, chained to a stone block, is dimly seen by the light of a small lamp that shines high up on the wall of a vaulted dungeon.

FLORESTAN. Dark! and always dark!
    (Ex. 1) How horrible the silence. (Ex. 2)
        Here in my lonely cell ne'er a living thing I see.
            O cruel fortune!
    (Ex. 3) Yet the will of God is righteous.
        I'll not complain, for all my suffering comes from Him.

Florestan's great aria now begins. Its melody may be seen in two different versions in my essay on the *Leonora* Overtures (Vol. IV, p. 33, Ex. 2). The version of *Fidelio* differs slightly from both.

> Ere my life is half completed
> All that gave me joy is flown.
> Words of truth too boldly spoken
> Brought me here to die alone.
> All my pain I gladly suffer;
> End my life without a groan.
> This alone consoles my sorrow,
> That my duty I have done.

Suddenly the aria closes into a bright foreign key; and soon from a state of 'half-dreaming' the starved prisoner passes into feverish exaltation—

Ex. 4.

Und spür' ich   nicht lin - de,   sanft säu - seln - de Luft?

Yet sometimes, half dreaming, I think I can see
A vision that rises before me;
An angel appearing in garments of light,
With soft words of comfort and love to restore me.
Or is it Leonora?
Leonora, my angel, my wife?

Ex. 5.

Le-o - no - ren, der Gat - tin so gleich,

Yes? Whom God sends to lead me to heavenly life.
I see her; she comes to me now,
To lead me to freedom and heavenly life.

He falls back exhausted. Footsteps are heard. Enter Rocco the jailer, and Fidelio, the youth who has come from nowhere, has entered his service, and has earned his whole-hearted approval as his prospective son-in-law. Their task is to dig up a part of the dungeon-floor that conceals an old well, so that the murderous commander of the fortress, Pizarro, may get rid of the body of his enemy Florestan before the arrival of the Prince, whom Pizarro has been secretly warned to expect as a surprise visitor.

Accompanied spoken dialogue.

FIDELIO. How cold it is in this underground vault!
ROCCO. Of course it is; it's a long way down.
FIDELIO (*trying to see her surroundings*). I thought we should never find the entrance.
ROCCO. There's the man.
FIDELIO. He seems not to move at all.
ROCCO. Perhaps he is dead.
FIDELIO. You think so?
    (*She tries to throw the light of her lamp on his face.*) (Ex. 5.)
ROCCO. No, no, he is only asleep. We must get to work at once; we have no time to lose.
FIDELIO (*aside*). It is so dark, I cannot distinguish his features.
        Oh, God help me if it is my husband.

(Quotations from a passage in Act I relevant to Rocco's next words.)

ROCCO. Somewhere here under this rubbish is the old well that I told you about. We shall not have to dig far to clear the opening.

Give me the pickaxe: you stand there and clear the stuff away. You're
shivering. Are you frightened?
FIDELIO. No, no; I'm only so cold.
ROCCO. Well then, set to work; that will soon make you warm.

Duet.

Musical quotations are not necessary for this movement, which
is a study in atmosphere, instrumentation, and declamation from
the first shadowy, vibrating chords to the stark unison phrase with
which it, and the gravediggers' task, ends. Rocco urges his fellow
worker in tones that have little more than the rise and fall of speech.
Fidelio replies in melody while at work, and the melody becomes
heroic during the aside in which the determination is formed to
save the prisoner, whoever he may be.

ROCCO. Come, set to work, for time is pressing;
There's not a moment to be lost.
FIDELIO. You ne'er shall say that I was idle,
Or left the task I had to do.
ROCCO (lifting a great stone). Here, come and help me lift this stone up.
Take care! and hold it fast.
FIDELIO. I'm holding it! Push below!
I'll do the best I can to move it.
{ ROCCO. 'Tis nearly out. It moves! Come, lift again!
{ FIDELIO. Take care! 'Tis nearly out. We have it now.
(*The stone rolls away.*)
ROCCO. Come, set to work: Pizarro's coming!
We must have done before he's here.
FIDELIO. A moment's rest and I am ready:
Not much remains for us to do.
(*aside*) That man, whoe'er he be, I'll save him,
I swear I will not let him die.
ROCCO. Come, come, I'll have no idling here.
FIDELIO. Indeed, sir, not one single moment will I waste.
ROCCO. Come, set to work, &c.
FIDELIO. You ne'er shall say, &c.

The mouth of the well is cleared. The prisoner awakens.
Fidelio (Leonora) recognizes him. Her quest is over: he is her
husband. But she must not reveal herself. She must remain in
her role of Fidelio until she can surprise Pizarro in the moment of
his murderous intention. Meanwhile the good-hearted Rocco, considering that Florestan's sufferings will soon be over, ventures to
answer the prisoner's questions at last. Florestan learns that he is
in the power of Pizarro, whose crimes he had two years ago discovered and tried to reveal. Rocco gives Florestan a draught of
wine.

Terzet.

Euch wer - de   Lohn in bes - sern   Wel - ten

FLORESTAN. Be this good deed in Heaven rewarded,
  For surely 'twas Heaven sent you here,
  My last remaining hours to cheer,
  Although by me with thanks alone rewarded.

ROCCO (*aside to Fidelio*). Poor soul, the wine I gladly give;
  Few moments more he has to live.

FIDELIO. My heart beats loud within my breast;
  With joy is, yet with pain, opprest.

FLORESTAN (*aside*). How strangely moved the lad appears;
  And even the man seems half in tears.

Together—

FIDELIO. One only hope to me remains,
  To die with him or break his chains.

FLORESTAN. And hope again returns to me
  That I may yet see liberty.

ROCCO. I have my duty here to do,
  But hate the deed no less than you.

FIDELIO (*aside to Rocco*). This piece of bread, may I not give him?
  He makes my heart with pity bleed.

ROCCO. A kindly thought that was indeed,
  But yet I know I must forbid it.

FIDELIO. Ah! yet you yourself this wine did give.

ROCCO. I have my orders to fulfil,
  I must obey my master's will.

FIDELIO. Few moments more he has to live.

ROCCO. Then give him what you will, I'll not refuse you.

FIDELIO. Then take, oh take this bread, oh hapless man!

FLORESTAN. Oh take my grateful thanks.

Together—

FIDELIO. Oh place your trust in Heaven above.
  You know not yet how near its help may be.

FLORESTAN. 'Twas surely Heaven that sent you here
  My dying hours to cheer.

ROCCO. Your sufferings filled my heart with pain,
  Although to help I was not free.

Together—

FLORESTAN.   'Tis more than I can e'er repay.
FIDELIO and ROCCO. 'Tis more than I can bear to see.

  All is now ready. Rocco gives a signal which brings down the
waiting Pizarro. He confronts Florestan and reveals himself.

Quartet.

Ex. 7.

PIZARRO. So die then! Yet before you perish,
I'd have you learn who strikes the blow.
No more I'll hide my secret vengeance.
My name you, ere you die, shall know.
Pizarro. Did you seek my ruin?
Pizarro. 'Twas your own undoing,
He stands before you, and wreaks his vengeance now.

FLORESTAN. So murder, not justice, is your end!

PIZARRO. 'Twas you alone who sought my overthrow,
One moment more is all you have to live.

(Fidelio rushes forward between Pizarro and Florestan.)

Together—
FIDELIO. No, no!
FLORESTAN. O God!
ROCCO. How now?

FIDELIO. You shall not, while I stand by his side.
You shall not wreak your vengeance
Till I for him have died.

Together—
FLORESTAN. O God, help me now.
PIZARRO. What, would you dare? Yes, you shall die for this.
ROCCO. Stand back! Would you dare?

FIDELIO. I am his wife.
FLORESTAN. My wife!
PIZARRO and ROCCO. His wife?
(We may now call Fidelio by her real name.)

LEONORA. Yes, I am Leonora.
I am his wife, and I will not let him die
For all your power.

Together—
LEONORA. His wrath I can defy, and all his power.
FLORESTAN. My heart stands still for joy!
PIZARRO. Does she my power defy?
ROCCO. My heart stands still for fear!

Together—
PIZARRO. Shall I before a woman tremble?
LEONORA. You shall not wreak your vengeance
While I stand by his side.

LEONORA *(presenting a pistol)*. Say but a word, I shoot you **dead**.

(A trumpet is heard from the tower, as in the Overture 'Leonora No. 3'
(see Vol. IV, p. 38, Ex. 9).)

Together—
LEONORA. Ah! You are delivered! Thanks to God!

FLORESTAN. Ah! I am delivered! Thanks to God!
PIZARRO.   Ah! That was the signal! All is lost!
ROCCO.   Oh! What is that sound? Thanks be to God!
            (*The trumpet sounds again.*)
A voice speaks from the top of the stairway.
Rocco! Rocco! The Prince is here! His outriders are at the gates!

Together—

LEONORA and FLORESTAN. Now strikes the hour of vengeance!

Your⎫
My ⎭ dangers are all past.

Through⎫
Your ⎭ courage and devotion

I'll⎫
Will⎭ set you free at last.

PIZARRO. Accurst who thwarts my vengeance!
          Not yet my hour is past.
          Despairing frenzy fills me;
          I'll have revenge at last!
ROCCO.   Now strikes the hour of vengeance.
          Are all his dangers past?
          Her courage and devotion
          May set him free at last.   (*Exeunt* PIZARRO and ROCCO.)

Duet.

Ex. 8.

O   na - men -, na - men - lo - se Freu-de!

LEONORA and FLORESTAN. Oh joy beyond expressing,
                        When heart finds heart again,
                        Our anguish all forgotten
                        In love's exultant strain.
LEONORA.   Once more within my arms I fold you!
FLORESTAN. By God's great mercy I behold you!

[Here the entry of the double-basses two octaves below the 'cellos is a *locus classicus* for an orchestral risk taken with sublime results.]

Ex. 9.   Du wie - der nun in mei - nen Ar - men,

&c.

LEONORA and FLORESTAN. O thank we Him whose tender care
                        Has given us now this joy to share.

Ex. 10.

My love! My life! Oh joy beyond expressing.

FLORESTAN. Leonora!
LEONORA.   Florestan!

Recapitulation.—One cannot help wishing that Beethoven could
have retained a glorious modulation of Ex. 10 into B flat, which
gave to the original recapitulation and coda of this duet a glow
which the excessive length and vocal strain of the sequel could not
weaken; but he is certainly right in now pressing on straight to
the end, though the composer of *Fidelio* in 1814 is undoubtedly
sometimes very severe in his treatment of the composer of *Leonora*
in 1805.

The finale of *Fidelio* is a delightful festive scene in the open
air, with exactly the right lightness of touch to bring us into the
mood for winding up matters less sublime, though not less human,
than Leonora's heroism. But in the concert-room we may at this
point most fitly rise to the height of what Beethoven had in 1814
discovered to be altogether too sublime for any conceivable
stage-music, and we may measure the happiness of Leonora and
Florestan by the musical values of the Overture *Leonora No. 3*,
letting it follow upon the duet without pause.

CCX. CANTATA, 'BECALMED SEA AND PROSPEROUS VOYAGE,'
OP. 112 (*Dedicated to Goethe*)

I venture to amend the English title of this work. *Calm Sea* misses
the point and suggests the poor land-lubber's *sine qua non* for a prosperous voyage. Goethe's little pair of poems deals with the oppres-
sion and terror of a sailing-ship becalmed, and the joy and relief
when the wind rises. A literal translation of the poems will run as
follows:

I. 'Deep silence broods on the waters; the sea reposes motion-
   less; and the mariner is troubled at the sight of smooth levels
   around him. No breath of air from any quarter; the deathly
   silence is terrible; throughout the enormous distance not
   a ripple stirs.'

II. 'The clouds are torn apart, the sky is clear, and Aeolus re-
   leases us from the bonds of fear. The winds rustle, the
   mariner bestirs himself; haste! haste! the waves part; the
   distance approaches; and now I see land.'

No musical quotations are necessary. In the severe medium of the chorus Beethoven illustrates his text naïvely and Beethovenishly from point to point, accomplishing in the 'becalmed' movement much of what Mendelssohn later achieved with the wider freedom of a purely instrumental 'tone-poem'. The outstanding feature here is his representation of the 'enormous distance'. The voices are singing in the anxious low tones with which they began, when suddenly the word 'Weite' bursts out as a long-sustained fortissimo cry on the top A of the sopranos: after which, of course, they subside with 'Reget keine Welle sich'. The late Mr. Edward Speyer possessed the original proofs of the pianoforte score with Beethoven's autograph corrections. The arranger, vainly ambitious of making enough noise on the pianoforte during the long cry of the chorus, has made the chord into a tremolo. This Beethoven roughly crosses out, and writes in the margin to the effect of telling the arranger to *look at the words! Reget keine Welle sich!*

Beethoven raises the wind by means of pianissimo scales crossing and recrossing in all parts of the harmony. Again I refrain from quoting the passage; but it might make an appropriate headpiece for appeals for the support of deserving musical schemes.

The rest of the 'prosperous voyage' is simple and jubilant, without making the mistake of trying to get an ambitious tone-picture from the chorus. In the proofs of the pianoforte arrangement, where 'the winds rustle', Beethoven takes umbrage at a besetting sin of the pianoforte arrangers of his day, an excessive use of tin-kettle high notes, and scrawls in the margin 'O you airy rabble! (O ihr luftiges Gesindel!)'.

SCHUBERT

CCXI. 'ERLKÖNIG'

For the last fifty years it has been supposed to show acumen to praise Loewe's very fine and exceedingly clever setting of *Erlkönig* at the expense of Schubert's. We are told, in particular, that Loewe's wonderful representation of the Erl-king's speeches by the notes of a mere major chord, is much more true to the facts than Schubert's pretty tunes, which we ought to regard as digressions into irrelevant ornament. Now it is true that Goethe's poem, like his *Iphigenie auf Tauris*, and like many other *aufgeklärt* poems of the period, is almost aggressively rationalistic; and that Goethe comes as near as anything short of literal statement can come to telling us that the child was delirious with marsh-fever, and that it accordingly died a natural death before it and its father reached the inn. But Goethe does not go so far as to make the delirious child see and hear no more than the things the father sees and hears. Goethe does not, like Loewe and the child's father, tell us that the *child* heard nothing but the wind whispering in withered leaves. He gives us the Erl-king's speeches in full, and they tell explicitly of golden raiment, of gay flowers, and of pretty games and dances. How can Schubert be wrong in following Goethe into the child's fevered fancies, and waiting until it is the father's turn to explain them away? Loewe's clever economy here is beautifully typical of the decline from a golden to a silver age. The fact is that the psychological critic and the psychological composer are alike inferior to Schubert in psychology as well as in music. They can neither construct nor understand large musical forms; and so they fail to see that a large musical form may interpret a poem so comprehensively that the criticism which can carp at the result is just as likely to discover with annoyed surprise that the poem is written in verse.

Schubert at the age of seventeen, when he wrote this masterpiece, had already formed the habit, equally sound as a principle of lyric art and of psychology, of determining what feature in the song should be present all the time. In the *Erlkönig* this feature is the galloping horse, on which the father rides in desperate endeavour to reach shelter before the marsh-fever has done its mischief. At first the horse, the rider, and the child in his arms are seen from the spectator's point of view. Then the father speaks, worried because his child hides his face. 'Father, don't you see the Erl-king there with his crown and train?' 'My son, that is only a streak of mist.'

But now Goethe and Schubert hear and see with the senses of the child. The immense stroke of genius here, as in the Erl-king's second speech, is the change in the galloping accompaniment. The galloping is no longer seen; it is felt in a troubled half-sleep, and felt mainly in the rhythmic rise of the rider pressing on his stirrups.

But when the Erl-king threatens to seize the child by force and then grasps him, the child is wide awake. The father presses on, but it is too late: when they reach the house the child lies dead in his arms.

VERDI

CCXII. REQUIEM IN MEMORY OF MANZONI

The genius of Verdi developed in ways that have provided many a pitfall for critics. For three-quarters of the nineteenth century Italian opera presented the phenomenon of a great tradition of singing, flourishing hectically on an orchestral tradition that had never been really alive and was not so much decadent as decayed.

You cannot allow dry-rot in the orchestra without eventually destroying vocal ideas also; and perhaps that is one reason why Italian
opera, which flourished as comedy in the spacious days of the
Barbiere (to say nothing of Mozart), needed, by the middle of the
century, to keep itself alive on blood-and-thunder tragedy. For this
tragic purpose it employed much the same orchestral habits and
melodic idioms that it had drifted into for comic purposes. If a
flute, a piccolo, two oboes, two clarinets, and all the violins faithfully
double the melody of the heroic tenor, he will get the credit for the
noise they are making. The necessary harmonic support may be
furnished by the whole mass of brass instruments playing thick-set
chords in dance-rhythms—for what other rhythms are there? In
the country that still possesses the most wonderful voices, and is the
historic ground of the Golden Age of Music that culminated in
Palestrina, this dramatic and operatic technique seemed, in the
mid-nineteenth century, to be common sense. In other countries,
especially Germany, other methods had arisen, but such foreign
fads were mere protestantisms and provincialities. Professor
Basevi, writing on the 28th of April 1858 in *L'Armonia* at Florence,
could, after referring respectfully to Mozart as *quell'animo tutto
melanconico*, stoutly maintain that since Rossini's *Guillaume Tell*
had been produced in 1832 '*non ha interamente progredito in Italia
l'Opera in musica*'. This is hard upon Verdi, who had produced
Rigoletto in 1851 and *Il Trovatore* and *La Traviata* in 1853, and
who was about to produce *Un Ballo in Maschera* in 1859. But in
some ways it was arguable; for the Parisians had roused Rossini up
to making his orchestration remarkably interesting, whereas Verdi's
orchestral habits changed slowly. And yet there are strokes of
genius, both dramatic and orchestral, in *Rigoletto* that are utterly
beyond Rossini's depth.

How is a composer going to rise to refinement, as well as to other
aspects of greatness, from post-Rossinian antecedents? And how is
criticism to deal, not only with the transitional stages, but with
the survivals in the mature style of practices that obviously have
a humble origin? One thing experience abundantly shows; that a
conflict between artistic civilizations on two different planes always
produces disagreeable effects, and will continue to do so long after
we have forgotten the origins of the works which show it. To use
the present psychological jargon, such works are bound to show an
inferiority complex, and this produces a squalid style in which the
elements belonging to the less highly-organized art are either feeble
or blatantly self-assertive against the others. Such a style is pain-
fully evident in Wagner even as late as *Lohengrin*; and it accounts
for some of the difficulty which his reforming principles had in
making their way. *Tannhäuser* and *Lohengrin* are Wagnerean

operas that owed some measure of popularity to the anti-Wagnerean music that they contain.

Now the remarkable thing in Verdi's later development is that it shows no conflict of style. Verdi once said of himself: 'I am not a learned composer, but I am a very experienced one.' That is the word of power. Walter Bagehot once divided men into those who have an experiencing nature and those who have not. Macaulay, who had the *'inexperiencing* nature' in a high degree, could never have fallen between two civilizations, and could never have extricated himself if he had been born between them. Wagner did extricate himself. Verdi never fell. All his experience went into his music and enlarged it, crowding out what it superseded, without demanding transplantation and without injuring its foundations. Not one of his habits did Verdi change as his style developed. Those that would have been weaknesses in his later art were crowded out: the rest became like material instruments. Their limitations were to be used, without inquiry as to the existence elsewhere of other stylistic instruments without these limitations. How, for instance, is Verdi going to extricate himself from the bad Italian valve-trombone technique, when his art rises to levels beyond the dreams of Italian mid-nineteenth-century music? The foreigner answers glibly that Verdi ought to learn the noble technique of Wagner's trombones, and to space out their harmony on true acoustic principles. That is not Verdi's solution. To him the Italian method is common sense, and his inspiration cannot wait for the process of reconstructing the common sense of his art. He uses his trombones in the old Italian way. They make lumps of heavy and hot chord low down in the harmony, and now and then burst out in ferocious barkings and sputterings, with a technique of fantastic agility. The only difference that Verdi's later art shows is the all-important fact that he now knows exactly what these effects mean. The result is that so great a composer and shrewd an observer as Richard Strauss regards Verdi's later treatment of brass as 'quite individual, though without the right feeling for the soul and true character of trumpet and trombone tone'. Correctly deducing this from the nature of the 'vulgar-toned valve-trombones', Strauss does not stop to ask whether Verdi was not justified in suiting his style to the nature of his instruments. The interesting point is that Strauss should describe as a style quite peculiar to *Falstaff* and *Otello* a method which differs from that of earlier Italian works in no particular, except that it is applied with imagination.

The reasoning that applies to this special case will account for more important aspects of the style of Verdi's *Requiem*. All his life Verdi had been a composer for the theatre. The ideals of church music realized by Palestrina three hundred years before him were never more absent from the European musical consciousness than in 1873, and nowhere more forgotten or more tardily recovered than in Italy. To expect Verdi to produce anything like an ecclesiastical music would be humanly absurd. It ill becomes us to dogmatize as to the limits of divine patience; but we may be very sure that Verdi's *Requiem* stands before the throne at no disadvantage from its theatrical style. As human documents go, this work is of a flaming sincerity. The language of the theatre was Verdi's only musical idiom; and our musical culture, resting securely on its foundation on Bach and Beethoven, can derive nothing but good from realizing that to object to the theatricality of Verdi's *Requiem* is about as profane as to point out that Beethoven lacked the advantages of a university education. When Verdi's *Requiem* shocked all Hans von Bülow's classical susceptibilities, the defence came from the purest classical aristocrat of the later nineteenth century. Brahms had no mercy on music that fell between two civilizations, and some of his judgements of musical half-breeds are not quotable in the smoking-room without apology. But his comment on Bülow's *Schand-Artikel* was: 'Bülow has given himself away (*hat sich blamirt*): Verdi's *Requiem* is a work of genius.'

To the memory of his friend, the poet Manzoni, Verdi devoted his greatest inspirations, with the whole resources that he had accumulated in *Aïda*. Manzoni died in 1873: Verdi had already written the *Libera me* for a memorial service for Rossini, who died in 1868. Early in 1871 Mazzucato, writing from Milan, where he was professor of composition, reminded Verdi of this piece. Verdi replied that Mazzucato should be more careful of his praises; for the *Libera me* already contains passages belonging to the *Dies Irae*; and such praises are dangerously near to an incentive to composing the entire *Requiem*, which would be a dreadful consequence of Mazzucato's thoughtlessness. But have no fear. Verdi does not care for useless matters. There are so many, many, *and* many *Messe da morto*. It is useless to add another.

Two years later, the death of Manzoni, 'the only great Italian left after Rossini', caused Verdi to finish what he had begun. It was no addition to 'many, many, *and* many works'. It is as unlike any other Requiem as its text permits. There is no trace of Mozart; and its theatrical language only accentuates its utter remoteness from the spirit of Berlioz's *Requiem*. Even the distant trumpets in the *Tuba mirum* have an almost opposite purpose to that of Berlioz's four sets of brass and drums at the north, south, east, and west of the concert-room. Berlioz wishes to astonish: while Verdi merely wants some trumpet-notes off-stage to get the actual fact of distance, without any attempt at a realistic treatment of a supernatural event.

I am not aware that Verdi ever encountered the kind of prig who would try to alter his ideas of religion, or of music, or even of religious music. But it might have been at least theoretically possible to point out that Mozart's *Requiem* (itself a very theatrical work from Palestrina's point of view) moves the listener by an architectural and vocal beauty which is itself unshaken; whereas Verdi's constant effort is to make the voices and structure express consternation and the abandonment of grief. And can we not see the great simple old Italian saying, with no mock modesty, that the great method of Mozart is not for him; but that consternation and the abandonment of grief he can and will express? In the last resort, his humble method achieves the greater qualities also. Verdi's *Requiem* is full of strokes of genius; and they are, one and all, architectonic features. Schumann's friend, Thibaut, who, in discovering the purity of Palestrina's style, took umbrage at the theatricality of all music since 1600, made much of the fact that Mozart, in setting the words *Liber scriptus proferetur*, uses the same musical language as that of the child Barbarina hunting for a lost pin in *Figaro*. Of course the real point of Mozart's musical vocabulary is the reverse of Thibaut's way of thinking: Barbarina sings the most tragic music in *Figaro*, because a child doesn't know the difference between losing a pin and facing the Day of Judgement. There are other pitfalls in these criticisms of an artist's vocabulary: for the languages of the arts develop and decline like other languages; words becoming loftier as they drop out of familiar use, until perhaps the heroic language becomes mock-heroic or even slang. And so theatricality itself is but a relative term; and I am not sure that Palestrina has not been quoted with a theatrical gesture in modern times.

All choral music, except movements that are worked out extensively on a single text, is best analysed by quoting the words in full, with whatever musical illustrations are necessary.

The first number of the *Requiem* corresponds to the Kyrie of the Mass, and ends with that text:

I. REQUIEM AND KYRIE

Requiem aeternam dona eis   Grant them eternal rest, O Lord:
Domine:

Ex. 1.

et lux perpetua luceat eis.   and let everlasting light shine on
                                            them.

The theme and harmony are in the instruments; the voices accompany with broken declamation in monotone. The characteristic
change from minor to tonic major, before the music can have
accomplished any action, is an Italian idiom which Schubert caught
from Rossini. It reverberates here both from Verdi's own traditions
and from his love of Schubert, which is often evident in his work.
The music closes unexpectedly into F major, where the unaccompanied chorus delivers the next clauses in a simple but sonorous
and devout paragraph.

Te decet hymnus, Deus, ex Sion,   To thee, O God, praise is meet
et tibi reddetur votum in Jeru-   in Sion, and unto thee shall the
salem. Exaudi orationem meam: vow be performed in Jerusalem.
ad te omnis caro veniet.   Hearken unto my prayer: unto
                                       thee shall all flesh come. Ps. 65.
                                       (The Bible and Prayer Book ver-
                                       sions differ from the Vulgate.)

The *Requiem* and *lux perpetua* passages are repeated. Then the
solo voices enter with the Kyrie, which is worked out in the most
moving passage in all Verdi's works; unquestionably one of the
greater monuments of musical pathos.

Kyrie eleison: Lord, have mercy upon us:
Christe eleison: Christ, have mercy upon us:
Kyrie eleison.   Lord, have mercy upon us.

II. DIES IRAE

The Dies Irae begins with the most naïve passage in the whole
work, a passage which recurs on several later occasions, and which
is always developed with great breadth. Eventually its powerful
stride carries us beyond our first impression of its *naïveté*, and we
recognize the great master of the Kyrie.

Ex. 5.

Dies irae, dies illa
Solvet saeclum in favilla
Teste David cum Sibylla.

The Day of Wrath, that day
shall dissolve the world in ashes,
as witnesseth David and the Sibyl.

The music dies away, without losing its swing, and the voices declaim in broken monotone the next terzina.

Quantus tremor est futurus
Quando judex est venturus
Cuncta stricte discussurus!

What trembling shall there be
when the Judge shall come who
shall thresh out all thoroughly!

Distant trumpets answer the trumpets of the orchestra in a crescendo which leads to the following text:

Tuba, mirum spargens sonum
Per sepulcra regionum,
Coget omnes ante thronum.

The trumpet, scattering a wondrous sound through the tombs of all lands, shall drive all unto the Throne.

Bass solo: slow declamation with long pauses, and broken rhythms in the lower registers of the orchestra.

Mors stupebit et natura
Cum resurget creatura
Judicanti responsura.

Death and Nature shall be astounded when the creature shall rise again to answer to the Judge.

Soprano solo: a long sustained slow movement, punctuated now and then by the chorus singing the words *Dies irae* in low monotone.

Liber scriptus proferetur
In quo totum continetur
Unde mundus judicetur.

A written book shall be brought forth in which shall be contained all for which the world shall be judged.

Judex ergo cum sedebit
Quidquid latet apparebit:
Nil inultum remanebit.

And therefore when the Judge shall sit, whatsoever is hidden shall be manifest; and naught shall remain unavenged.

Suddenly the orchestra flares up and the chorus bursts out with the latter portion of the Dies irae movement, just before its diminuendo. This now leads to a trio for soprano, mezzo-soprano, and tenor, in adagio 6/8 time, G minor (the key of the Dies irae as a whole). It is worked out as a long sustained pathetic movement, and is a *locus classicus* for its combination of voices and upper strings with a solo bassoon as an expressive flowing bass.

Quid sum miser tunc dicturus,
Quem patronum rogaturus,
Cum vix justus sit securus?

What shall I say in my misery? Whom shall I ask to be my advocate, when scarcely the righteous may be without fear?

At last the three voices ask their questions one by one alone. Then the basses of the chorus thunder out the beginning of the next movement, an adagio maestoso in C minor, of which I quote the third line, which the solo voices sing, and which is developed to one of the principal emotional climaxes in the work.

Ex. 6.

Sal - va me, fons pi - e - ta - tis

Rex tremendae majestatis
Qui salvandos salvas gratis;
Salva me, fons pietatis.

King of awful majesty, who freely savest the redeemed; save me, O fount of mercy.

Duet for soprano and mezzo-soprano.

In the same tempo (which is Verdi's fundamental tempo for Church music; common time with crotchets ranging between 72 and 88 to the minute) the *Recordare* deals with the next terzina in a broad lyric movement. The childlike rhythmic figure of the wind instruments recalls, perhaps not accidentally, the cries of *salva me* in the preceding movement.

Ex. 7.

Re - cor - da - re,   Je - su pi - e

Recordare, Jesu pie,
Quod sum causa tuae viae
Ne me perdas illa die.

Remember, merciful Jesu, that I am the cause of thy journey, lest thou lose me in that day.

The next lines are those which Dr. Johnson sometimes tried to quote, but never without bursting into tears. The first line I take to allude to the woman of Samaria.

Quaerens me sedisti lassus;
Redemisti crucem passus.
Tantus labor non sit cassus.

Seeking me didst thou sit weary: thou didst redeem me, suffering the cross: let not such labour be frustrated.

Juste Judex ultionis	O just Judge of vengeance, give
Donum fac remissionis	the gift of remission before the day
Ante diem rationis.	of reckoning.

In an almost recitative-like passage the tenor interpolates the next terzina before proceeding to another lyric movement.

Ingemisco tanquam reus:	I groan as one guilty; my face
Culpa rubet vultus meus.	blushes at my sin. Spare, O God,
Supplicanti parce, Deus.	me, thy suppliant.

Then follows a movement in E flat with two themes, both intensely Italian, of which the second (accompanied by high tremolo violins) comes at the lines beginning *Inter oves*.

Qui Mariam absolvisti	Thou who didst absolve Mary,
Et latronem exaudisti,	and didst hear the thief's prayer,
Mihi quoque spem dedisti.	hast given hope to me also.

Preces meae non sunt dignae,	My prayers are not worthy, but
Sed tu, bonus, fac benigne,	do thou, good Lord, show mercy,
Ne perenni cremer igne.	lest I burn in everlasting fire.

Inter oves locum praesta	Give me place among thy sheep
Et ab haedis me sequestra,	and put me apart from the goats,
Statuens in parte dextra.	setting me on the right hand.

If proof were yet needed that Verdi's theatrical language is of untainted sincerity, good evidence might be found in the fact that the next terzina is still given to a solo voice, and that the stress is laid not on the obvious contrast between the first pair of lines and the third, but on the contrite prayer which follows.

Confutatis maledictis	When the damned are con-
Flammis acribus addictis,	founded and devoted to sharp
Voca me cum benedictis.	flames, call thou me with the
	blessed.

An interesting document in the history of modern harmony is the following passage, which (like the treatment of *omnis terra veneretur* in Verdi's last work, the *Te Deum*) shows that to him the negation of classical part-writing expressed by the series of consecutive fifths is appropriate to the sentiment of utter self-abasement:

Oro supplex et acclinis,	I pray, kneeling in supplication,
Cor contritum quasi cinis,	a heart contrite as ashes, take thou
Gere curam mei finis.	mine end into thy care.

Ex. 8.

Finally the voice seems to be closing in E minor; but, by one of the greater architectonic strokes of this work, Verdi makes the chord resolve into G minor, and the chorus resumes the opening of the Dies irae, with the whole text of the first terzina (Ex. 5).

This dies away into the dark key of B flat minor, where the final movement carries out its solemn design. The melody of the Lacrimosa is naïve enough for *Il Trovatore*.

Ex. 9.

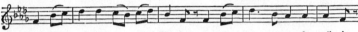

Lac - ri - mo - sa di - es　　il - la qua re - sur - get ex fa - vil - la

Lacrimosa dies illa　　　　　　　Lamentable is that day on which
Qua resurget ex favilla　　　　　guilty man shall arise from the
Judicandus homo reus.　　　　　ashes to be judged.

Those to whom Verdi's style is a stumbling-block may feel some relief that the first two bars of Ex. 9 were followed by other figures instead of immediately repeating themselves. But, as Bülow might have said before his noble recantation in 1892, *das fehlte noch*; and it does happen later, but not until a fine arch of counterpoint is stretched over it by the solo voices when the chorus proceeds to the last lines, which mark the end of the hymn by adding a fourth line to the previous terzina (*huic* is two syllables), and concluding with two short rhymeless lines and an Amen.

Huic ergo parce, Deus.　　　　　Spare then this one, O God,
Pie Jesu Domine:　　　　　　　merciful Lord Jesu: give them
Dona eis requiem. Amen.　　　　peace. Amen.

The Amen is one of the subtlest and most impressive strokes of genius in all Verdi's work, being unexpectedly on a chord of G major; after which the orchestra ends with the chord of B flat major.

III. OFFERTORIO

The whole of this important section is set as a solo quartet. The main movement is an andante mosso in 6/8 time and the key of A flat major. A quiet introduction for the violoncellos and a few wind instruments gradually arrives at the main figure—

Ex. 10.

to which the soprano and tenor add, in broken phrases, the invocation. The bass then completes the sentence, using the theme of Ex. 10, and the movement develops in a flowing style, to the following words, the terrors of which are unable to prevail over the calm of faith expressed by the music.

Domine Jesu Christe, Rex gloriae, libera animas omnium fidelium defunctorum de poenis inferni et de profundo lacu; libera eas de ore leonis; ne absorbeat eas Tartarus, ne cadant in obscurum.

O Lord, Jesu Christ, King of glory, deliver the souls of all the departed faithful from the torments of hell and from the bottomless pit; deliver them from the mouth of the lion; lest Tartarus swallow them; lest they fall into the darkness.

Now the soprano enters. This is one of the great moments.

Sed signifer Sanctus Michael repraesentet eas in lucem sanctam—

But let Saint Michael the standard-bearer bring them forth into the holy light—

Then the music breaks into a quick almost alla-breve tempo, treating with simple lyric fervour a text that has almost always been set as a fugue. But nothing in Verdi's *Requiem* is an addition to the *tante tante e tante* Requiems written before it.

Quam olim Abrahae promisisti et semini ejus.

which thou didst once promise unto Abraham and his seed.

The climax leads suddenly to a quiet slow movement in a bright key.

Ex. 11.

Hos - ti - as et pre - ces ti - bi, Do - mi - ne

Hostias et preces tibi, Domine, laudis offerimus. Tu suscipe pro animabus illis quarum hodie memoriam facimus. Fac eas, Domine, de morte transire ad vitam.

To thee, O Lord, we render our offerings and prayers with praises. Do thou receive them for those souls which we commemorate today. Make them, O Lord, pass from death unto life.

The *Quam olim Abrahae* is repeated in full as the completion of the sentence. This time it leads back to the original 6/8 movement, and the quartet, in octaves, with impressively sombre scoring, concludes with Ex. 10, to the words *libera animas*, &c.; adding *fac eas de morte transire ad vitam*.

IV. SANCTUS

Sanctus, sanctus, sanctus Domine Deus Sabaoth. Pleni sunt coeli et terra gloria tua. Hosanna in excelsis. Benedictus qui venit in nomine Domini. Hosanna in excelsis.

Holy, holy, holy, Lord God of Sabaoth. Heaven and earth are full of thy glory. Hosanna in the highest. Blessed is he that cometh in the name of the Lord. Hosanna in the highest.

The most unexpected of all features in this extraordinary work
is the Sanctus. For reasons probably liturgical and certainly
beyond my information, the Sanctus of every Requiem known to
me is very much shorter and slighter than the Sanctus which forms
the central feature of an ordinary Mass. Verdi gives no exception
to the rule, but he achieves a vivid contrast to the rest of the work.
After some trumpet-calls the chorus, divided into two choirs, sings
the whole Sanctus, Pleni, Benedictus, and Hosanna in one un-
broken double fugue, which, like most post-classical Italian fugues,
revolves in four-bar periods.

Ex. 12.

But the effect is not stiff, and if it is dance-like, the dance is that of
the Sons of the Morning. Towards the end the words *pleni sunt
coeli et terra* recede into distance with the Hosannas, becoming
slow, quiet, and vast, while the orchestra dances on. Then suddenly
the music blazes out again and comes to a brilliant end.

V

The Agnus Dei is another strange and unique conception. Two
solo voices, unaccompanied, give out a melody of twice seven bars,
grouped as 4 and 3. Here are the first seven bars:

Ex. 13.

Ag - nus De - i, Ag - nus De - i, qui . . . .

tol - lis pec - ca - ta mun - di.

This is repeated by the chorus in a lower octave, also unharmonized,
but accompanied in unison by most of the orchestra. The solo pair
repeat it harmonized in a minor variation; the chorus replies with a
fully harmonized major variation. (I speak of variation in reference
to the accompaniment: the vocal melody never alters, except in as
far as it was put into the minor.) Then comes the passage, quoted in
every book on instrumentation, where three flutes surround the two
voices with a flow of counterpoint. The chorus repeats the last
six bars with a new harmonization, and a short coda in echoing
dialogue on the words *requiem sempiternam* ends the movement.
Liturgically the idea is that the prayer is uttered three times, and

the last time with the addition of the word *sempiternam*, so that it should be set forth as follows:

Agnus Dei qui tollis peccata mundi: dona eis requiem.
Agnus Dei qui tollis peccata mundi; dona eis requiem.
Agnus Dei qui tollis peccata mundi; dona eis requiem sempiternam.

Lamb of God, that takest away the sins of the world: give them rest, . . . give them eternal rest.

VI. LUX AETERNA

A trio for mezzo-soprano, tenor, and bass. Below a soft high tremolo starting in B flat major, but modulating mysteriously, the mezzo-soprano declaims the whole text. Then the bass interpolates the text *Requiem aeternam*, over a dark chord of B flat minor (roll on drums in fifths, and low trombone-chords). In G flat major the unaccompanied vocal trio again deals with the rest of the text. The dark B flat minor passage returns, with the addition of the upper voices, and at last the movement settles to a lyric melody in B flat major, exquisitely scored.

Ex. 14.

et . . .   lux   per - pe - tu-a

Lux aeterna luceat eis Domine cum Sanctis tuis in aeternum quia pius es. Requiem aeternam dona eis Domine, et lux aeterna, &c.

Let everlasting light shine on them, O Lord, with thy Saints for ever; for thou art merciful. Grant them, O Lord, eternal rest and let everlasting light, &c.

VII. LIBERA ME

When Verdi replied to Mazzucato in 1871 that the *Libera me* written for Rossini already contained a recapitulation (*riepilogo*) of the *Requiem aeternam* and *Dies Irae*, he showed that the order of composition did not interfere with the logic of his ideas. When the time came to write the whole work, everything led up to the incidents of the already finished *Libera me* as cause to effect. The design begins with an introduction in which the soprano solo and the chorus declaim the words sometimes on a mere reciting note, sometimes in dramatic recitative-like phrases.

Libera me, Domine, de morte aeterna in die illa tremenda quando coeli movendi sunt et terra; dum veneris judicare saeculum per ignem.

Deliver me, O Lord, from eternal death in that awful day when the heavens and the earth shall be moved: when thou shalt come to judge the world by fire.

Then the soprano settles down, though in broken phrases, to a formal movement, which the orchestra holds together with a flowing accompaniment.

Tremens factus sum et timeo, dum discussio venerit atque ventura ira, quando coeli movendi sunt et terra.	I am become trembling, and I fear the time when the trial shall approach and the wrath to come; when the heavens and the earth shall be moved.

The voice dies away. After a pause the *riepilogo* of the Dies Irae (Ex. 5) crashes in. The text, however, is not the same. For one thing, it is not metrical. (Was this, then, an older part of the liturgy, and the hymn written after it and suggested by it?)

Dies irae, dies illa calamitatis et miseriae, dies magna et amara valde.	A day of wrath, that day of calamity and woe, a great day and bitter indeed.

The diminuendo is more impressive than on any previous occasion, which shows how Verdi, in the heat of inspiration for the rest of the work, could hold in reserve what had already been written to come at the end. And now comes the most moving and most architectonic stroke in the whole work. The *riepilogo* of the *Requiem aeternam* (in B flat minor and major) gives to the unaccompanied chorus, led by the solo soprano, the music which at the outset of the work was given only by the orchestra, the voices having nothing but broken monotone. The effect, which Mazzucato thought unsurpassable in itself, seems now to depend on the whole weight and dimensions of the complete work. (See Exx. 1 and 2.)

Requiem aeternam dona eis, Domine, et lux perpetua lucat eis.	Grant them, O Lord, eternal rest, and may light everlasting shine upon them.

With a startled tremolo on the violins the soprano resumes the text *Libera me*, and the work concludes with a fugue.

Ex. 15.

Li - ber-a me, Do - mi - ne, de mor - te ae - ter - na . .
. . . in die il - la tre - men - da

Classical practice is not in favour of full closes in fugal expositions, but Verdi likes them well enough to mark them with the full orchestra. They are in keeping with the rest of his style; and a

fugue that would satisfy examiners might not so easily satisfy Verdi.
Yet this fugue is no poor example of resources, contrapuntal and
dramatic. The subject is inverted—

Ex. 16.

&c.

and, later on, augmented at the entry of the soprano solo, a passage
of high pathos; and the whole movement expands on lines of form
as near to Beethoven's as anything so completely Italian could be.
The quiet end is perfect in its poetry and solemnity.

CCXIII.   SCENA FROM ACT III OF 'OTELLO'
(THE WILLOW SONG)

There was a core of truthfulness in Verdi's art from its crudest
beginnings, when it was struggling through the most degenerate
conventions of the facile Rossinian tradition, to the almost Chinese
refinement of *Falstaff*, the product of his eighty-first year. One of
the astounding things in that refinement is that, except for the
actual art of phrasing and composition, there is no change from
Verdi's earliest habits. From *Aïda* onwards the instrumentation
becomes extremely interesting, bold and subtle. Yet the trombones
remain the tinny little Italian valve-trombones treated as a lump
of dull red-hot leaden close harmony of brutal quality. The only
difference is that Verdi has learnt to appreciate its brutality. And
this is the nature of his wonderful later refinement in all things.
He has not changed his language: he has learnt to use it accurately.
The hero declaims tragically with all the energy of *Il Trovatore*,
but he is no longer accompanied by the rhythm of a bolero. Verdi,
by thus sternly dismissing irrelevancies, has set his imagination
free in all directions; and what he seems to have learnt in each later
work is immeasurable. In the treatment of the voice he had not
so many irrelevancies to dismiss, and consequently not so much to
learn. But there was an *Otello* before Verdi's; and Rossini's
Desdemona expired in roulades, as the Mock-Turtle's schoolmates
fainted in coils. Yet even in Rossini's interpretation the tragic
power of Shakespeare proved such that a Covent Garden *habitué*,
who had never before noticed what was happening in the action
of any opera, started out of his seat at the catastrophe, exclaiming
'Good heavens! the Tenor is murdering the Soprano!'

Boito's libretto is astonishingly close to Shakespeare in details
of language, though the non-musical lover of literature will grieve
at the drastic simplification of the drama in the interests of music.

The English translator, Francis Hueffer, writing in 1887 to Boito,
gives an admirable apology for the compromises he must sorrow-
fully make between Shakespeare's language and Verdi's music;
and points out how remarkable it is that he is able to reproduce
such a large proportion of Shakespeare's salient words. This is,
indeed, so far the case that instead of giving Hueffer's admirable
translation I can here give the relevant lines of the original Shakespeare throughout the present scene; premising that Boito has,
very rightly from the musician's point of view, proceeded straight
from Shakespeare's Act IV, Sc. iii, to Act V, Sc. ii.

In concert-performances it is as well to omit Desdemona's life-
like orders to Emilia ('Lay by these,' 'No, unpin me here'), as well
as Emilia's words. With excellent judgement Boito has selected
from these details just so much as will carry on the action through
the music. Boito, for reasons arising from compression elsewhere,
transfers the first words from Emilia to Desdemona as a request.

Emilia.   I have laid those sheets you bade me on the bed.
(Act IV,   'Prithee, to-night Lay on my bed my wedding sheets.')
Sc. ii, ...

Desdemona.   If I do die before thee, prithee, shroud me
               In one of those same sheets. . . .
               My mother had a maid call'd Barbara;
               She was in love, and he she lov'd prov'd mad
               And did forsake her; she had a song of 'willow';
                    . . . that song to-night
               Will not go from my mind. . . .

               The poor soul sat sighing by a sycamore tree,
                    Sing all a green willow;
               Her hand on her bosom, her head on her knee,
                    Sing willow, willow, willow:
               The fresh streams ran by her, and murmur'd her moans
                    Sing willow, willow, willow:
               Her salt tears fell from her, and soften'd the stones;
                    Sing willow, willow, willow.
               Sing all a green willow must be my garland,

               .   .   .   .

               Hark! who is it that knocks?
Emilia.   It is the wind.

Boito does not venture upon the profoundest touch of pathos in
the whole scene. Shakespeare, writing in the style of an old ballad,
makes poor Barbara's faithless lover reply coarsely to her reproaches;
and Desdemona, who winces at the rough-shod sympathy with
which poor Emilia harps on Othello's unbearable language, can
sing the coarse line as simply as she can sing 'willow, willow,

willow'. The modern poet must be more decorous, and he manages very well with—

He was born for his own glory, and I for love.

Desdemona.   So get thee gone; good night. Mine eyes do itch;
Doth that bode weeping?

She bids Emilia good night, and, as Emilia turns to go, cries out in passionate farewell. Whether this is or is not Shakespearean, it is one of the greatest and simplest things in music-drama.

The whole scene takes place in Desdemona's bedroom. There is an altar of the Madonna, before which she kneels and recites an Ave Maria (translated into Italian), followed by a prayer for intercession for herself, for the sinner and the innocent, for the oppressed weak, and for the mighty who also is miserable and needs mercy; and for her whose forehead is bowed beneath an evil fate (Dys-daemona); for us (both) on the threshold of death.

She resumes the Ave Maria, of which we now hear only the first and last words and an Amen.

Verdi has set the whole of this prayer-scene in a different key, and in complete contrast to the Song of the Willow. It is usual in concert-performances to add a fundamental note to the last chord. I prefer to leave it floating where Verdi leaves it before that most terrible moment in all music-drama, the entry of Othello to the deepest sounds of the four-stringed double-basses.

BRAHMS

CCXIV. 'REQUIEM', OP. 45

The great choral work which brings all the resources of Brahms's art to maturity is a Requiem only in the most general colloquial sense, and has no connexion with any liturgical office. The full original title is *Ein Deutsches Requiem, nach Worten der heiligen Schrift*: a German Requiem with scriptural text. It was composed in memory of the fallen in the war of 1870[1]; and, in glaring contrast to the *Triumphlied* which followed it, has no hint of earthly warfare in its contents. Brahms's knowledge of the Bible was exhaustive. On the other hand, it is extremely unlikely that he knew anything about the liturgy of the Church of England, and quite certain that he had no other liturgy, Protestant or Roman, in mind, when he selected words that so frequently remind English listeners of the Church of England Order for the Burial of the Dead. One thing we may be sure of, that his mind was always alert to the context of every sentence he chose; and that, while it would be fantastic to

[1] Wild nonsense: it was performed in its entirety in 1868, except for No. V.—D.F.T.

draw inferences from his omission and inclusion of this doctrine
and that, we can hardly exaggerate the completeness and intensity
of his poetic insight into the words he has chosen, and the depth of
the musical symbolism of his setting. Some of the finer detail is lost
by translation. The best available English will not always bring the
rhetorical point where the music puts it; and some of the repetitions
of English words, where Brahms had no such stammering in his
setting of the German, should make us consider whether the
certain foolish mannerisms in nineteenth-century English church-
music may not have originated in the assumption that the inspiration of the foreign composer extends to the translation of his text.
Brahms is not responsible for saying, 'For the trumpet, the trumpet
shall sound'; nor, on the other hand, does he give two notes of
melody to one syllable without some rhetorical point. Where such
irritating things happen with an English version, we must realize
that Brahms would have composed the English text differently.
Some of the finest passages are barely intelligible as rhetoric with
the English text; and it is a sad fact if nobody cares. A Master of
Balliol once said that 'the British schoolboy generally believes in
his heart that no nonsense is too enormous to be a possible translation of a classical author'; and so there will always be people, and
even composers, who combine a correct appreciation of Brahms's
treatment of the words 'sorrow and sighing' with a failure to see
anything queer about his terrific emphasis on 'shall flee, shall flee
FROM THEM, FROM THEM!' But the German words are '*wird weg
müssen*', an idiom which is both Lutheran and colloquial at the
present day. We may not render it 'shall hence must'; but we can
sing it and hear it with much greater conviction when we know that
that is the shape of the phrase.

In my musical quotations I shall give the German text only; but
the analysis will be an almost tabular arrangement of the themes as
they occur in the course of the words. I take the words from the
Authorized Version and the Prayer Book, omitting further reference to the makeshifts of their adaptation to the music.

No. I

An orchestra without violins plays, in the solemn veiled tones
of violas and violoncellos, a ritornello which adumbrates several
important themes, as my quotation indicates by citing the words
hereafter set to this music.

The chorus, after adapting the first bars of the ritornello to the words 'Selig sind', gives out the whole Beatitude,

Blessed are they that mourn, for they shall be comforted (Matt. v. 4),

to the following theme—

Ex. 2.

which is then continued in dialogue with the orchestra, so as to make a large musical paragraph, at the echoing close of which the figure marked (c) becomes prominent. The last orchestral close plunges into the dark warm key of D flat, where a new theme appears with a new text.

Ex. 3.

They that sow in tears: shall reap in joy (Ps. cxxvi. 5).

The contrast between the two clauses is grandly expressed. At the close the orchestral basses descend in utter darkness to the note of the opening. The whole prelude, with very slight change, is now recapitulated as a setting of the first clause of Ps. cxxvi. 7:

He that now goeth on his way weeping, and beareth forth good seed—

This now leads to D flat with Ex. 3, wherewith (the orchestra slightly varying the beginning of the theme) the whole clause is set:

—shall doubtless come again with joy, and bring his sheaves with him.

This is now followed in D flat by the preamble 'Selig sind', which modulates back to F major. The Beatitude is now resumed, a short version of the theme (Ex. 2) being given to soft wind instruments in a high octave, while the altos and tenors sing its bass. This solemn device is followed by a full recapitulation of the whole section, including the dialogue between voices and orchestra, the parts of which are at first interchanged. A coda introduces a new treatment of figure (b).

Ex. 4.

(a)

The voice parts seem here to be a mere neat counterpoint, but, like many apparently accidental things in art and nature, their new figure bears a mountain of meaning afterwards revealed.

No. II

The orchestra plays a solemn march in a triple time, which implies some grave dance-measure, since plain marching is possible only in duple rhythms. The impression of a dance is confirmed by a second theme which, rising up plaintively in the dominant major, resembles a Viennese *Ländler* clearly enough to have given great offence to some critics even among Brahms's contemporary supporters. Now a Viennese *Ländler* is, at its best, a very pretty thing. So is a Dresden Shepherdess, and so are the human dancers of *Ländlers* and models of Dresden Shepherdesses. And can you realize the pathos and tragedy of death if you confine your attention to its most sublime victims? There are two main types of failure in the Grand Style: one is the sentimental confusion between the Sublime and the Pretty; the other is the ambition to achieve the Sublime in relation to nothing else. And the second error is the graver, for everybody thinks himself warned against sentimentality, while the ambition to achieve the Sublime is universally believed to be a fine strenuous motive.

Whatever issues of taste may be involved, there are no oversights in Brahms's Requiem. His march theme proves to be a counterpoint to a solemn iambic hymning of the text (1 Peter i. 24):

For all flesh is as grass, and all the glory of man as the flower of grass.

Here is the combination—

Ex. 5.

And with the rest of the verse Brahms gives us the crowning touch of pity for the withering of flowers that in life made no claim to be among the more pompous glories of man.

Ex. 6.

Das   Gras   ist ver - dor - ret

The grass withereth, and the flower thereof falleth away.

In a second strain the orchestra prepares a mighty crescendo on a dominant pedal, which brings back the whole chant with full unison chorus, closing with Ex. 6 in the tonic.

Then, like a trio to the march, a quiet middle section in lighter rhythm deals with a new text. Here again it is possible to misjudge the melody by assuming that a comparative lightness is an absolute defect. When a master who knows the foundation of hope advises one in deep grief to be patient, his tone at once achieves its aim whilst it jars by its lightness.

Ex. 7.

So   seid nun ge - dul - dig, lie - ben Brü - der,

Be patient therefore, brethren, unto the coming of the Lord (James v. 7).

If, after repeating this, Brahms had nothing broader to give, then there would be a lapse of style; but there is no such danger. As the rest of the text expands, so does the music, without making the mistake of becoming heated, though it is most poetically descriptive.

Behold, the husbandman waiteth for the precious fruit of the earth, and hath long patience for it, until he receive the early and latter rain.

The chorus dies away reiterating 'so seid geduldig', the echoes of which drop downward to the key of the march, which is repeated in full.

When it is over the full chorus bursts out solemnly in massive major chords with the conclusion, deferred till now, of St. Peter's quotation from Isaiah:

But the word of the Lord endureth for ever.

Through the massive chords the trumpets build up the figure (*a*) of the main theme of the ensuing chorus:

And the ransomed of the Lord shall return and come to Zion with songs—(and)

Ex. 8.

Brahms's text has a different punctuation from our Authorized Version, giving the remaining clause as a new sentence (completed by the bracketed words):

   —everlasting joy [shall be] upon their heads (Isa. xxxv. 10).

This he sets in a mighty musical sentence in the dominant, which comes to a wonderful soft close. The middle section of the chorus begins with a new theme curiously combined with itself in 'augmentation' (like Handel's 'Let all the angels of God worship him').

Ex. 9.

They shall obtain joy and gladness, and sorrow, and sighing shall flee away.

The 'sorrow and sighing' plunge into keys infinitely remote; and the German idiom 'wird weg müssen' enables Brahms to shoo them away with his 'müssen' right round the harmonic sphere, while the omnipresent figure (a) of Ex. 8 summons the ransomed of the Lord from all points of the compass and all beats of the measure, until the whole theme expands itself in the tonic with enormous energy, concluding therein with the sentence about 'everlasting joy'.

This reverberates quietly in a great solemn coda on a tonic pedal, over which the omnipresent figure (a) builds itself up in orchestral columns and architraves, among which separate voices wander here and there until they gather themselves together in a cadence expressive of yearning hope.

No. III

So far we have listened to the parable of the seed which must die before it can live. Except for the opening Beatitude, the whole of the text has been in parables, and its application is not to ourselves, but to those for whom we mourn. Now comes the direct and literal message; and it concerns ourselves. There are similes in plenty till the end of the work, but the teaching is no longer by parables.

A baritone solo teaches the chorus the following verses of the thirty-ninth Psalm, the first of which I must translate literally from Luther's Bible, which differs from our Authorized Version and Prayer Book version to an extent that influences Brahms's musical conception:

4. Lord, teach me that there must be an end of me: that my life has a term and I must hence.

6. Behold, thou hast made my days as it were a span long; and mine age is even as nothing in respect of thee.

Brahms represents the 'span' by a swift journey right round the harmonic world, and the chorus repeats the journey in a steeper ascent to a great climax, after which the baritone solo recapitulates the first strain (Ex. 10), the chorus intervening at the end. Then the orchestra crashes in with a burden derived from Ex. 11 (b).

With tragic irony the next section begins in the tonic major. The English text does not quite accurately correspond to the change of tone, partly because the adapter has skipped half a verse, and partly because, even if the right clause had been chosen, the German version of our A.V., 'at his best state,' is 'die doch so sicher leben', which means 'who nevertheless live so sure of themselves'.

Ex. 12.

Ach, . . . wie   gar   nichts   sind   al - le   Men - schen

Verily every man at his best state is altogether vanity.

In the next verse the music alludes to Ex. 10 in a fragmentary inconclusive style exactly expressing the sense of the words, which Brahms would never have set to the broad melodic pathos of Ex. 12.

Surely every man walketh in a vain show: surely they are disquieted in vain: he heapeth up [riches], and knoweth not who shall gather them.

Into this the chorus bursts with Ex. 12 in F major. Then the baritone solo resumes its allusion to Ex. 10 with the words best represented in the Prayer Book version:

And now, Lord, what is my hope?

This the chorus takes up in great excitement.

Ex. 13.

Nun Herr,   wess soll ich mich trös - ten?   &c.

(a)

Nun Herr, wess soll ich mich trös - ten?

When the climax has died away on a sobbing chord, there arises from the depths a glorious choral cadenza in the major, to the words

My hope is in Thee.

This closes into a fugue the unique features of which, like every musical phenomenon in the work, are profoundly symbolical of the text.

The souls of the righteous are in the hand of God, and no torment shall come nigh unto them.

Ex. 14.

Der Ge - rech - ten See - len   sind   in   Got - tes

Hand und kei-ne   Qual rüh - ret sie an

This is really a double fugue, not in the usual sense of a fugue on a pair of subjects, but in this way, that the chorus sings a complete fugue which the orchestra accompanies with another almost complete instrumental fugue. As the quotation shows, the vocal and the instrumental subjects imitate each other, but the two fugues are none the less remarkably independent in their completeness. Below them both is a thundering organ-point, holding the two simultaneous fugues from the first note to the last through their widest modulations and most crowded stretti (overlapping of subject with answer). Never has musical symbolism been more powerful and more unmistakable.

No. IV

In a key far away, yet easily connected with that of the last number, the orchestra announces a yearning phrase which, inverted, becomes a broad lyric melody.

Ex. 15.

Wie lieb - lich sind dei - ne Woh - nun - gen.

O how amiable are thy dwellings: thou Lord of hosts! (Ps. lxxxiv. 1).

A second theme is set to the same text, the tenors imitating the violins, and the basses *at the same pitch* imitating the tenors with a beautiful and rare contrast of tone.

Ex. 16.

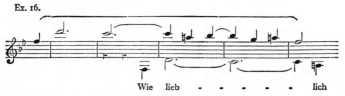

Wie   lieb -   -   -   -   lich

A widely modulating middle section or development sets the next verse to appropriate phrases:

My soul hath a desire and longing to enter into the courts of the Lord: my heart and my flesh rejoice in the living God (Ps. lxxxiv. 2).

Brahms's modulations lead him back to the tonic for a recapitulation of Exx. 15 and 16. The latter is now a regular 8-bar tune in one plane, first on the orchestra, and then on the chorus. It now has a text of its own:

> Blessed are they that dwell in thy house (Ps. lxxxiv. 4),

the second part of which is set to a triumphant double fugue—

Ex. 17.

out of the climax of which a quiet coda on the words and music of Ex. 15 arises, and comes to a close with a wonderful device of vocal octaves. Once, when Joachim was deploring the growing tendency of composers to reduce choral writing to a lazy, degenerate mass of chords doubled in octaves, Brahms said in reference to this passage, 'Ah, I set them a bad example there!'

No. V.

Some time after the Requiem was completed and performed, Brahms lost his step-mother, to whom he was devoted. Her monument is here.[1]

The orchestra establishes the key of G major with the figure given in quavers in Ex. 18, whereupon a soprano solo enters with a broad and melodious declamation, all on the dominant, giving the first clauses of the text their true force as a mere concessive preamble to the promise introduced by the word 'but'.

> And ye now therefore have sorrow: but—

Ex. 18.

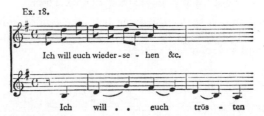

I will see you again, and your heart shall rejoice, and your joy no man taketh from you (John xvi).

For convenience I quote, in Ex. 18, the combination of themes as it occurs in the recapitulation when both are in the tonic; but the

---

[1] More nonsense: the step-mother died some time after this movement was added. The death of Brahms's mother in 1865 was the most probable inspiring cause of the whole Requiem.—D. F. T.

wonderful 'augmentation' which the chorus utters like a voice from the grave, is first heard as a 'second subject' in the dominant. Its text is:

As one whom his mother comforteth, so will I comfort you
(Isa. lxvi. 13)—

and that is the text of the chorus throughout, including the new theme which it contributes to the widely modulating middle section and the coda.

Ex. 19.

Ich will euch trös - ten

During this middle section the soprano sings:

Look upon me. A little while I have had tribulation and labour, and have found great comfort.

No. VI

In harmonies and melody, which, without going beyond the limits of a modal freedom of key, shift vaguely as the words imply, the chorus announces the following theme—

Ex. 20.

Denn wir ha - ben hie kei - - - ne blei - ben - de Statt

For here we have no continuing city, but we seek one to come (Heb. xiii).

The key of C minor, around which the harmony hovers, is instantly relegated to extreme distance by the baritone solo, whose message the chorus repeats in an awakening dream.

Ex. 21.

Sie - he, ich sa - ge euch ein Ge - heim - - - - niss.

Wir wer - den nicht alle ent-schla - - - - - - - - fen

(The resemblance of its preamble to the main figure of Ex. 8 is accidental: a theme cannot purposely refer across five intervening movements to a declamatory formula without collateral evidence in the context.)

Behold, I shew you a mystery: We shall not all sleep, but we shall all be changed, in a moment, in the twinkling of an eye, at the last trump.
(1 Cor. xv. 51, 52.)

Brahms, like Beethoven, attempts no realistic trumpet-sounds, though he uses the brass grandly. It is the voices, with their triplet flourish and their grand modulation (unquoted here) from C minor to E minor, who make poor Berlioz's four brass bands at their four points of the compass as harmless as that once famous pianoforte piece *The Battle of Prague*.

Ex. 22.

Denn es wird die Po - sau - ne schal - - - - len

For the trumpet shall sound, and the dead shall be raised incorruptible, and we shall be changed.

The baritone resumes (with its recitative preamble adapted to triple time):

Then shall be brought to pass the saying that is written—

The chorus recapitulates Ex. 22 to the new text:

Death is swallowed up in victory—

and then drives Death into a corner by a series of rising modulations—

Death, where is thy sting? Grave, where is thy victory?

At last the revelation bursts forth. Its import lies not so much in the text of the grand subject as in those of the countersubjects, which bring 'the ransomed of the Lord' and 'the souls of the righteous' under the Fatherhood of 'all created things'.

Ex. 23.

(a)   (b)

Herr, du bist wür - dig zu neh - men Preis und Ehre . . . und Kraft

Thou art worthy, O Lord, to receive glory and honour and power: for thou hast created all things, and for thy pleasure they are and were created (Rev. iv. 11).

Although Brahms naturally sets this as a fugal exposition, it is no part of his intention to write a fugue. His plan is that of a series of spacious episodes in which often a single vocal part floats through the orchestra in a manner characteristic of Handel, but almost totally neglected by other composers. Thus every clause of the text becomes clearly emphasized, and then the voices gather together on the main theme, first piling up figure (*a*) in close stretto, and then making Jacob's-ladder sequences on figure (*b*).

The stretti on (*a*) are systematically ranged in order of rhetorical force, the first notes of each entry successively making a climbing series, now in thirds (as G, B, D, F; it makes no difference whether these be rising thirds or falling sixths as a lower or an upper voice leads), now in fourths (with reckless modulating, as C, F, B flat, E flat), and lastly in rising steps (G, A, B, C, D, E, F). The Jacob's-ladder device culminates in two stupendous examples on the following model—

Ex. 24.

after each of which the clause 'for thou hast created all things' is set to an almost lyric expression of the loving Fatherhood of the Creator.

No. VII

The great theme which opens the final chorus is scored in a way which shows that Brahms is thinking of its context. The sopranos reverberate through a surging accompaniment that reaches from the depths to the heights of the orchestra, and their theme is answered by the basses. 'I heard a voice from heaven, saying unto me, Write'—

Ex. 25.

Blessed are the dead which die in the Lord from henceforth.
(Rev. xiv. 13.)

The basses having answered in the dominant, the whole chorus expands the text in a massive paragraph in that key, coming to a

quiet close. Upon this the orchestra utters a terse cadence theme
ending in a rising scale.

Ex. 26.

A solemn rhythmic dialogue, almost in monotone, between low
voices and brass tells us:

> Yea, saith the Spirit, that they may rest from their labours—

and this text is taken up in a gentle cantabile in the bright key of
A major—

Ex. 27.

dass . . . sie . . ru - hen von ih - rer Ar - beit

the new theme concluding the text in the dominant:

> and their works do follow them.

Then the solemn rhythmic dialogue with the brass modulates to a
remote key, from which the return to A is achieved quietly by a
swift stroke of genius, the tenors leading the theme and its conclusion being brought into the tonic of A.

Suddenly the tonic of F breaks through, and the first section
(Blessed are the dead) is recapitulated, the main theme (Ex. 25) by
the tenors, and the full choral paragraph in the tonic.

The orchestra gives the terse cadence theme (Ex. 26), but the
chorus joins in its final scale, which leads astonishingly and
abruptly up to E flat, the key a tone below our tonic. This is a
relation used by great composers only where it may appropriately
convey a sense of something seen through a veil, whether of
memory or of distance. And so in E flat we hear, to the next text
('Blessed are the dead'), the theme of the first chorus (Ex. 2) as it
appeared in the coda when altos sang its bass below high soft wind
instruments.

With an effort the harmony is wrested back to F, and the scale
rises again to a remoter chord from which we reach D flat, the key
of the middle section of the first chorus. From this key the chords
that were used to effect its original return to the tonic are naturally
available, and so now the whole work closes (to the present text) in

the full daylight of its key, F major, with the original close of the first chorus. But who would have thought that the gentle accessory vocal detail of Ex. 4 was to be the main figure in the theme of the mighty voice from Heaven?

CCXV. RHAPSODIE FOR ALTO VOICE, MALE CHORUS, AND ORCHESTRA, OP. 53

(Literal translation)

But who goes there apart?
In the brake his pathway is lost,
Close behind clash
The branches together,
The grass rises again,
The desert engulfs him.

Who can comfort his anguish,
Who, if balsam be deathly?
If the hate of men
From the fulness of love be
  drained?
He that was scorned, turned to a
  scorner,

Lonely now devours
All he hath of worth
In a barren self-seeking.

But if from thy psaltery,
All-loving Father, one strain
But come to his hearing,
Oh, enlighten his heart!
Lift up his o'er-clouded eyes
Where are the thousand foun-
  tains
Hard by the thirsty one
In the desert.

Goethe's *Harzreise im Winter* is an ode in which the poet uses the winter scenery of the Harz Forest as a background for the figures of huntsmen and foresters happy in the brotherhood of their crafts, contrasted with the solitary misanthrope whose embittered soul has poisoned all that human loving-kindness can do for him. A God has appointed to each man his path; the happy man runs his course swiftly to its joyous end; but he whose heart misery has contracted, struggles in vain against the iron bonds which only the bitter shears of fate shall sever at last. It is easy to follow the carriage which Good Fortune drives, as the leisurely cavalcade on the new-levelled road follows the Prince's entry in state.

At this point Brahms begins his interpretation of the poem, selecting with a musician's insight the three middle stanzas which, without rising to the Pindaric ecstasy of the climax, contain in a completeness of their own the poet's heartfelt prayer to the Father of Love to restore the soul of the lonely hater of men. With shudders the orchestra presents an introductory picture of the slow steps of the recluse, the springing back of the bushes through which he breaks, the slow rise of the tall grass he has trodden, and the solitude that engulfs him. Then the alto gives words to the description, following the tracks through wider modulations, and thus rounding off this introduction with great musical breadth and simplicity.

The next stanza, which tells the history of the misanthrope's soul, is treated with equal breadth and simplicity in a sustained lyric melody.

Ex. 1.

The cross-rhythm (3 × 2 against 2 × 3) is very characteristic of Brahms, and I cannot illustrate the continuity of musical history better than by the strokes which I add at the normal rhythmic divisions, on a plan which proves to be convenient in displaying to modern singers the cross-rhythms of Palestrina.

By repeating the first four lines after the other four, so as to get a da capo after a middle section, Brahms does no violence to the poetic sense, though he thereby gains a perfect and purely musical form. He even brings out the highest refinement of poetic interpretation by his choice of another key (the dominant major) for its close, which thus approaches the prayer of the third stanza with a growing dawn of hope.

The psaltery of the All-loving Father is materially suggested by the harp-like pizzicato accompaniment of the violoncellos; and the tone which shall reach the ear of the self-tortured misanthrope swells gently upward in men's voices beneath the glorious melody of the alto.

Ex. 2.

This melody alternates with another, in which a modulation, near and yet infinitely far, brings out the full pathos of the prayer to open his clouded sight to the thousand springs that surround him athirst in the wilderness.

Ex. 3.

With perfect musical form Brahms combines the minute illustrative accuracy of the vocal music of the sixteenth century. Modern criticism is apt to disbelieve this, for want of realizing that true musical forms are means of expression not less direct and characteristic than details of harmony, instrumentation, and declamation.

CCXVI. 'SONG OF DESTINY' ('SCHICKSALSLIED'), FOR CHORUS AND ORCHESTRA, OP. 54

Friedrich Hölderlin's poem is set by Brahms in a form which has been thought to go beyond the mandate of its text in a fundamental matter. I think that on mature reflection we shall find that the setting does no such thing, but that we are apt to forget or ignore the privilege of music to treat the time-direction in a way of its own, retracing the past and grasping the future without regard to the way in which human life is confined to one order of events. Brahms, the last great master of sonata forms, could not be expected to ignore that privilege; and Wagner committed himself to no assertion of personal immortality when he made Isolde die beside the corpse of Tristan to the music of their love-duet, nor when he made Siegfried die to the music of Brünnhilde's awakening.

A literal translation of Hölderlin's poem can bring out the meaning more closely than can be managed in a singable version. The otherwise excellent version of Troutbeck may be sung, with a change in one detail where that eminently musical translator lost faith in Brahms's rhythm and, counting the bar-periods wrongly, assumed that the German text was wrongly accented, whereas it is perfectly correct. Instead of Troutbeck's ' At last do we pass away ' I read ' In doubt and darkness . . . we fall '.

An orchestral introduction expresses the most wistful longing—

Ex. 1.

A solemn rhythm in the drums pervades most of this paragraph.

The close anticipates the first theme of the chorus, which is announced by the altos and repeated in full harmony—

Ex. 2.

Ihr wan-delt dro - ben im Licht auf wei-chem Bo-den, se - li - ge Ge - ni - en

Ye walk on high in light, upon soft ground, ye spirits blest! (*selige Genien*).

Gleaming breezes divine lightly stir you as the artist stirs the sacred harp-strings with her fingers.

Ex. 3.

Violins.

The *glänzende Götterlüfte* are represented by a new figure that
modulates in subtle chords divided among antiphonal groups of
voices, wood-wind, and brass; while the *heilige Saiten* are represented by Ex. 3.

The next stanza freely recapitulates the music of the first, to
words of the following purport:

(Ex. 2) Free from Fate, as a sleeping babe at the breast, the heavenly
ones draw their breath: chastely guarded in its modest bud, their spirit
blooms for ever; (Ex. 3) and their hallowed eyes gaze in calm eternal
clearness.

The orchestra resumes the close of its introduction. Suddenly
there is a new chord, ambiguous and ominous. Upon this the
orchestra flares out in wild agitation, and the chorus re-enters,
bewailing the helpless state of man in his darkness and doubt—

Ex. 4.

Doch uns   ist   ge - ge - ben auf kein - er Stät - - te   zu ruh'n.

But to us it is given to find rest nowhere: suffering mankind dies away
and falls blindly from hour to hour, like water hurled from rock to rock,
year in, year out, down into the unknown.

Brahms develops this theme and these words in a huge movement which goes again and again through its cycle of despairing
thoughts, finding no way out except by sheer exhaustion. Yet, like
the representation of Absence in Beethoven's Sonata *Les Adieux*,
the movement is not inordinately long, and its form is perfectly
clear. The simile of water hurled from rock to rock is graphically
represented by the cross-rhythm—

Ex. 5.

Wie Was - ser   von   Klip - pe   zu   Klip - pe   ge - wor - fen,

and when this point is reached again in recapitulation, the key is
unexpectedly remote. In the final stages of exhaustion the rhythm
of Ex. 4 becomes—

Ex. 6.

and the orchestra has dying flickers of energy, with a pathetic
augmentation of its figure of accompaniment—

Ex. 7.

When no thought is left except that of the dark unknown, the
longing for light arises again. In ruthless beauty the orchestral
prelude returns, in C major. At first the drums are silent; and
nothing darkens the '*stiller, ewiger Klarheit*' of the melody with
which the flute soars up. Towards the end the drums are heard,
but their rhythm is not so solid as at first. We may not know that
because this vision rouses our longing it is an answer to our doubts
and fears. It must suffice us that music is capable of such visions.

JOACHIM

CCXVII. MARFA'S SOLILOQUY, FROM SCHILLER'S UNFINISHED DRAMA 'DEMETRIUS', SET FOR MEZZO-SOPRANO AND ORCHESTRA, OP. 14

Since the revival of Moussorgsky's operas, whether in Rimsky-
Korsakov's tidied-up versions or in their original form, we have
become more familiar with the subject of the false Demetrius
than any audience to whom Frau Joachim can have sung the great
scena which Joachim wrote for her at some time in the 'sixties,
probably before Moussorgsky had begun to think of *Boris Godunov*,
and certainly at least ten years before that opera was first produced.
Even when, early in the present century, Joachim made one of his
last visits to England and took part in the Leeds Festival, playing a
double concerto with his quondam pupil Arbòs, and conducting
this scena, its subject was still known only to the few who had read
either Schiller's fragment or Pushkin's poem. And probably there
were as yet more English readers of Schiller than of Pushkin. The
Moussorgsky revival did not reach this country for another ten
years or so.

Schiller's fragment is very interesting, in itself, in its subject,
and in the prolonged efforts Goethe made to arrive at a possible
plan for finishing it. He eventually gave up the idea; but not before
a considerable mass of literature had been accumulated, what with
his discussions and Schiller's posthumous sketches. This mass
fills a stout volume, not of Schiller's works, but of the collected
Schriften der Goethegesellschaft. In this volume the Demetrius
fragment fills some 80 pages. The subject interested Joachim
deeply, and he wrote an overture to it which he did not publish.

After Brahms's death, Joachim was pleased and not a little touched to find that Brahms, who had so carefully destroyed every scrap of his own immature or unfinished works, had made an arrangement of this overture for two pianofortes which he had carefully preserved, together with a similar arrangement of Joachim's acknowledged and published Overture to *King Henry the Fourth*. Joachim showed me both the arrangement and the original score of the Demetrius Overture, saying with glee, 'It's awful!—an attempt at psychological music!' I did not find it very awful; and the psychology of it was good enough to prove that Joachim understood Liszt and his Weimar group of revolutionaries through and through before he renounced their ways. I well remember a passage in which a theme grew, by 'augmentation', to a gigantic size, in a way vividly suggestive of the horror of the self-deceived impostor as he found both his power and his helplessness growing to his own destruction.

But this soliloquy of Marfa, written not long after that overture, is set in a style which has the deeper psychological truth of classical forms. The words are in the singer's mouth, and not in some literature that must be read elsewhere. And it was as a mature master of orchestration that the young Joachim so soon felt that he must openly part company with the devotees of a histrionic style that seemed to him extravagant. Neither these devotees nor their leaders could be satisfied without avowals of sympathy; and on the other side there was a confusion, not confined to one group, nor to one country, nor even to one art—a disastrous confusion between matters of taste and subjects of moral judgement. It is ridiculously easy to see this now. We need not take the slightest trouble to find out what the protagonists of these struggles were worrying about; knowledge and principles are irrelevant encumbrances to us when we take upon ourselves to pronounce verdicts of aesthetic history.

The soliloquy of Marfa takes place in a convent by the lake of Belofero. Marfa is the widow of Ivan the Terrible, and the mother of his heir Demetrius, who perished in infancy: according to some reports, by murder at the instigation of Tsar Boris. As in Pushkin's poem and Moussorgsky's opera, a young monk has become persuaded (by various early memories and certain tokens, such as a jewel that hung round his neck when he was adopted by the monks as a foundling) that he is the lost heir. Boris goes far to support this rumour by the terror he shows at the progress of the impostor. Such is Marfa's own view when Boris sends messengers to her retreat to warn her against lending herself to the deception. A certain desire for revenge for her own injuries at the hands of Boris adds zest to her will to believe in the restoration

of her son. The messengers, alarmed by her attitude, have retired
in consternation; and she breaks out with—

Ex. 1.

'It is my son; I will harbour no doubts.

'The wild tribes of the very desert are arming for him: the proud
Pole, the Palatine, ventures his own daughter on the pure golden
security of his case; and shall I, his mother alone reject him?
Shall I alone not be shaken by the storm of joy that overwhelms all
hearts and shakes the earth?

'He is my son! I believe in him: I *will* believe. I grasp with
lively faith the rescue that Heaven sends me!

'It is he; he comes with his armed forces, to deliver me, to avenge
my shame.

Ex. 2.

'Hark to his drums, his war clarions!—

'Ye nations, come from the East and the South, come from your
steppes, from your immemorial forests; come, ye of all tongues,
of all garbs; bridle your horses, your reindeer, your camels; come
unnumbered as the waves of the sea, and crowd unto your king's
banner!

(*Recitative*). 'O, why am I cramped here, bound, limited when
this illimitable feeling stirs me?—

Ex. 3.

Du ew' - - - ge Son-ne, die den Er - den-ball um - kreist

'Thou eternal sun, circling round the world, be thou the mes-
senger of my desires! Thou all-pervading, unconfined air that
swiftly dost accomplish the vastest journeyings, bring thou to
him the message of my burning longing.

(*A quicker movement, bringing back the figure of Ex. 1.*)

Ex. 4.

Ich ha - be nichts als mein Ge - bet und Fleh'n

'I have nothing but my prayers and supplications, which I delve
in flames from the depth of my soul: I send them on wings to the
heights of heaven; I send them like an army to meet thee!'

PARRY

CCXVIII. 'AT A SOLEMN MUSIC', FOR CHORUS AND ORCHESTRA

Parry's setting of Milton's Ode was produced in 1887, and though it is not his first important choral work it marks an epoch in British musical history. It represents classical choral writing at the height of maturity and natural resource. There was plenty of good English choral writing before it; the musical discipline of our old-fashioned University degree examinations has retained, though in a sadly debased form, many vestiges of sixteenth-century culture: and British musicianship was throughout the nineteenth century too much concentrated on the training of church choirs to remain ignorant of the practice as well as the theory of vocal harmony. We were, no doubt, in a sad and stagnant backwater of musical culture, but, as a modern poet has remarked,

'All is not false that 's taught at public schools,'

and our knowledge of vocal writing has been a real enough thing as far as it went. It ought to be quite easy to see how immensely further Parry's work has taken it. We have only to consider the experienced writer of words for music, the musical journalist who purveyed oratorio-libretti to the Festival composer with one hand, while with the other he wrote hostile criticisms of the composers who preferred Milton and Robert Bridges; and we shall soon see what was needed to rescue British music from its contentment with that state of culture to which it pleased Mr. Chorley to call it. Let us begin by reading the first sentence of Milton's poem:

> Blest pair of Sirens, pledges of Heav'n's joy,
> Sphere-born harmonious Sisters, Voice and Verse,
> Wed your divine sounds, and mixt power employ
> Dead things with inbreath'd sense able to pierce,
> And to our high-rais'd phantasy present
> That undisturbed Song of pure concent,
> Aye sung before the sapphire-colour'd throne
> To Him that sits thereon,
> With Saintly shout and solemn Jubilee,
> Where the bright Seraphim in burning row
> Their loud uplifted Angel trumpets blow,

There; that is not the whole sentence for it ends only with a comma, but it is the first possible stopping-place after telling what Voice and Verse are to do. The style is not in the least long-winded; the clauses are thoroughly varied in length and none of them clumsy. But the composer who would set this to music must be able to produce a musical paragraph of the same structure. Not only that,

but if his musical paragraph is merely declamatory it will be no paragraph at all, however just the emphasis. Many a talented and culti-
vated musician has taken the greatest pains to give the right emphasis
to each and every word of a passage of prose or verse; and in so doing
has arrived at something which sounds, in the first place, as if the
singer was talking right across the beautiful instrumental accompaniment which contains all the real musical sense, and, in the
second place, was delivering these words as instructions to a well-
meaning but rather stupid servant. The greatness of Parry's life-
work is shown here in the fact that his mass of pure eight-part
harmony sweeps through this whole verse-paragraph in a perfectly
natural flow of melody. There is no nonsense of the kind so familiar
to conventional musicians, where words are repeated when there
are too many notes for them in the tune, and notes are repeated
where there are too many syllables for the tune in the words. The
only clause which Parry repeats here is the line 'And to our high-
rais'd phantasy present'; and this is no vain repetition, nor is it
a rhetorical point to emphasize those words. It does not emphasize
them; it does not even suggest that anybody is saying them twice
over. The eight-part chorus is broken up into its main divisions,
and we hear these words in one group of voices after another till
they gather together again in 'That undisturbed Song of pure concent,' thus throwing into relief the meaning of the word 'concent'.
Now let us proceed a stage further with this verse-paragraph:

> And the Cherubick host in thousand quires
> Touch their immortal Harps of golden wires,
> With those just Spirits that wear victorious Palms,
> Hymns devout and holy Psalms
> Singing everlastingly:

And so after broadening to a great climax in the bright foreign key
in which this passage has been set, the orchestra bursts in with its
introductory theme, which will be heard for the third and last time
at the very end of the work.

Milton has not yet come to a full stop, and Parry, in holding the
immense structure together by this return of the orchestral introduction, does not violate Milton's continuity, for the orchestra has
not played more than eight bars when the chorus, without interrupting the symphony or diverting its course, re-enters with a counterpoint of its own, singing in octaves for the first time. This use of
plain octaves carries our musical consciousness back to the ages
when the octave was the only 'perfect concord' accepted; and it is
the exact translation of Milton's notion of 'undiscording voice' and
'perfect diapason'. Parry knew his musical history as Milton knew
his classical scholarship, but it follows no more in his case than in
Milton's that he worked this all out quasi-etymologically with

no direct instinct to inspire him. We may not rashly put the composer on the same supreme plane as the poet; but it is not too
much to say that the failure to appreciate Parry will generally be
found to coincide with a failure to appreciate Milton. One negative
thing is obviously instructive in Parry's treatment of his text; and
most people would call it by the misleading name of 'reserve'.
I well remember the indignation of a contemporary of mine, full of
the resources of modern orchestration, when he found that Parry
used no such measures as might be taken by forced notes on stopped
horns to illustrate the 'harsh din' which 'broke the fair musick'. But
Parry has given it perfectly adequate vocal expression for a chorus
that is deploring the fact instead of describing it; nor did Parry see
reason to interest himself in any orchestration beyond what is suited
for supporting and relieving his chorus. Otherwise, no doubt, instead
of letting the chorus sing in peace about the Cherubic host touching
'their immortal harps of golden wires', he might have directed our
attention to all sorts of glissandos and harmonics on half a dozen
mortal harps with cat-gut 'wires'; an obviously more important
matter than the continuity of Milton's paragraph. A change of
rhythm to triple time, a change of mode to the key of G minor, and
a sufficiently but not extravagantly high chord on the words 'harsh
din', are exactly to the point as Parry uses them. The words stand
out as if there were no musical artificialities whatever to come
between them and us. Parry's devices are adequate in exactly the
same way as Milton's unexpected pauses in the long line 'Jarred
against nature's chime, and with harsh din'. Let us finish the verse-
paragraph from the point where the symphony was resumed:

> That we on Earth with undiscording voice
> May rightly answer that melodious noise;
> As once we did, till disproportion'd sin
> Jarred against nature's chime, and with harsh din
> Broke the fair musick that all creatures made
> To their great Lord, whose love their motion sway'd
> In perfect Diapason, whilst they stood
> In first obedience, and their state of good.

Here is Milton's first full stop! And here, too, in spite of (or rather
because of) his beautifully clear form, is Parry's first real full stop;
for the orchestra now enters with a new theme and thus carries the
mind definitely away from any longer retrospect over what has been
so firmly welded together. The new theme (it is only a single figure)
rises and falls in wistful sequences. At last it dies away in the
depths; and the sopranos re-enter with a melodious cantabile
in a common time considerably quicker than that of the first part.
This is answered by the tenors and soon brought into four-part
harmony; whereupon, with a further quickening of time, a final

theme bursts out and is developed in a stirring fugato rising from climax to climax until the orchestra crowns the last chords by the third and final allusion to its opening theme. The words consist of the four remaining lines of the Ode; they bear repetition because they are clearly the summary and object of the whole poem; and they need repetition because with them, and especially with the last line (the theme of the fugato), lies the possibility of making a musical climax that shall balance the rest of the music, as these four lines in themselves balance the huge verse-paragraph which has led to them:

> O may we soon again renew that Song,
> And keep in tune with Heav'n, till God ere long
> To his celestial consort us unite,
> To live with him, and sing in endless morn of light!

ETHEL SMYTH

CCXIX. MASS IN D, FOR CHORUS AND ORCHESTRA

Modern settings of the words of the Mass raise two questions. First, are they liturgically convenient; that is to say, do they emphasize at moderate length the climax of the ritual and lose no time in disproportionately elaborating the rest? Secondly, are they religious music?

It is difficult to solve the first problem with the resources of a full orchestra. The text of the Gloria and Credo contains things which a full orchestral accompaniment must illustrate emphatically if it is to justify its existence at all; and the illustration of these texts tends to overshadow all the rest. And so Beethoven's *Missa Solemnis* in D is, *pace* the liturgiologists, after all a liturgical work— for the installation of a Royal Archbishop.

But when we talk of liturgical music we mean something more ordinary. After all, as Queen Victoria remarked, it is not *every* day that one marries the eldest daughter of the Queen of England; or is installed Archbishop. At all events, one may safely say that a Mass on the scale of Beethoven's or Dame Ethel Smyth's is not in any normal sense liturgical.

But religion, where it exists, is an everyday affair. And, if music and language have meaning, Dame Ethel Smyth's Mass is religious music. There is no 'religiosity' about it; and the prayers of the Kyrie and Agnus Dei are far from expressing a mood of resignation. But the music is throughout, like Spinoza, God-intoxicated; and, while it certainly does not acquiesce in the belief that in this best of all possible worlds everything is a necessary evil, it expresses an all-pervading joy in the things told by the text.

The almost constant prevalence of the key of D, which provokes criticism, is a material element in the mood of the whole work; which is otherwise signally free from the kind of monotony or tautology that could be considered an oversight. The vocal writing, though sometimes difficult, inspires enthusiasm in the singers; and the score should become a *locus classicus* for the whole duty and privileges of choral orchestration. The composer has realized the truth, almost forgotten since Handel, that high notes, though exciting at a climax, are not the most sonorous for sustained final chords in a chorus.

No choral work within modern times is more independent of all classical or modern antecedents except those of artistic common sense. The classical Mass that evidently agrees most nearly with the composer's outlook is Beethoven's *Missa Solemnis*; but in no single point is the treatment of the text similar. Yet in listening to either Mass the text seems to be treated in the only possible way: impressively, with tremendous emphasis; but without trace of eccentricity or paradox.

KYRIE

English Prayer-Book Version.

(Ex. 1) Kyrie eleison.	Lord, have mercy upon us.
(Ex. 2) Christe eleison.	Christ, have mercy upon us.
Kyrie eleison.	Lord, have mercy upon us.

Dame Ethel Smyth treats the Kyrie as a cry *de profundis*. The following theme pervades it as a ground bass—

Ex. 1.

It rises in the upper parts, and at the *Christe eleison* makes a tremendous climax with the aid of new figures—

Ex. 2.

Christe eleison.

The passion subsides into a mood which, if resigned, is a tragic resignation.

In concert performances the composer wishes to proceed from this to the Credo.

CREDO.

(Ex. 3) Credo in unum Deum, Patrem omnipotentem, factorem coeli et terrae, visibilium omnium et invisibilium;

Et in unum Dominum Jesum Christum, Filium Dei unigenitum et ex Patre natum ante omnia saecula, Deum de Deo, lumen de lumine, Deum verum de Deo vero, genitum, non factum, consubstantialem Patri per quem omnia facta sunt;

(Ex. 4) Qui propter nos homines et propter nostram salutem descendit de coelis,

(Ex. 5) Et incarnatus est de Spiritu Sancto ex Maria Virgine, et homo factus est;

(Ex. 6) Crucifixus etiam pro nobis, sub Pontio Pilato passus et sepultus est;

Et resurrexit tertia die secundum Scripturas;

Et ascendit in coelum; sedet ad dexteram Patris, et iterum venturus est cum gloria judicare vivos et mortuos, cujus regni non erit finis;

(Ex. 7) Et in Spiritum Sanctum Dominum et vivificantem, qui ex Patre Filioque procedit, qui cum Patre et Filio simul adoratur et conglorificatur, qui locutus est per Prophetas. Et in unam sanctam catholicam et apostolicam ecclesiam. Confiteor unum baptisma in remissionem peccatorum, et exspecto resurrectionem mortuorum,

(Ex. 8) Et vitam venturi saeculi. Amen.

I believe in one God the Father Almighty, Maker of heaven and earth, And of all things visible and invisible:

And in one Lord Jesus Christ, the only-begotten Son of God, Begotten of his Father before all worlds, God of God, Light of Light, Very God of very God, Begotten, not made, Being of one substance with the Father, By whom all things were made: Who for us men, and for our salvation came down from heaven, And was incarnate by the Holy Ghost of the Virgin Mary, And was made man, And was crucified also for us under Pontius Pilate. He suffered and was buried, And the third day he rose again according to the Scriptures, And ascended into heaven, And sitteth on the right hand of the Father. And he shall come again with glory to judge both the quick and the dead: Whose kingdom shall have no end.

And I believe in the Holy Ghost, The Lord and giver of life, Who proceedeth from the Father and the Son, Who with the Father and the Son together is worshipped and glorified, Who spake by the Prophets. And I believe one Catholick and Apostolick Church. I acknowledge one Baptism for the remission of sins. And I look for the Resurrection of the dead, And the life of the World to come. Amen.

The opening, without competing with that of the Gloria, strikes a joyous enough note of contrast to the Kyrie, and maintains it with unfailing enthusiasm through all the eleven or twelve defining epithets that follow—

Ex. 3.

Pa - trem om - ni-po-ten - tem.

As with Beethoven, though in a very different musical language, the thought of the Godhead becoming human inspires a note of deep tenderness and warmth.

Ex. 4.

Qui pro - - - - pter nos ho - mi-nes

The mystery of the Incarnation is sung in strains of such spirituality as Palestrina would have approved if he had been brought into touch with our orchestral language. Yet there is no trace of Beethoven's modal treatment here. As throughout the Mass, the musical idiom is as personal as it is normal and classical.

Ex. 5.

Andante.

&c.

Profoundly sorrowful, and entirely without histrionic elements in its style, is the close-knit fugue which tells of the Crucifixion.

Ex. 6.

Cru - ci - fix - us

The Resurrection and Ascension are sung with the same joyousness as the opening, and on the same material. The effect is excellent as well as adequate, and it leaves the composer with forces in reserve by which one of the supreme things in Christianity may be treated in better proportion to the rest of the creed than has hitherto been the case with orchestral Masses. For it is a singular fact that this is the first Mass since Palestrina in which the composer has laid stress on the clauses which most of all would seem fitted to inspire anybody to whom religion is an experience at all. The structural difficulties of a big orchestral Credo are such that these clauses, coming just after those of the Resurrection and the Day of Judgement, usually leave the composer in the position of dealing with an anti-climax in a long series of doctrinal details which serve for little more than a period of relaxation before the final climax, *et vitam venturi saeculi.*

But here the clauses, from *Et in Spiritum Sanctum* onwards, make one of the great moments in the Mass. A theme, in a mysteriously bright key, not less ethereal than that of the Incarnatus—

Ex. 7.

alternates with energetic short fugatos for full chorus (*Dominum et vivificantem*, &c.), as if to show the mighty works that man can achieve when the Spirit moves him.

At last, after the word *mortuorum* has reverberated in solemn darkness, the hope of a life to come is breathed faintly, and then sung triumphantly in a fugue on one of the grandest of themes.

Ex. 8.

SANCTUS.

(Ex. 9) Sanctus, sanctus, sanctus, Dominus Deus Sabaoth. (Ex. 10) Pleni sunt coeli et terra gloria tua; Osanna in excelsis.

(Exx. 11, 12) Benedictus qui venit in nomine Domini. Osanna in excelsis.

Holy, holy, holy, Lord God of hosts, heaven and earth are full of thy glory. Hosanna in the highest.

Blessed is he that cometh in the name of the Lord.

Hosanna in the highest.

Very solemn and quiet is the opening of the Sanctus—

Ex. 9.

and the first expression of the words *Pleni sunt coeli* has the kind of warmth that shows that to the composer the Divine Glory is a matter that concerns humanity—

Ex. 10.

Soon the glory grows to a triumphant climax, to reverberate once more in the quiet of the devout human heart.

The Benedictus, beginning mysteriously in a momentary divergence into a remote key, is in the mood of the Incarnatus.

Ex. 11.

A semi-chorus of sopranos and altos softly accompanies the soprano solo; and a cor anglais has a counterpoint (or main theme) in a deeper tone.

Ex. 12.

At the Hosanna a trumpet joins the soprano, and enhances with its triumph the pure spiritual ecstasy of the mood.

AGNUS DEI.

(Ex. 13) Agnus Dei qui tollis peccata mundi, miserere nobis.

Agnus Dei qui tollis peccata mundi,

(Ex. 14) Dona nobis pacem.

O Lamb of God, Who takest away the sins of the world, have mercy upon us.

O Lamb of God, Who takest away the sins of the world, give us peace.

The Agnus Dei begins in something like the tragic mood of the Kyrie—

Ex. 13.

but this passes, without any despairing crisis, naturally into the confidence that the prayer for peace will be granted—

Ex. 14.

GLORIA.

(Exx. 15, 16) Gloria in excelsis Deo

(Ex. 17) Et in terra pax hominibus bonae voluntatis.

Laudamus te, benedicimus te, adoramus te, glorificamus te; gratias agimus tibi propter magnum gloriam tuam; Domine Deus, Rex coelestis, Deus pater omnipotens.

(Ex. 18) Domine Fili unigenite Jesu Christe; Domine Deus, agnus Dei, filius Patris;

Qui tollis peccata mundi, miserere nobis. Qui tollis peccata mundi, suscipe deprecationem nostram. Qui sedes ad dexteram Patris, miserere nobis;

(Ex. 19) Quoniam tu solus sanctus, tu solus Dominus, tu solus altissimus Jesu Christe, cum Sancto Spiritu in gloria Dei Patris. Amen.

Glory be to God on high, and in earth peace, good will towards men. We praise thee, we bless thee, we worship thee, we glorify thee, we give thanks to thee for thy great glory, O Lord God, heavenly King, God the Father Almighty.

O Lord, the only-begotten Son Jesu Christ; O Lord God, Lamb of God, Son of the Father, that takest away the sins of the world, have mercy upon us. Thou that takest away the sins of the world, have mercy upon us. Thou that takest away the sins of the world, receive our prayer. Thou that sittest at the right hand of God the Father, have mercy upon us.

For thou only art holy; thou only art the Lord; thou only, O Christ, with the Holy Ghost, art most high in the glory of God the Father. Amen.

All the chimes in Christendom could not ring a more joyous peal than the orchestral opening of the Gloria.

Ex. 15.

The voices, without effort, maintain the note of triumph.

Ex. 16.

Glo - ri - a in ex - cel - sis

Nothing in this Mass is more original and more impossible to forget than the change of time and the radiant melody at *Et in terra pax.*

Ex. 17.

Et . . . in ter - ra pax ho - mi - ni-bus

The mood of the *Qui tollis* is asserted where grammatical logic most demands it, already at the words *Domine Fili unigenite.*

Ex. 18.

One of the greatest passages in the Mass is the penultimate transition to *Quoniam tu solus sanctus*. The final movement has many themes, of which the most important hovers for a long while, dove-like, in the oboes before it takes shape in the full chorus.

Ex. 19.

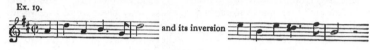

DEBUSSY

CCXX. 'THE BLESSED DAMOZEL'

Debussy's setting of *The Blessed Damozel* was sent by him to the Section des Beaux-Arts from Rome after he had obtained the Prix de Rome in 1884. It shocked professors by its unorthodoxy; and the biographers have ever since pointed out how history repeated itself after similar events in the early career of Berlioz. There is really no close parallel, for Berlioz was a difficult subject whose mastery in certain directions contrasted with such clumsiness in other directions as would bewilder the judgement of the best of critics in the best of circumstances; his *Mort de Cléopatre* (which caused all the trouble) is a work which nobody cares to revive, except for a single passage which Berlioz himself incorporated in a riper work, itself unproducible nowadays. Sir Henry Hadow has pointed out that the harmonic progression which most shocked the judges can be found in Mozart's pianoforte works; so that, while on the one hand it was not so much the work itself as the subsequent fame of Berlioz that stultified the judges of his day, there is little or no question of its containing anything nearly as revolutionary as they seem to have thought it. In short Berlioz's rejected work was not a masterpiece and was not epoch-making, though it was admittedly the best sent in for the competition. Debussy appears to have had no difficulty in obtaining the Prix de Rome for his cantata *L'Enfant Prodigue. La Damoiselle Élue* shocked the Institute because it was throughout based consistently on principles for which they were unaccustomed to legislate. There is no question whatever that it is a masterpiece; there is also no

question that it could never have fallen in with the requirements
of a body of examiners proceeding on known principles. With
our experience of Debussy's later works we are able to recognize
in it a wide range of resources in common with older music.
Debussy had not as yet reduced his harmonic and melodic
schemes to an alternation between whole-tone and pentatonic
scales; nor had he consistently excluded all chord-progressions
that depend on polyphonic principles. But he already freely used
progressions that explicitly deny the polyphonic principles; that
is to say, progressions in which a chord simply moves up and
down the scale as a primitive sensation instead of behaving as if
each of its component notes were part of an independent line. In
other words it was possible for an exceptionally stupid critic to
point out that he wrote consecutive fifths, as it was possible for
Artemus Ward to point out that Chaucer, though a man of 'con-
siderble literry parts, could not spel'. But I do not think this was
the attitude of Debussy's judges, nor do I see any parallel between
his case and Berlioz's. *The Blessed Damozel* is a masterpiece, but
it was possible to rule that its music is no more eligible for prize
competition purposes than the poem would be eligible for the
Newdigate. What really damned the Parisian adjudicators of
Debussy and Berlioz was what always betrays itself in such cases,
the clumsy admission that the condemned work was really the
best sent in.

The hardships of this work of genius did not cease with its
recognition as not only the early work of a master but a masterpiece in itself. What Debussy set to music was a faithful and
singable translation into French of the poem in its original form.
The editor of the score with English text has tried to fit the
music to Rossetti's deplorable later attempt to reproduce his
poem from memory, whereas not only the sense of the French
translation but its rhythm correspond fairly accurately both to
Debussy's music and to Rossetti's original version of 1850; but
throughout the printed copies the English words have been set
under Debussy's notes in a very crude fashion with many clumsy
repetitions, and there is dire necessity for a completely new edition
of the vocal score with English words.

The orchestra begins with the figure of plain triads—

Ex. 1

which afterwards becomes associated with the fifth of the selected
stanzas ('The sun was gone now', &c.), reappearing at the end of
the work, and serving generally to indicate the vast calm of space

in which this vision of Heaven is seen. Soon there follows a calm devout theme, not unlike those in *Parsifal* expressive of faith.

Ex. 2.

We meet with this in stanza 3 (. . . 'lovers, . . . Spoke evermore among themselves Their heart-remembered names'); stanza 6 ('Are not two prayers a perfect strength?'); stanza 11 ('angels meeting us shall sing To their citherns and citoles'); and finally in the last stanza but one ('Her eyes pray'd, and she smil'd').

These two themes expand broadly in the manner of a great introduction. Still profoundly calm, but at a slightly quickened pace, a new theme appears to which all the introduction has been leading.

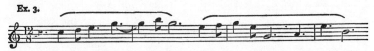

Ex. 3.

It may be taken as representing the Blessed Damozel herself; and it underlies all the stanzas that describe her: stanzas 2 and 4, and (in combination with Ex. 1) stanza 5 ('And now She spoke through the still weather'); also stanza 10 ('Our love, Not once abashed or weak') and stanza 12 ('Only to live as once on earth With Love'); and lastly in the final two stanzas ('She gazed and listened . . . And laid her face between her hands'). The chorus for the most part goes straight through the words in very simple declamation with exquisitely coloured harmonies. When the Blessed Damozel herself speaks, she begins with a phrase—'I wish that he were come to me'—

Ex. 4.

I   wish   that   he   were   come   to   me
All   this,   all   this   is   when   he comes

which, in itself merely an appropriately musical declamation, first reveals its depth fully when we hear it again, to her last words 'All this is when he comes'. One other theme may be quoted, that which belongs to the words 'There will I ask of Christ the Lord Thus much for him and me', and to 'That living mystic tree Within whose secret growth the Dove Is sometimes felt to be', since it is

remembered with such moving effect *pianissimo* at the very end
of the work.

Ex. 5.

For the rest, it will be found that the work can be easily followed
by reading the selected stanzas of the original poem as given here
with the marginal references to the musical examples. Every
detail in the orchestra illustrates the words which Debussy had
before him. In spite of all that can be done short of preparing a new
English edition of the music, there are still some annoying misfits
and one or two ineradicable repetitions of words in the setting.
For these Debussy is in no wise to blame. His French declamation
is supremely natural, and he has no repetitions whatever; but there
are unfortunately far more syllables in the French text than in
Rossetti's.

THE BLESSED DAMOZEL

The blessed damozel leaned out
   From the gold bar of Heaven;
Her eyes were deeper than the depth
   Of waters stilled at even;
She had three lilies in her hand,
   And the stars in her hair were seven.

(Exx. 1, 3)   Her robe, ungirt from clasp to hem,
   No wrought flowers did adorn,
But a white rose of Mary's gift,
   For service meetly worn;
Her hair that lay along her back
   Was yellow like ripe corn.

     .   .   .   .

Around her, lovers, newly met
   'Mid deathless love's acclaims,
(Ex. 2)   Spoke evermore among themselves
   Their heart-remembered names;
And the souls mounting up to God
   Went by her like thin flames.

And still she bowed herself and stooped
   Out of the circling charm;
(Ex. 3)   Until her bosom must have made
   The bar she leaned on warm,
And the lilies lay as if asleep
   Along her bended arm.

     .   .   .   .

(Ex. 1) The sun was gone now; the curled moon
                  Was like a little feather
           Fluttering far down the gulf; and now
(Exx. 1, 3)   She spoke through the still weather.
           Her voice was like the voice the stars
                  Had when they sang together.

       .   .   .   .   .

(Ex. 4) 'I wish that he were come to me,
                  For he will come,' she said.
           'Have I not prayed in Heaven?—on earth,
                  Lord, Lord, has he not pray'd?
(Ex. 2) Are not two prayers a perfect strength?
                  And shall I feel afraid?

           'When round his head the aureole clings,
                  And he is clothed in white,
           I'll take his hand and go with him
                  To the deep wells of light;
           As unto a stream we will step down,
                  And bathe there in God's sight.

       .   .   .   .   .

           'We two will lie i' the shadow of
                  That living mystic tree
           Within whose secret growth the Dove
(Ex. 5)   Is sometimes felt to be,
           While every leaf that His plumes touch
                  Saith His Name audibly.

       .   .   .   .   .

           'We two', she said, 'will seek the groves
                  Where the lady Mary is,
           With her five handmaidens, whose names
                  Are five sweet symphonies,
           Cecily, Gertrude, Magdalen,
                  Margaret and Rosalys.

       .   .   .   .   .

           'He shall fear, haply, and be dumb:
                  Then will I lay my cheek
           To his, and tell about our love,
(Ex. 3)   Not once abashed or weak:
           And the dear Mother will approve
                  My pride, and let me speak.

           'Herself shall bring us, hand in hand,
                  To Him round whom all souls
           Kneel, the clear-ranged unnumbered heads
                  Bowed with their aureoles:
(Ex. 2) And angels meeting us shall sing
                  To their citherns and citoles.

(Ex. 5) 'There will I ask of Christ the Lord
  Thus much for him and me:—
 Only to live as once on earth
(Ex. 3) With Love,—only to be,
 As then awhile, for ever now
  Together, I and he.'

(Ex. 3) She gazed and listened and then said,
  Less sad of speech than mild,—
(Ex. 4) 'All this is when he comes.' She ceased.
  The light thrilled towards her, fill'd
 With angels in strong level flight.
  Her eyes pray'd, and she smil'd.

 (I saw her smile.) But soon their path
(Ex. 3) Was vague in distant spheres;
 And then she cast her arms along
  The golden barriers,
 And laid her face between her hands,
  And wept. (I heard her tears.)
(Exx. 5, 1)

GRANVILLE BANTOCK

CCXXI. 'SAPPHO', PRELUDE FOR ORCHESTRA AND NINE
FRAGMENTS FOR CONTRALTO

Prelude.
I. Hymn to Aphrodite.
II. I loved thee once, Atthis, long ago.
III. Evening Song.
IV. Stand face to face, friend.
V. The moon has set.
VI. Peer of God he seems.
VII. In a dream I spake.
VIII. Bridal Song.
IX. Muse of the golden throne.

There are any number of technical methods of setting words to music; and, until the thing has been done, there is no means of knowing whether the method is right. When the method is demonstrably correct or ingenious we may nevertheless feel that we might prefer to think of other methods. When the words are great poetry this feeling is very likely to disturb us. But when the music is worthy of great poetry we have no leisure to attend to anything else. Great music has often idealized very inferior poetry, turning false sentiment into the truths the poetaster was misquoting; and if the composer can ignore the imperfections of the poet, so can we. The composer's ideas are realities suggested by the words and adequately expressed by him. If the words and the music are alike great, so much the better: nor is there anything to prevent several totally different settings being alike perfect compositions of the same poem. No two people ever see the same rainbow, and no two people ever read the same poem; but the angle of incidence is equal to the angle of reflection, and where the eye receives the light it receives a complete rainbow. Now there is this phenomenon about a great musical setting of a great poem—that the better you know the music the less conscious are you of anything extraneous to the words. The whole resources of the composer's art seem to pour themselves into the words, which become vivid not by any process of illustration but by a peculiar and direct intensifying force. Nor need this depend on the selection the composer makes of the possible aspects and elements of the poem. Both Schubert and Brahms, for instance, show a vivid sense of the form of the poem: so that if you know the poem first through their music no great surprise awaits you when you afterwards read the poem without the music. On the other hand, you might know the greatest things in Handel's *Samson* by heart (and they are very great indeed) without ever tracing either the original metres of Milton's *Samson Agonistes* or the mess Handel's librettist has made in his adaptation of it. Nor would you easily guess from Bantock's music how much poetic form Lady Bantock has preserved in her text. But the music gives the words so directly and forcibly that except for the orchestral prelude there might seem to be nothing to say here but to present the words and recommend the listener to follow them. This excellent advice certainly cannot mislead the listener; but it does not tell him everything. You may have a wonderful capacity for reading lyric poetry with a vivid idea of its force; but I question whether any reader except Bantock ever realized, for example, that when Sappho said of Atthis, 'Thou art nought to me,' she said it twice with fury and then, saying it a third time, her voice failed and betrayed her.

This is no demonstrably correct or ingenious method of setting words: it leaves no room for other possibilities. Other possibilities may become such realities in other great settings of the poem; but we know nothing of them while we listen to this. It is the truth: and each of these nine vocal pieces embodies an idea of this order of reality. The forms are completely free; in the 'Hymn to Aphrodite' it is appropriate that the first stanza of invocation should be reproduced at the end; accordingly this number ends in the key in which it began: and so does the tiny 'Evening Song': otherwise the opening key of each number (including even the Prelude) is merely its most convenient harmonic starting-point. There is only one way by which a composer can arrive at such settings as these compositions of Bantock. It cannot be done by illustrating the words. Sometimes a phrase will be graphically illustrated, as for instance (in the 'Hymn to Aphrodite') 'Beautiful, fleet thy sparrows drew thee hither': sometimes a word which many a composer would regard as highly coloured will be left without change of tone, as (in No. II) 'Scornful wert thou, none like to thee'. Bantock has no safe and ingenious method: he understands Sappho herself. Her imagery implies illustration: her passion must be sung, not merely orchestrated.

It is enough, and not too much, to say of these compositions that they can inspire a British music-lover with the direct conviction that Sappho's poetry is among the greatest things in art.

I will now leave the rest to the text, giving first in the following nine quotations the principal themes in the Prelude which are used in the songs, with the words which they foreshadow. This list does not include more detailed allusions—

Ex. 1.

First five chords = No. IX. 'Muse of the golden throne, O raise that strain.'

Ex. 2.

No. V. 'I yearn and seek—I know not what to do.'

Ex. 3.

No. V. 'Fatal creature, bitter-sweet, yea, Eros shakes my soul.'
[For the inner trumpet-part compare Ex. 8.]

Ex. 4.

No. V. 'A wind on the mountain falling on the oaks.'

Ex. 5.

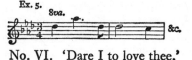

No. VI. 'Dare I to love thee.'

Ex. 6.

No. IV. Instrumental passage preceding and illustrating, 'Ah! a hue as honey pale o'erspreads thy cheek'.

Ex. 7.

No. VI. 'Sight have I none nor hearing', &c.

Ex. 8.

Last two bars = No. VII. 'Death is evil,—the Gods have so judged', &c.

Ex. 9.

No. VII. 'Delicate Adonis is dying', &c.

GUSTAV HOLST

CCXXII. 'THE HYMN OF JESUS,' OP. 37

The Hymn of Jesus is a poem found in the apocryphal Acts of St. John. Holst has set an English version of it for two full choruses, a semi-chorus of trebles and altos, and orchestra. The score is very full, and the resources of its style range through all the centuries in which music has been intelligible to western ears down to the present day. There is no essential novelty in the musical aesthetics of Strauss, nor in the diametrically opposite musical aesthetics of Ravel, which may not be found in this score, and found in its clearest and simplest form. There is no musical truth known to Palestrina that is not also to be found here, if our analysis is broad enough and deep enough to reach the fundamental principles. There are older truths still, truths of musical resonance that are older than Palestrina's classical harmony. These lie deeper than that treatment of complex chords as mere primitive sensations which we find in

Debussy and Ravel. It would therefore be entirely mistaken to ascribe to French influence the rising triads in the oft-repeated Amen in the semi-chorus. Generally speaking, the work gives no temptation for question as to its musical origins. I shall not easily forget the first impression I had on merely reading it. The whole of the music seemed to have projected itself into the words and vanished. Or, rather, the words seemed to shine in the light and depth of a vast atmosphere created by the music. But nobody, having once read the music, could say whether the poem by itself would have made the right impression at all. It is obviously inspired by the profoundest emotional sense of the Eucharist and all that that implies; and in its archaic symbolism it evidently demands to be rendered into the simplest English without regard for any prejudices against plain words. Accordingly the only way to describe it is to set out the words and mention here and there the mode and tempo of their musical treatment.

The work begins with an orchestral prelude. Trombones declaim freely (as if uttering the words) the plain-chant hymn *Pange lingua* (see Ex. 3 below).

The last note becomes a far-off chord which fades into other mutually remote chords on various groups of the orchestra. Again the *Pange lingua* is declaimed by a cor anglais, and this dies away into slow swinging chords on three flutes, below which long-drawn impassioned cries resound in falling modulations.

Ex. 1.

Lento.

The chords float down, and from the deepest organ pedals the first line of another hymn (*Vexilla Regis*, see Ex. 2) slowly leads to a note from which soft chords in slow 4/4 time mount like clouds of incense to vast heights, and swing on indefinitely while a distant choir of sopranos sings a stanza of the *Vexilla Regis*:

Ex. 2.

Vex-il-la re-gis pro-de-unt, Ful-get Cru-cis mys-te-ri-um

Quo car-ne car-nis Con-di-tor   Sus-pen-sus est pa-ti-bu-lo

The King's banners come forth; shines the Cross's mystery,
Whereby in the flesh the Creator of all flesh is hung upon the gibbet.

This is answered by tenors and basses with the first stanza of *Pange lingua*:

Ex. 3.

Pan - ge lin-gua glo - ri - o - si   Prae - li - um cer - ta - mi - nis   Et su - per cru -

- cis tro-phae-um Dic tri-umphum no - bi - lem   Qua - li - ter Re-demp-tor or - bis

Im-mo - la - tus   vi - ce - rit.   A - men. . . . .

Rehearse, O tongue, the battle of glorious strife, and above the trophy of the Cross tell out the noble triumph, how the World's Redeemer, being sacrificed, hath vanquished.

The Amen is echoed by a few instruments in the orchestra; the slow swinging chords die away; there is a silent pause, and then the Hymn begins with the full double chorus, answered at each clause by *Amen* from the distant semi-chorus.

THE HYMN OF JESUS

Double Chorus   .   .   Glory to Thee, Father!
Semi-Chorus (*distant*)   .   Amen.

Throughout the work the *Amen* is of the following type, of which I give the three main versions:

Ex. 4.
I.

A - - - - - men.

8va basso.

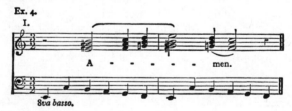

II.   III.

A - - - men.   A - - - men.

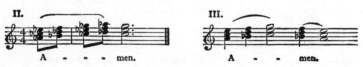

Double Chorus   .   .   Glory to Thee, Word!
Semi-Chorus   .   .   .   Amen.

Double Chorus (softly)	.	Glory to Thee, O Grace!
Semi-Chorus	. . .	Amen.
Double Chorus (dispersedly, spoken)	. . .	Glory to Thee, Holy Spirit

(The spoken words reverberate like the Gift of Tongues through a distant sound as of a mighty rushing wind)

Semi-Chorus	. . .	Amen.
Double Chorus (singing, building up the harmony part by part,	. .	Glory to Thy Glory,
antiphonally)	. .	We praise Thee, O Father, We give thanks to Thee, O Shadowless Light! Amen.

This is the exordium to the Hymn, which now begins; telling of mysteries which the anthropologist recognizes as older than Christianity, and the Christian recognizes as before all worlds.

Andante 4/4

Chorus II	. . .	Fain would I be saved:
Chorus I	. . .	And fain would I save.
Semi-Chorus	. . .	Amen.
Chorus II	. . .	Fain would I be released;
Chorus I	. . .	And fain would I release.
Semi-Chorus	. . .	Amen.

Now the two choruses begin to overlap:

Chorus II	. . .	Fain would I be pierced;
Chorus I	. . .	And fain would I pierce.
Chorus II	. . .	Fain would I be borne;
Chorus I	. . .	Fain would I bear.
Chorus II	. . .	Fain would I eat;
Chorus I	. . .	Fain would I be eaten.
Chorus II	. . .	Fain would I hearken;
Chorus I	. . .	Fain would I be heard.
Chorus II	. . .	Fain would I be cleansed:
Chorus I	. . .	Fain would I cleanse.
Chorus I and II	. .	I am Mind of All!
Semi-Chorus	. . .	Amen.
Chorus I and II	. .	Fain would I be known.

Allegro 5/4—two unequal beats in the bar:

Semi-Chorus	. . .	Divine grace is dancing;
Chorus I	. . .	Divine grace is dancing.
Chorus II	. . .	Fain would I pipe for you,
Chorus I and II	. .	Dance ye all.
Semi-Chorus	. . .	Amen.

Chorus II   .   .   .   Fain would I lament:
Chorus I and II   .   .   Mourn ye all.
*Chorus I, II, and Semi-
Chorus* (dispersedly)   .   Amen.

Ex. 5.

Heav'n - ly   Spheres   make   mu - sic   for   us

Chorus I and II   .   .   The Heavenly Spheres make music for us,
Semi-Chorus .   .   .   Amen.
Chorus I and II   .   .   The Holy Twelve dance with us;
                                              All things join in the dance.

Short orchestral tutti:

Chorus I and II   .   .   Ye who dance not, know not what we are
                                              knowing;
Semi-Chorus .   .   .   Amen.
Chorus I and II   .   .   Fain would I flee;
                                              And fain would I remain.
Semi-Chorus .   .   .   Amen.
Chorus II   .   .   .   Fain would I be ordered;
Chorus I   .   .   .   And fain would I set in order.

The rhythm here begins to broaden; alternating 5/4 with 5/2:

Chorus II   .   .   .   Fain would I be infolded;
Chorus I   .   .   .   Fain would I infold.
Chorus II   .   .   .   I have no home;
Chorus I   .   .   .   In all I am dwelling.
Chorus II   .   .   .   I have no resting-place;
Chorus I   .   .   .   I have the earth.
Chorus II   .   .   .   I have no Temple;
Chorus I   .   .   .   And I have Heaven.

The rhythm has now become a slow and solemn 5/2:

Ex. 6.

doubled in lower 8ves.

To   you   who   gaze,   a   Lamp   am   I . . . .

doubled in lower 8ves.

These discords, frightful if played on two pianofortes, are aston-

ishingly natural and clear on the double chorus, their principle
being as obvious as Mozart's way of emerging from unison, thus:

Mozart. K.V. 575.

&c.

&c.

Chorus I and II	. .	To you who gaze, a Lamp am I:
Semi-Chorus .	. .	Amen.
Chorus I and II	. .	To you that know, a Mirror:
Semi-Chorus .	. .	Amen.
Chorus I and II	. .	To you who knock, a Door am I:
		To you who fare, the Way.
Semi-Chorus I and II	.	Amen.
Chorus I and II (to the first		
line of *Pange lingua*)	.	Give heed unto my dancing: (see Ex. 3)
		In Me who speak, behold yourselves:
Semi-Chorus .	. .	Amen.
Chorus I and II	. .	And beholding what I do, keep silence on
		my mysteries.

   The first line of *Vexilla Regis* is faintly heard on the organ pedals; and
then the orchestra takes up the swaying chords of the introduction.

Chorus I and II   .   .   Divine ye in dancing what I do;
                            For yours is the passion of man that I go
                            to endure.

   Sound of distant trumpets with strange harmonies are heard, answered
by the *Vexilla Regis*, rapidly intoned in the thin high tenor of the bassoons. The sopranos of both choruses in unison take it up exultantly,
without words, to the martial sound of side-drums. It dies away suddenly into the cloudy chords which we heard in the three flutes, with
the long-drawn impassioned cry resounding below them, towards the
end of the prelude (see Ex. 1). The double chorus re-enters above an
enormously deep pedal note:

Chorus I and II   .   .   Ye could not know at all;
                            What thing ye endure,
                            Had not the Father sent Me to you as a
                            Word.

   Ex. 1 is resumed as accompaniment to an impassicned new
theme which is developed to a tremendous climax.

Ex. 7.

Be-hold-ing what I suf - fer,   ye know Me   as the   Suf - fer - er.

Chorus I and II	. .	Beholding what I suffer, ye know Me as the Sufferer.
		And when ye had beheld it, ye were not
crescendo and		unmoved;
accelerando		But rather were ye whirled along,
		Ye were kindled to be wise.
Chorus I and II	. .	Had ye known how to suffer,
		Ye would know how to suffer no more.
Lento		Learn, and ye shall overcome.
		Behold in Me a couch:
pianissimo		Rest on Me!

Soft common-chord of C in the Double Chorus, with the bell-tolling scales of Ex. 4, I, in the extreme bass and the Amen of Ex. 4, III, in the Semi-Chorus. And so the Burden fell from Christian's shoulders.

Semi-Chorus .	. .	Amen.
Chorus I and II	. .	When I am gone, ye shall know who I am;
		For I am in no wise that which I seem.
		When ye are come to Me, then shall ye know:
		What ye know not will I myself teach you.
Semi-Chorus .	. .	Fain would I move to the music of holy Souls! (A slow and soft version of Ex. 5 in A flat.)
Chorus I and II	. .	Know in Me the Word of wisdom.

With closed lips at the end of the word 'wisdom' the double chorus holds the mysterious but not harsh dissonance of the notes of the whole-tone scale—

and, after a silent pause, ends with a shortened recapitulation of the exordium, substituting 'Holy Spirit' for 'Grace'.

Chorus I and II	. .	And with Me cry again
		Glory to Thee, Father!
Semi-Chorus .	. .	Amen.
Chorus I and II	. .	Glory to Thee, Word!
Semi-Chorus .	. .	Amen.
Chorus I and II	. ,,	Glory to Thee, Holy Spirit!
Semi-Chorus I and II	.	Amen.